CI Marketing, cimprint@msn.com

ISBN-13: 978-1517597849

ISBN-10: 1517597846

BISAC: REL046000 RELIGION / Christianity / Church of Jesus Christ of Latter-day Saints (Mormon)

The Great Awakening

a sequel to

The Great Gathering

by

Mechelle "Shelle" McDermott

This book is dedicated to the like-minded Ninja Preppers
found Among LDS Friends. We have spent countless hours together,
planning, studying and preparing
for one the most amazing times in history.
This book is because of your relentless pursuit of knowledge. Your insights,
your connections and your faith created a community
of family, love and peace.

Contributors

Lory Van Valkenburg - Chapter 2, Economic Collapse. Lory is a temple ordinance worker, lives in South Jordan, Utah, loves all things prepping.

James Vierra - Chapter 6, Earthquakes and Appendix, Faraday Cages. James is a FEMA Certified for post-earthquake building evaluations, also EMP subject matter expert. He loves to spend time with his family.

Dawn Norton – Chapter 7, Secret Combinations. Dawn is a wellness consultant, teaches and loves gospel doctrine. She lives in Arizona.

Nathan Coffey – Chapter 9, Persecution & Apostasy. Nathan is a web development project manager, loves motivating others to prep and lives in Austin, Texas.

Sara Low – Chapter 11, Visions. Sara is an executive assistant and student of the gospel…she lives in Salt Lake City, Utah.

Terrell Kukla – Chapter 11, Visions. Terrell is a spa owner, loves teaching in the healing arts and lives in Mesa, Arizona.

Elaine Thompson – Chapter 11 Visions. Elaine is a retired school teacher, a student of the end-times and lives in Morgan, Utah.

Sheli Cunningham – Chapter 12, Famine. Sheli is a wife mother grandmother loves to spend time with loved ones. She lives in Idaho.

P.K. Smith – Chapter 13, Iniquity. P.K. is a private investigator, loves study the gospel and lives in the Salt Lake Valley.

Margene Nielsen – Appendix, DIY Preparedness Articles. Margene is a Social Media and Content Writer. She loves to help people get prepared. She's lived in Oregon and Utah.

David Randall Smith – Appendix, The Musing of President Monson, False Prophets, Parallels to Nauvoo and David's Prepping Tips. David is a military analyst, loves to make pizza and ice cream, and lives near Colorado Springs, Colorado.

Lorrie Lou Anderson – Appendix, author of "The Spirit and Purpose of Gathering". Lorrie is an avid reader and homeschooler who lives in Lake Oswego, Oregon.

Cynthia Ligouri – Appendix, Jewish Calendar and Signs. Cindy is a grandma, a semi-retired social worker and a convert to the Church. She has many interests including gardening, learning, her family and studying the gospel and lives in Vestal, New York.

Credits: **Jen Sanchez,** Editor **Kate Butler**, Book Title

The Great Awakening
Table of Contents

Introduction

A Continuation

The Great Awakening is a continuation of the book, ***The Great Gathering*** by the same author; both are free as downloadable files at **www.nofearpreps.com**. The second book builds on the material presented in the first, so it is recommended that you read them in order.

Once again, this second book relies on the quotes and speeches of ancient and modern-day prophets, the scriptures, and visions from members of the Church of Jesus Christ of Latter-Day Saints and non-members alike, to bring additional insights.

This book was written to be a resource manual, a workbook and even a place for personal journaling as we explore the amazing events at our very doorstep! After each topic presented there will be extra space for the reader to record additional sources he or she discovers along their personal journey of studying, watching, praying, and preparing.

Our generation has a mission.

The "end times" officially opened when Joseph Smith restored the gospel of Jesus Christ and the Priesthood was once again restored to the earth. This particular dispensation was set aside for the work of preparing the earth to receive the Savior and ushering in the Millennium, and preparing the billions of souls who have ever graced the planet for the final judgment through temple work.

This time has been foreseen and recorded by every single prophet in every previous dispensation of time! It is an exciting time, but it is also a time of cleansing and preparing.

> **President Ezra Taft Benson** (March 4, 1979)
>
> *"For nearly six thousand years, God has held you in reserve to make your appearance in the final days before the Second Coming of the Lord... God has saved for the final inning some of His strongest and most valiant children, who will help bear off the kingdom triumphantly.* ***That is where you come in, for you are the generation that must be prepared to meet your God."***

Our leaders are "a voice of warning"

Recent comments made by LDS leadership indicate that we are fast approaching the tribulation period mentioned in the scriptures. There are more of these references in volume one, The Great Gathering.

Elder Kim B. Clark, Seminary and Institute Broadcast, August 4, 2015

"Whatever level of spirituality we now enjoy in our lives, whatever degree of faith in Jesus Christ we now have, whatever strength of commitment and consecration, whatever degree of obedience or hope or charity is ours, whatever level of professional skill and ability we may have obtained, it will not be sufficient for the work that lies ahead.

Brothers and sisters, you and I need to be much better than we are now.
<u>The scriptures teach us that the world is now and will be in commotion.</u>
Wickedness and darkness will increase.
Yet in that darkening world there will be increased divine light.

The Lord Jesus Christ has a great work for us to do with the rising generation. It is a greater work than we have ever done before. The Lord is working in power to strengthen teaching and learning in his true and living church. <u>He is hastening His work and He is preparing the earth, His kingdom, and us for his return."</u>

Elder Neil L. Anderson, April 2015 General Conference

We live, brothers and sisters, <u>in the days preceding the Lord's Second Coming</u>, <u>a time long anticipated</u> by believers through the ages.
We live in days of wars and rumors of wars, days of natural disasters, days when the world is pulled by confusion and commotion.

Elder Dallin H. Oaks, April 2004 General Conference

We are living in the prophesied time 'when peace shall be taken from the earth', when 'all things shall be in commotion' and 'men's hearts shall fail them'. ....<u>We need to make both temporal and spiritual preparations for the events prophesied at the time of the Second Coming.</u>

We have been admonished to watch for the signs.

This book is not about predicting the precise timing of the Second Coming of the Lord, but it is about deliberately watching for the signs of His return as we have been commanded to do, so we will not be caught unaware.

Matthew 24: 42-44

42 Watch therefore: for ye know not what hour your Lord doth come.

43 But know this, that if the goodman of the house had known in what watch the thief would come, he would have watched, and would not have suffered his house to be broken up.

44 Therefore be ye also ready: for in such an hour as ye think not the Son of man cometh.

D&C 68:10-11

10 And he that believeth shall be blest with signs following, even as it is written.

11 And unto you it shall be given to know the signs of the times, and the signs of the coming of the Son of Man;

Luke 21:36

36 Watch ye therefore, and pray always, that ye may be accounted worthy to escape all these things that shall come to pass, and to stand before the Son of man.

D&C 45:38-40

38 Even so it shall be in that day when they shall see all these things, then shall they know that the hour is nigh.

39 And it shall come to pass that he that feareth me shall be looking forth for the great day of the Lord to come, even for the signs of the coming of the Son of Man.

40 And they shall see signs and wonders, for they shall be shown forth in the heavens above, and in the earth beneath.

All Eyes on Israel

One of the defining prophesies given by Christ himself in Matthew 24:32 is one of the most significant passages that indicates that we are very close to the Savior's return.

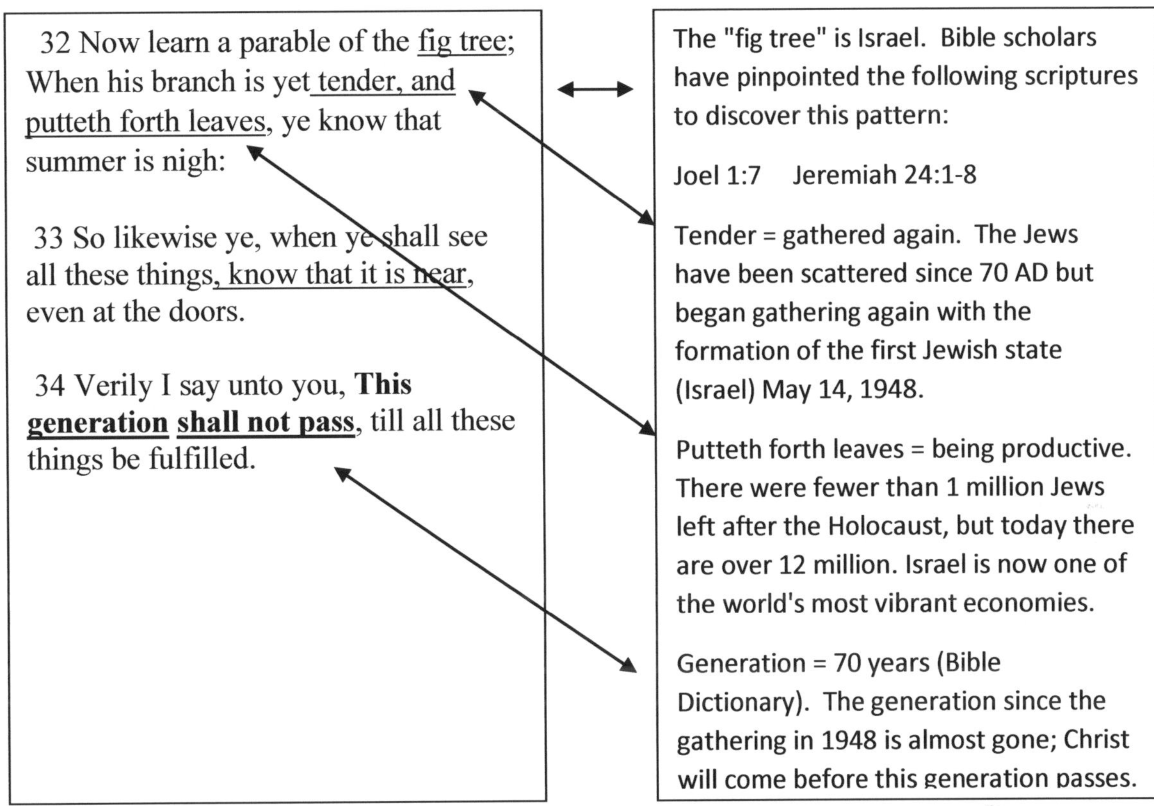

When Christ "comes again", it will first be to the Jews, when he will rescue them from the world's army during "Armageddon". His coming to the world is a few years later, as Revelation tells us Armageddon is 3 1/2 years into the tribulation period.

The country of Iran has long been committed to the destruction of the neighboring Jewish state of Israel and annihilation of her people, but has been slowed in its efforts by long-standing U.S. government involvement through our policies that protect them as an official political ally. But in 2015, changes in U.S. foreign policy (the nuclear deal signed by President Barack Obama) allowed the country of Iran to legally obtain nuclear materials. This deal was without any input from Israel and included no protections for Israel. Her prime minister spoke out loudly against it, and Jews throughout the world have mourned its passage. It was a very significant shift not only because it allows Iran the means to more easily take out Israel, but also because this is the first time in U.S. history that that our nation did not support Israel.

http://www.americanthinker.com/articles/2015/08/iran_nuclear_deal_what_now.html

This policy shift will bring the condemnation spoken of in the scriptures to our country.

Numbers 24:9 "Blessed is he that blesseth thee (Israel), and cursed is he that curseth thee."

Isaiah 54:17 "No weapon that is formed against thee (Israel) shall prosper; **and every tongue that shall rise against thee in judgment thou shalt condemn**.

Signs in heaven that have been prophesied are starting to appear.

Genesis 1:14

And God said, Let there be lights in the firmament of the heaven to divide the day from the night; and let them be for signs, and for seasons, and for days, and years.

TETRAD - BLOOD MOONS

The term "blood moon" generally refers to a lunar eclipse, and individually they are not very rare. However, four blood moons in one year --that also fall on four Jewish holidays-- is extremely rare, and should be considered a "sign". This series of four in a row is called a **Tetrad**.

This year, in September 2015, *we are finishing a Tetrad.*

- There have only been **7** tetrads since the birth of Christ. *Each time there was a tetrad, the Lord was delivering the Jews from something.*
- The last tetrad was during the Six Day War in 1967. The one before that was the Holocaust in 1948. *We are not scheduled for another tetrad for 500 years.*

TOTAL SOLAR ECLIPSE - Revelations 6:12-13

The gentile calendar is based on sun cycles and is also called the Gregorian calendar. There was a total solar eclipse in March of 2015! There is one more September 13, 2015. No one but God can manipulate the cosmos.

STAR OF BETHLEHEM

On June 30, 2015 the Star of Bethlehem reappeared after 2,000 years!
http://www.cbsnews.com/news/jupiter-venus-to-converge-in-star-of-bethlehem-moment/

CONSTELLATION VIRGO CLOTHED Revelations 12

https://www.youtube.com/watch?v=Rvkzpy7tOsQ&feature=share

"King Planet" goes inside Virgo womb then comes out 41 weeks later (gestation period for human birth). Exits September 2017

PLANET X Fly By   Luke 21:11

Estimated for March 2016. This "mysterious" planet is thought to be the cause behind the earth's geological disturbances, earthquakes, tsunamis, floods, volcanoes, and more. The planet is being perturbed by another larger planet somewhere and affecting earth.

https://www.youtube.com/watch?v=rX7S-dzOmYE&feature=share

Additional Jewish Signs have shown up in 2015

SHEMITAH

The year 2015 is also a **Shemitah** year for the Jews! It concludes September 2015.

Every 7 years the Jews were to observe the Shemitah or be cursed. There was to be a "release" from the oppression of the massive debt and slavery to "Babylon" (Deuteronomy 15:2, 20:19).

This Shemitah is the "fall of Babylon in an hour" (Revelations 18:10, 17, 18) "for in one hour thy judgment is come...so great riches have come to naught...for in one hour is she (Babylon) made desolate.

What does all this mean?

Seven years ago in the month of September (2008) was a stock market collapse and a housing market collapse. Seven years before that (2001) in September was 9/11 and a stock market collapse. Both were Shemitah years. This sign is not date specific, but it a caution for what is about to happen.

JUBILEE

Every seven Shemitah's is a **Jubilee**. What are the odds that a Jubilee is being celebrated this September!!

SUPER JUBILEE

Finally, 70 Jubilees is a **Super Jubilee**. There have been 70 Jubilees since the birth of Christ. Guess what this September is? A Super Jubilee!

Previous Super Jubilees: Birth of Abraham, The Exodus of the Jews from Egypt, Dedication of Solomon's temple and The Birth of Christ.

The Jewish elders have stated this year, 2015 is the opening of a tribulation period.

The odds of a Tetrad, a Shemitah, a Jubilee and a Super Jubilee all falling on the same month in the same year are truly astronomical! The lining up of these events seems to indicate that something significant is about to happen, and we would be wise to prepare for a great shift in our society.

In volume one, The Great Gathering, one of the more popular chapters was an event-line based on a collection of quotes, scriptures, and visions. It was a pattern of events that we could expect during a cleansing period (also called the tribulation period) just prior to the Savior's Second Coming. This book will continue that research in more detail.

Some of the events listed in the scriptures during this cleansing period, which will help prepare the earth for the Millennium, are as follows:

- Worldwide Economic Collapse
- Famine, Pestilence, and Drought
- War, chaos, violence
- Earthquakes
- Plagues

In addition to the scriptures, we have visions in the church archives and visions from members of the church. We are reminded in Joel that visions will be common during the end times.

Visions for our time

We know from **Joel 2:28** that dreams and visions will be given in the last days to help us prepare for what is coming.

> **28 And it shall come to pass afterward, that I will pour out my spirit upon all flesh; and your sons and your daughters shall prophesy, your old men shall dream dreams, your young men shall see visions:**

We know that the Lord has given us multiple resources to help us understand the signs of the times. His promise that common people would receive important dreams and visions is an example of one of the avenues we can use as we study this important topic. There have been literal volumes of personal dreams and visions published that are interesting and can provide insight into what may happen in different places and to different people in the near future. As we study them, we start to see **patterns** emerge. When the events predicted this way also line up with revealed scriptural patterns and current events we can begin to predict when, or the order in which, the future happenings are likely to unfold.

Because visions are a personal spiritual gift, we should not regard them as new doctrine, and we certainly do not replace our current leadership in the church with those who have had visions! The visions are for consideration only and can be very helpful as we dissect them to find important patterns and possible insights.

We need the spirit to see some things.

Some things are difficult to share. Some things are sacred and require the spirit to confirm truth to us.

Members of the Church of Jesus Christ of Latter-Day Saints generally have an understanding that the Holy Ghost is able to teach and witness to each of us individually in ways that are both significant and personal. As we study the signs of the times, we can ask for and receive confirmation and enlightenment from the Spirit.

Dreams and visions are not a source that we use to "prove" things, and aren't meant to give a solid evidence like some sort of indisputable, scientifically-based fact. They are like another puzzle piece, and provide source material through which the Lord can teach us what we each need to know.

D&C 77:116-118

116 Neither is man capable to make them known, for they are only to be seen and understood by the power of the Holy Spirit, which God bestows on those who love him, and purify themselves before him;

117 To whom he grants this privilege of seeing and knowing for themselves;

118 That through the power and manifestation of the Spirit, while in the flesh, they may be able to bear his presence in the world of glory.

Some will miss the signs.

Brigham Young, Journal of Discourses 8:115

When He again visits this earth, He will come to thoroughly purge His kingdom from wickedness, and, as ruler of the nations, to dictate and administer to them as the heir to the kingdom; and the Gentiles will be as much mistaken in regard to his second advent as the Jews were in relation to the first.

On the next page is a proposed timeline, compiled through significant study of hundreds of dreams and visions. The chapters of this book follow the same order, and supporting evidence for each event is found detailed within each correlating chapter.

Proposed Timeline Using the Visions

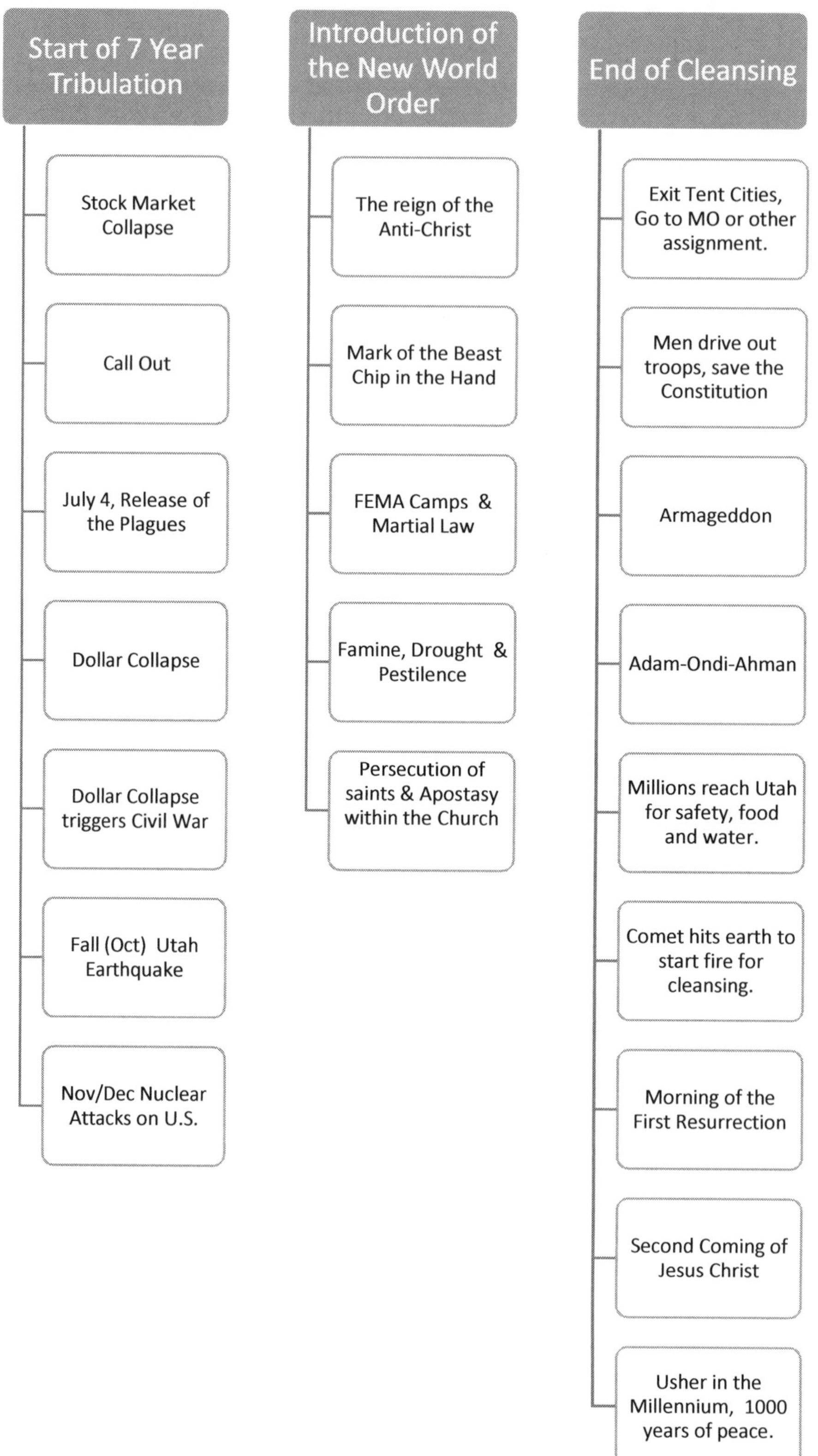

Positive Mindset

Although the events foreseen in the end-times are in many ways frightening and indicate some very difficult times are ahead, we must remember that we were foreordained to be here now, during one of the most exciting times in the history of the world! We have been instructed over and over to **not fear**. If we are keeping the commandments and aligning ourselves with God, we will be protected and miracles will abound to help us survive this time. Believing that Christ has the power to save us will make a difference in our ability to move forward with faith.

Awakening to the reality of the coming events and their timeframes is a wonderful thing, if we use this knowledge to commit now to do the following things: 1) We have been commanded to store up every needful thing. 2) We have been commanded to follow the prophet. If we choose to do these things, we will have what we need and be able to participate in the Lord's plan to lead His people to places of safety and refuge.

The Lord will preserve the righteous

1 Nephi 22:16-17

16 The time soon cometh that the fulness of the wrath of God shall be poured out upon all the children of men, for he will not suffer that the wicked shall destroy the righteous.

17 Wherefore, he will preserve the righteous by his power, even if it so be that the fulness of his wrath must come, and the righteous by his power, even if it so be that the fulness of his wrath must come, and **the righteous be preserved**, even unto the destruction of their enemies by fire. Wherefore the righteous need not fear, for thus saith the prophet, they shall be saved, even if it so be as by fire.

Perhaps if we keep the end goal in mind, we can find the much-needed inspiration we will need to endure. In Revelation we read where John is being asked who those people are, that are dressed in white surrounding God's throne?

Revelation 7:13-15

13 And one of the elders answered, saying unto me, What are these which are arrayed in white robes? and whence came they?

14 And I said unto him, Sir, thou knowest. And he said to me, **These are they which came out of great tribulation, and have washed their robes, and made them white in the blood of the Lamb.**

15 Therefore are they before the throne of God, and serve him day and night in his temple: and he that sitteth on the throne shall dwell among them.

Additional Sources & Notes

Economic Collapse

"It appears that we have gathered many to Zion who do not fully appreciate the great work of these days—namely, to place the people of God in a condition that they can sustain themselves, against the time that **Babylon the Great shall fall.** Some will say that it is ridiculous to suppose that Babylon, the "Mother of Harlots" is going to fall. Ridiculous as it may seem, the time will come when *no man will buy her merchandise*, and when the Latter-day Saints will be under the necessity of providing for themselves, or going without. This may be a wild idea, but it is no more wild or wonderful than what has already transpired, and that before our eyes.

When we are counseled to "provide for your wants within yourselves" we are only told to prepare for that day. When we are told, "unite your interests and establish every variety of business that may be necessary to supply your wants," we are only told to lay a plan to enjoy liberty, peace, and plenty.

George Albert Smith, May 6, 1870

Scriptures

Revelation 18:2

2 And he cried mightily with a strong voice, saying, **Babylon the great is fallen, is fallen**, and is become the habitation of devils, and the hold of every foul spirit, and a cage of every unclean and hateful bird.

Revelation 18:10-11, 17, 18

10 Standing afar off for the fear of her torment, saying, Alas, alas, that great city Babylon, that mighty city! for in one hour is thy judgment come.

11 And the merchants of the earth shall weep and mourn over her; for no man buyeth their merchandise any more:

17 For in one hour so great riches is come to naught. And every shipmaster, and all the company in ships, and sailors, and as many as trade by sea, stood afar off,

18 And cried when they saw the smoke of her burning, saying, What city is like unto this great city!

Helaman 13:21, 23

21 Behold ye, the people of this great city, and hearken unto my words; yea, hearken unto the words which the Lord saith; for behold, he saith that ye are cursed because of your riches, and also are your riches cursed because ye have set your hearts upon them, and have not hearkened unto the words of him who gave them unto you.

23 For this cause hath the Lord God caused that a curse should come upon the land, and also upon your riches, and this because of your iniquities.

Quotes About Economic Problems by Church Leaders

Thomas S. Monson, "Models to Follow" General Conference October 2002

"A just man and perfect in his generations," one who "walked with God," was the prophet Noah. He warned that failure to heed his message would bring floods upon those who heard his voice, and yet they hearkened not to his words. Noah heeded God's command to build an ark, that he and his family might be spared destruction. He **followed God's instructions**...Said President Spencer W. Kimball: "As yet **there was no evidence** of rain and flood, were **warnings considered irrational**... but **time ran out**. The disobedient were drowned. Noah had the unwavering faith to follow God's commandments. May we ever do likewise. May we remember that the wisdom of God oft times appears as foolishness to men; but the greatest lesson we can learn in mortality is that when God speaks and we obey, we will always be right."

M. Russell Ballard, "Standing for Truth and Right" General Conference October 1997

"The Book of Mormon teaches that secret combinations engaged in crime present a serious challenge, not just to individuals and families but to entire civilizations. Among today's secret combinations are gangs, drug cartels, and organized crime families. The secret combinations of our day function much like the Gadianton robbers of the Book of Mormon times. They have secret signs and code words. They participate in secret rites and initiation ceremonies. Among their purposes are to "murder, and plunder, and steal, and commit whoredoms and all manner of wickedness**, contrary to the laws of their country** and also the **laws of their God**." If we are not careful, today's secret combinations can obtain power and influence just as quickly and just as completely as they did in the Book of Mormon times. Do you **remember the pattern?** The secret combinations began among the "more wicked part" of society, but eventually "seduced the more part of the righteous" until the whole society was polluted.

L. Tom Perry "Be the Best of Whatever You Are", BYU Speeches March 12, 1974

The final area I would like to touch on is our obligation to the earth and the nation in which we live. I have just returned from one of the great nations of the world. This country is in one of its most difficult periods. After suffering during World War ll, the people went into a great rebuilding program. As they accomplished and things became easy again, they started to relax and wanted only to enjoy life. Their great interest became the pub and the television. If an industry was in difficulty, rather than attempting to solve the problem, it was much easier and more secure to turn it over to the government and nationalize it. One by one, the government found itself operating more and more businesses. ...The **economic pressures caused the government to fall** and a general election was called. Unfortunately, the election just highlighted problems rather than solving them. There had been such a lack of interest for so long that the elections failed to turn up new leadership. The vote was split between the two major parties; Neither had the majority to rule. A small third party was now in control and could bargain for the best deal. The ability to organize the government rested in its hands. Radical leaders could now demand positions of importance and power in the new government far beyond what they were entitled to as representatives of the people. This is a classic example, to me, of what occurs when complacency and the desire for security supersede the desire for freedom and the willingness to sacrifice for its preservation. **We currently find ourselves in a situation where we have experienced a period of unprecedented prosperity**. It has caused us to become soft and spoiled. We have again reached the point where we demand much more than we are willing to give and have become self-centered and worldly. We turn to things of man rather than to things of God. **We know the ultimate outcome of such a course**.

Marion G. Romney, General Conference October 1973

Unfortunately, there has been fostered in the minds of some an expectation that when we experience hard times, when we have been unwise and extravagant with our resources and have lived beyond our means, we should look to either the church or government to bail us out. Forgotten by some of our members is an underlying principle of the church welfare plan "that **no true Latter-day Saint will, while physically able, voluntarily shift from himself the burden of his own support**."

Teachings of Ezra T. Benson, pg 638-639

The pending **economic crisis** that now faces America is painfully obvious. If even a fraction of potential foreign claims against our gold supply were presented to the Treasury, we would have to renege on our promise. We would be forced to repudiate our own currency on the world market. Foreign investors, who would be left holding the bag with American dollars, would dump them at tremendous discounts in return for more stable currencies, or for gold itself. The American dollar both abroad and at home would suffer the loss of public confidence. If the government can renege on its international monetary promises, what is to prevent it from doing the same on its domestic promises? How really secure would be government guarantees behind Federal Housing Administration loans, Savings and Loan Insurance, government bonds, or even Social Security? Even though American citizens would still be forced by law to honor the same pieces of paper as though they were real money. Instinctively, they would rush and convert their paper currency into tangible material goods which could be used as barter, as in Germany and other nations that have previously done just that.

Brigham Young, June 5, 1853 Journal of Discourses Vol 1, pg 250,

The time will come that gold will hold no comparison in value to a bushel of wheat. Gold is not to be compared with it in value. Why would it be precious to you now? Simply because you could get gold for it? Gold is good for nothing, only as men value it. It is no better than a piece of iron, a piece of limestone, or a piece of sandstone, and it is not half so good as the soil from which we raise our wheat, and other necessities of life. The children of men love it, are greedy for it, and are ready to destroy themselves, and those around them, over whom they have influence, to gain it."

Ezra Taft Benson "Prepare Ye", Ensign Magazine, Jan 1974

We must do more to get our people prepared for the difficult days we face in the future. Our major concern should be their spiritual preparation so they will respond with faith and not fear, 'if ye are prepared ye shall not fear' (D&C 38:21). Our next concern should be for their temporal preparation. **When the economies of nations fail**, when famine and other disasters prevent people from buying food in stores, the saints must be prepared to handle these emergencies. This is a matter of concern for area, region, and stake councils.

President J. Rueben Clark, Jr.

Let us avoid debt as we would a plague...Let every head of every household see to it that he has on hand enough food and clothing, and, where possible, fuel also, for at least a year ahead...Let every head of household aim to own his own home, free from mortgage. Let us clothe ourselves with these proved and sterling virtues—honesty, truthfulness, chastity, sobriety, temperance, industry, and thrift; let us discard all covetousness and greed."

Elder Neal A. Maxwell

An economic depression would be grim, but it would not change the reality of immortality. The inevitability of the second coming is not affected by the unpredictability of the stock market. ... A case of cancer does not cancel the promises of the temple endowment.

All that matters is gloriously intact. The promises are in place. It is up to us to perform. (*"Notwithstanding My Weakness,"* Salt Lake City: Deseret Book Co., 1981, p. 57.)

Dreams & Visions of Economic Problems

Bishop Koyle Summary

- The U.S. government will keep propping up the economy as if it were on stilts, until finally it would suddenly collapse overnight.
- Taxes will become oppressive and almost impossible to pay.
- The United States will experience interest rates which will finally reach 20% to 24% after a period of 10% to 14%."
- There will be an overnight price crash. Wages and prices will be 20 cents on the dollar.
- Near the end, many of the General Authorities will become quite old. Troubles will start when three leaders will die in close proximity to one another.
- This time of trouble will be ushered in by a financial crash; we go to bed at night and awake in the morning with no light, water, gas or heat. The money will become worthless, not worth the paper it is written on, an armful would not buy a loaf of bread.
- Something will cause the Church welfare program to be inadequate at the end.
- Wall Street will have a major drop sometime before the total failure.
  See http://woodyoubelieveit.blogspot.com/2009/08/john-koyle-prophecies-dream-mine.html

A. Milton Musser

"My brother Noah Packard says that he heard the Prophet Joseph say that the next great U.S. civil war, after the war of the rebellion, (the civil war of the 1860's between the North and South) would commence in a little town now called Chicago, but at that time it would have grown to be a very large city. And another brother told me that the Prophet said that the cause of the next great trouble of the United States would be the **depreciation of the currency** of the United States. I believe I have given you all the facts in as short and concise a manner as possible." -LDS church archives, letter from Nephi Packard to A. Milton Musser, July 24, 1896.

Gayle Smith Summary August 26, 1997

October the 10th and the 29th are significant days, but the year has not been revealed. She also said that a worldwide **economic collapse** that would take place in the month of October, and it starts in the United States. It will literally happen overnight or over a weekend like Friday to Monday. http//www.greaterthings,com/nde/GayleSmith/vision.htm

Renae Lee, September 18, 2000

"It was as if I was at the NYSE. I saw two men in a tug of war over money. Then others joined in from all sides, and they all started pulling. The money was stretching more and more and getting thinner and thinner…then the stretched out money tore right down the middle…everyone landed on their backs and their hands were empty, they stood up, brushed themselves off and looked around. All the money was gone. Then again I saw the house of cards, it had fallen and the cards were laying everywhere in disarray on the NYSE floor."

"Then I was in New York City. I saw a man getting out of a taxi holding a brief case. He looked up at a very large stark grey building. I knew it was somehow connected to the World Bank. Then I saw a meeting inside this building. Several individuals were sitting at a large table, and there was a lot of yelling. There was a man standing with his back to the others, looking out a window and talking on a cell phone. He was negotiating with the World Bank in England. They were shifting funds to stop the worldwide meltdown of banks. He was speaking of two banks they were very concerned about. One was here in the United States, and very large, the other was in the UK and connected to the royalty. Both banks were ready to fall and one had to be sacrificed to save the other. It was like a power tug of war. If the royal bank were to fail it would affect the political stability in Europe. All of the European banks were scrambling. Even the royal family was concerned. Next I saw that it was decided to sacrifice the US bank."

"Next I saw the Whitehouse. The president was in the oval office and got the news. He then called for a meeting of the Joint Chiefs of Staff and a special session of congress. He had no more moves to make and was following orders…back at the meeting at the White House everyone looked down. There was nothing they could do. They had worked all day to save the **economy** and it was gone. Next I saw the NYSE just before the closing bell. There were some people who had connections and rumor of the bank closure was affecting everything. I saw the market drop 1,200 points just before things closed. Next I saw the President's face as he picked up the phone. Then he was on a news broadcast and declared a **nationwide/global emergency**."
http//groups.yahoo.com/group/greaterthings/message/642

Sarah Menet, *There is No Death*, NDE

"The next thing that came to me was more felt than seen. It was the understanding that shortly after the crashing of the buildings in New York City, commerce ceased. Shopping and buying seemed to stop and the economy failed throughout the world. Few had any money at all, and those who did have it could not buy anything. Gold and silver and other commodities had value and could be traded."

Charles Fuchs, LaVerkin, Utah

"...At that point, President Smith quite abruptly stopped and turned in the seat so that he was facing my brother and related to him what sounds basically like the same vision that Brother David Horne related. Everything that my brother wrote down in his journal....
However, Pres. Smith did tell him to look specifically for the day when the American Dollar was so worthless that no other country would allow payment in dollars, for that would signal the beginning of such a severe depression that only LDS people who had their food supplies and clothing supplies and whatever they needed for heat and to cook with would be able to survive."

"Spencer", *Visions of Glory*, pp. 116-117

"I saw that whenever this time was that I was being shown, the financial structure of the world had completely collapsed. Every bank had closed down and money was worthless. People were learning to trade and barter. ... In Salt Lake City, there had been a massive earthquake in that area in the fall of the year."

Hector Sosa, *A Change is Coming* (Interview with Lory Val Valkenburg, August 2015)

Question: Were you shown anything in your experiences regarding a financial or economic collapse in the United States?

Answer: Yes, not only in the U.S., but worldwide.

Question: When do you foresee an economic issue?

Answer: Things started in July with Greece failing to meet their financial obligations. Now Puerto Rico and others, including the U.S. are in trouble.

Question: What and when do you see a marked change economically for the U.S.?

Answer: In September of this year, 2015. I see a drastic drop in the stock market, like nothing we have ever seen. Try as we might, we will not recover.

Question: What makes you think there will be a drastic drop in the market?

Answer: Many people think that things come to me out of the blue, but that is not true. I not only receive revelation, but I study and search out information regarding issues brought to my mind. It helps me better understand what I am seeing and learning about when the Lord teaches me. I have talked with hundreds who have seen just what I have seen. I know that thousands of people have experienced what I have and seen what I have. There are multiple witnesses, not just mine. It also coincides with the Shemitah year in the Hebrew calendar. That series of seven cycles has proven to be accurate.

Question: Do you see more than a drop in the markets in September regarding the economy?

Answer: Yes, I see great challenges in the transportation industry. I see a marked change regarding inflation. Gas prices will raise dramatically. Food prices will soar; I see milk going to $6.00 a gallon. The availability of products will be a difficulty. The collapse of the dollar will come later. I don't know when, but it will come in the midst of other trials.

Question: What do you see next on the horizon dealing with the US economy?

Answer: There will be other events that affect the economy. I believe an earthquake will happen, affecting travel of products and goods. I see another trend of escalating unemployment.

Question: When do you think this rate of inflation will occur?

Answer: It's hard to tell exactly. Things will happen right on top of each other and one event will trigger another. I fear that if people don't have their supplies they won't be able to afford to get them. We really need to have some food on hand. Just recently a law was passed in New York making it against a "hoarding" law to store any food.

Question: It looks like more than food will be affected then. What else could happen?

Answer: With the cost of gasoline getting high it will affect everything. Transporting goods will be very difficult. I see a real challenge with health care access as well. I believe that people will not be able to get government assistance either. The funds will not be available that once were.

Question: Do you see things getting any better once the stock market drops?

Answer: There will be a short period of hope, but it won't last. It's only the beginning of much harder days to come. The dollar will collapse after but I don't know when. I just know it's after a period of time.

Question: What can you tell me about the collapse of the economy in general?

Answer: Brazil, Russia, India, and China are all preparing for a new world currency. They will present it to the world in October. They will have the IMF "run" the program. The dollar is not what they want to maintain a standard by any more, it's too weak. They have been "dumping" the dollar and purchasing the bulk of available gold. **The most important advice I can share is to get prepared if you aren't already, and continue preparations if you have already started**. I have felt a great sense of urgency for quite some time now. Those of us who are in a position to add additional food and water to our storage have no excuse not to do so. The available resources through church and local agencies will be taxed in their efforts to assist those who genuinely do need extra help. A change IS coming, in fact, it's already here if one chooses to look and acknowledge it. "You ain't seen nothing yet".

Additional Commentary & Resources:

SHEMITAH EXPOSED: Financial Crisis Planned For September 2015

https://www.youtube.com/watch?v=rkELgi6EkNo#t=80

Demise of the Petrodollar and the End of American Power

https://www.youtube.com/watch?v=KmVeDeav0DI

MESSAGE FROM JONATHAN CAHN

https://www.youtube.com/watch?v=HbCIPFktGWU&feature=youtu.be

Forbes Magazine, November 24, 2014, "Central Banks, Complexity, and Economic Collapse" Niall Ferguson

Wall Street Journal, first quarter 2015, "US jobless claims rose 270,000"

Washington Post, June 2015, "Markets fall as twin defaults loom in Greece, Puerto Rico"

Forbes 2/19/2015, "China buys more gold than the world produces"

OilPrice.com, January 15, 2015, "Russia abandons Petrodollar by opening reserve fund."

Additional Sources & Notes

The Gathering

D&C 45:71-72

71 And it shall come to pass that
the righteous shall be gathered out
from among all nations, and shall
come to Zion, singing with songs
of everlasting joy.

72 And now I say unto you, keep
these things from going abroad
unto the world until it is expedient
in me, that ye may accomplish
this work in the eyes of the
people, and in the eyes of your
enemies, that they may not know
your works until ye have
accomplished the thing which I
have commanded you;

Scriptures

(Please refer to volume one The Great Gathering for the first set of scriptures.)

Isaiah 57:1

1 The righteous perisheth, and no man layeth it to heart: and merciful men are taken away, none considering that the righteous is taken away from the evil to come.

2 Nephi 30:10

10 For the time speedily cometh that the Lord God shall cause a great division among the people, and the wicked will he destroy; and he will spare his people, yea, even if it so be that he must destroy the wicked by fire.

Matthew 24: 40-42

40 Then shall two be in the field; the one shall be taken, and the other left.

41 Two women shall be grinding at the mill; the one shall be taken, and the other left.

42 Watch therefore: for ye know not what hour your Lord doth come.

Revelation 18:4

Come out of her my people . . . that ye receive not of her plagues.

Note: In the Greek translation, the word here translated as "come out" literally means

Alma 26:5-8

Yea, they shall not be beaten down by the storm at the last day; yea, neither shall they be harrowed up by the whirlwinds; but when the storm cometh they shall be gathered together in their place, that the storm cannot penetrate to them:

Isaiah 26: 20 -21

20 Come, my people, enter thou into thy chambers, and shut thy doors about thee: hide thyself as it were for a little moment, until the indignation be overpast.
21 For, behold, the Lord cometh out of his place to punish the inhabitants of the earth for their iniquity: the earth also shall disclose her blood, and shall no more cover her slain.

D&C 84:2

2 Yea, the word of the Lord concerning his church, established in the last days for the restoration of his people, as he has spoken by the mouth of his prophets, and for the gathering of his saints to stand upon Mount Zion, which shall be the city of New Jerusalem.

Isaiah 40: 9

9 ¶O Zion, that bringest good tidings, get thee up into the high mountain; O Jerusalem, that bringest good tidings, lift up thy voice with strength; lift it up, be not afraid; say unto the cities of Judah, Behold your God!

D&C 101:64-67

64 That the work of the gathering together of my saints may continue, that I may build them up unto my name upon holy places; for the time of harvest is come, and my word must needs be fulfilled.

65 Therefore, <u>I must gather together my people, according to the parable of the wheat and the tares,</u> that the wheat may be secured in the garners to possess eternal life, and be crowned with celestial glory, when I shall come in the kingdom of my Father to reward every man according as his work shall be;

66 While the tares shall be bound in bundles, and their bands made strong, that they may be burned with unquenchable fire.

67 Therefore, a commandment I give unto all the churches, that they shall continue to gather together unto the places which I have appointed.

D&C 63:54

54 And until that hour there will be foolish virgins among the wise; and at that hour <u>cometh an entire separation of the righteous and the wicked</u>; and in that day will I send mine angels to pluck out the wicked and cast them into unquenchable fire.

Zephaniah 2:1-3

1 Gather yourselves together, yea, gather together, O nation not desired;

2 Before the decree bring forth, before the day pass as the chaff, before the fierce anger of the Lord come upon you, before the day of the Lord's anger come upon you.

3 Seek ye the Lord, all ye meek of the earth, which have wrought his judgment; seek righteousness, seek meekness: it may be ye shall be hid in the day of the Lord's anger.

D&C 45:68-71

68 And it shall come to pass among the wicked, that every man that will not take his sword against his neighbor must needs flee unto Zion for safety.

69 And there shall be gathered unto it out of every nation under heaven; and it shall be the only people that shall not be at war one with another.

70 And it shall be said among the wicked: Let us not go up to battle against Zion, for the inhabitants of Zion are terrible; wherefore we cannot stand.

71 <u>And it shall come to pass that the righteous shall be gathered out</u> from among all nations, and shall come to Zion, singing with songs of everlasting joy.

Leadership Quotes

Orson Pratt, June 15, 1873, Journal of Discourses, Vol 15, p. 79

We find, in the 40th chapter of the prophecies of Isaiah, that the people of Zion are to be raised up preparatory to the second advent of the Son of God. Isaiah uses an exclamation something like this—"O Zion, that bringest good tidings, get thee up into the high mountain." It seems by this, that the people called Zion, wherever they might be, were to be removed from the regions they originally inhabited, and were to be located in a high mountain, or in a very elevated region. If you wish to know the time which this prophetic exhortation to the people of Zion had reference to, read the whole of the 40th chapter of Isaiah, and you will find that, at that period, the glory of God is to be revealed and all flesh is to see it together, evidently referring to the great day when the Son of God shall come in his glory, when every eye shall see him, and they also who pierced him, and all people, nations and tongues under heaven, who are spared unto that day, shall behold him descend in power and majesty to this earth. In his 40th chapter, the Prophet Isaiah has told us that then the mountains shall be broken down, the valleys exalted, the rough places made smooth, the glory of the Lord revealed and all flesh see it together. Then the iniquities of ancient Israel will have been sufficiently punished, for the Lord will have rewarded them double for all their sins. When that time arrives the people called Zion will be required to go into the high mountains, and they shall bring good tidings unto the inhabitants of the earth.

Heber C Kimball, Life of Heber C. Kimball, p. 450

How is it now? You have the First Presidency, from whom you can get counsel to guide you, and you rely on them. The time will come when they will not be with you. Why? Because they will have to flee and hide up to keep out of the hands of their enemies. You have the Twelve now. You will not always have them, for they too will be hunted and will have to keep out of the way of their enemies. You have other men to whom you look for counsel and advice. Many of them will not be amongst you, for the same reason. You will be left to the light within yourselves. If you don't have it you will not stand; therefore seek for the testimony of Jesus and cleave to it, that when the trying time comes you may not stumble and fall."

Neal A. Maxwell, BYU Speeches September 5, 1982

Furthermore, whether you realize it or not, you are a generation drenched in destiny. If you are faithful, you will prove to be a part of the winding-up scenes for this world, and as participants, not merely as spectators, though on later occasions you might understandably prefer to be the latter. …

Though we have rightly applauded our ancestors for their spiritual achievements (and do not and must not discount them now), those of us who prevail today will have done no small thing. The special spirits who have been reserved to live in this time of challenges and who overcome will one day be praised for their stamina by those who pulled handcarts.

George Q. Cannon, Journal of Discourses, Vol. 26 p. 250

We have these circumstances to contend with. We are mixed with the wicked. The tares and the wheat grow together, and will grow until the harvest. This seems to be designed in the providence of our Father. But the time will come when there will be a separation, a final separation, of the righteous from the wicked, and that separation will be brought about by the exercise of the Priesthood which God has bestowed. That Priesthood will draw up from the earth the pure, the holy, the worthy. It will draw them up to the society of God. Everything that is not pure will be left behind. Then we will feel and know the value of that tie.

Joseph F. Smith, Journal of Discourses, Vol.19, p. 193, September 30, 1877

In various dispensations there are various differences in regard to certain requirements of the Gospel. For instance, in the day of Noah, when he preached the Gospel to the antediluvian world, he was given a special commandment, to build an ark, that in case the people would reject him and the message sent unto them, that himself and all who believed on him might be saved from the destruction that awaited them. In this dispensation there is a principle or commandment peculiar to it. What is that? It is the gathering the people unto one place. The gathering of this people is as necessary to be observed by believers, as faith, repentance, baptism, or any other ordinance. It is an essential part of the Gospel of this dispensation, as much so, as the necessity of building an ark by Noah, for his deliverance, was a part of the Gospel of his dispensation. Then the world was destroyed by a flood, now it is to be destroyed by war, pestilence, famine, earthquakes, storms, and tempests, the sea rolling beyond its bounds, malarious vapors, vermin, disease, and by fire and the lightnings of God's wrath poured out for destruction upon Babylon. The cry of the angel unto the righteous of this dispensation is, "Come out of her O my people, that ye partake not of her sins, and that ye receive not of her plagues."

John Taylor, *The Government of God*, Chapter 11

Before the Lord destroyed the old world, he directed Noah to prepare an ark; before the cities of Sodom and Gomorrah were destroyed, he told Lot to "flee to the mountains," before Jerusalem was destroyed, Jesus gave his disciples warning, and told them to "flee out of it;" and before the destruction of the world, a message is sent; after this, the nations will be judged, for God is now preparing his own kingdom for his own reign, and will not be thwarted by any conflicting influence, or opposing power. The testimony of God is first to be made known, the standard is to be raised, the Gospel of the kingdom is to be preached to all nations, the world is to be warned, and then come the troubles. The whole world is in confusion, morally, politically, and religiously; but a voice was to be heard, "come out of her, my people, that you partake not of her sins, and that ye receive not of her plagues."

Harold B. Lee Conference Report, April 1948

Thus, clearly, the Lord has placed the responsibility for directing the work of gathering in the hands of the leaders of the Church to whom he will reveal his will where and when such gatherings would take place in the future.

It would be well before the frightening events concerning the fulfillment of all God's promises and predictions are upon us, that the Saints in every land prepare themselves and look forward to the instruction that shall come to them from the First Presidency of this Church as to where they shall be gathered and not be disturbed in their feelings until such instruction is given to them as it is revealed by the Lord to the proper authority.

Heber C. Kimball, August 2, 1857, Journal of Discourses, Vol. 5, p. 134

A great many suppose that when they get there they will be perfectly safe. You will, if you keep the commandments of God; but if you cannot learn to keep the commandments of God in Great Salt Lake City, how can you learn to keep them when you have to flee to the mountains? And if you cannot keep them here, how do you expect to keep them in Jackson County? For we are as sure to go back there as we exist.

Orson Pratt, Journal of Discourses, Vol. 18, p 67July 25, 1875

Read the fortieth chapter of Isaiah, where he speaks of the glory of the Lord being revealed, and all flesh to see him when he comes the second time and how the mountains and hills should be lowered and the valleys be exalted; and in the same chapter the Prophet also says that, before that great and terrible day of the Lord, Zion is required to get up into the high mountains. Isaiah predicts this. Says he, in his fortieth chapter—"Oh Zion, thou that bringest good tidings, get thee up into the high mountains."

Thus you see that the people who organize Zion through the everlasting Gospel which the angel brings, have good tidings to declare to all the inhabitants of the earth. But these people are required, according to this prophecy, to get up into the high mountains.

Brigham Young, Journal of Discourses, Vol. 3, p. 153, May 6, 1855

It would be pleasing if all the Saints had strong faith and confidence, but sometimes many seem to falter in their feelings. I do not know how many I might find in this congregation who would have faith enough to believe that we could live on the tops of these high mountains, which are 6, 619 feet higher than the Temple Block, in case we're called to go up there and live, and there was no other place for us; I do not know whether a great many in this congregation could have faith to believe that we could live there.

Joseph Smith, Documentary History of the Church, Vol. 1

Verily, Verily, saith the Lord, your Redeemer, even Jesus Christ... Verily, I say unto you, that the day of vexation and vengeance is nigh at the doors of this nation, when wicked, ungodly, and daring men will rise up in wrath and might, and go forth in anger, like as the dust is driven by a terrible wind; and they will be the means of the destruction of the government and cause the death and misery of many souls; but the faithful among my people shall be preserved in holy places during all these tribulations.

(Source: Revelation given to Joseph Smith, July 17, 1831, west of Jackson County, Missouri, contained in a letter from W. W. Phelps to Brigham Young, dated August 12, 1861, Joseph Smith Collection, Church Historian's Office.)

Joseph Smith, Prophecy of Joseph Smith (1833):

And now I am prepared to say by the authority of Jesus Christ, that not many years shall pass away before the United States shall present such a scene of bloodshed as has not a parallel in the history of our nation; pestilence, hail, famine, and earthquake will sweep the wicked of this generation from off the face of the land, to open and prepare the way for the return of the lost tribes of Israel from the north country. (Source: Documentary History of the Church, Vol.1, p. 315-316, January 4, 1833)

Heber C. Kimball

After a while the Gentiles will gather by the thousands to this place, and Salt Lake City will be classed among the wicked cities of the world. A spirit of speculation and extravagance will take possession of the Saints, and the results will be financial bondage.

Persecution comes next and all true Latter-day Saints will be tested to the limit. Many will apostatize and others will be still, not knowing what to do. Darkness will cover the earth and gross darkness the minds of the people. The judgments of God will be poured out on the wicked to the extent that our Elders from far and near will be called home, or in other words the gospel will be taken from the Gentiles and later on carried to the Jews.

The western boundary of the State of Missouri will be swept so clean of its inhabitants that as President Young tells us, when you return to that place, there will not be left so much as a yellow dog to wag his tail.

Before that day comes, however, the Saints will be put to a test that will try the integrity of the best of them. The pressure will become so great that the more righteous among them will cry unto the Lord day and night until deliverance comes.

Source: First Counselor in the First Presidency, May 1868, in Deseret News, 23 May 1931; see also Conference Report, Oct. 1930, p. 58-59

Dreams & Visions

Samuel Whitney Richards, March 1846

I went to my Seventies Quorum meeting in the Nauvoo Temple. The whole quorum being present consisting of fifteen members. ... Dressing ourselves in the order of the Priesthood we called upon the Lord, his spirit attended us, and the visions were opened to our view. I was, as it were, lost to myself and beheld the earth reel to and fro and was moved out of its place. Men fell to the earth and their life departed from them. ... And great was the scene of destruction upon all the face of the land, and at the close thereof, there appeared a great company as it were of saints coming from the west, as I stood with my back passing to the east and the scripture was fulfilled which saith, "Come; see the desolation which the Lord hath made in the earth;" and the company of saints who had been hid as it were, from the earth; and I beheld other things which were glorious while the power of God rested down upon me. Others also beheld angels and the glory of God. ... The sacrament was administered. Our joy increased by the gift of tongues and prophecy by which great things were spoken and made known to us.

Sarah Menet, *There is No Death*

As I looked upon this scene of chaos, smoke, and destruction, I noticed there were small pockets of light scattered over the US, perhaps 20 or 30 of them. I noticed that most of the locations of light were in the western part of the US with only three of four of them being in the East. These places of light seemed to shine brightly through the darkness and were such a contrast to the rest of the scene that they caught my full attention. I focused on them for a moment and asked, "What is this light?"

I was then able to see these points of light were people who had gathered together and were kneeling in prayer. The light was actually coming from the people, and I understood that it was showing forth their goodness and love for each other. They had gathered together for safety and contrary to what I had witnessed elsewhere, were caring more for each other than for themselves. Some of the groups were small with only a hundred people or so. Other groups consisted of what seemed to be thousands.

I realized that many, if not all, of these places of light, or "cities of light" had somehow been established just before the biological attack and they were very organized. In these places were relative peace and safety. I noticed the gangs made no threats on these groups. However, the people within had defenses and God was with them.

The Cardston Prophecy (excerpt), Cardston, Canada Temple, 1923

I saw further on, instructions given whereby places of refuge prepared quietly but efficiently by inspired elders. I saw Cardston and the surrounding foothills, especially north and west for miles, being prepared for your people quietly but quickly. I saw the fuel resources of the district develop in many places and vast piles of coal and timber stored for future use and building. I saw the territory carefully surveyed and mapped out, for the camping of a great body of the people of the church. I saw provisions also made for a big influx of people who will not at first belong to the church, but who will gather in their tribulation. I saw these things going on practically unknown to the Gentile world.

I saw the inspired call sent forth to all the church, to gather to the refuges of Zion. I saw the stream of your people quietly moving in the direction of their refuge. I saw your people moving more quickly in larger numbers until all the stragglers were housed. I saw the wireless message flashed from Zion's refuge to Zion's refuge in their several places that all was well with them, and then the darkness of chaos closed around the boundaries of your people, and the last days of tribulation had begun.

Anonymous (Dreams & Visions, Vol. II p.124) (JENN NOTE: Is this one person, or several?)

I would note that during this part of the dream, when we initially left, there was no sense of panic or urgency. We were hurrying to get going because we didn't want to be left behind. Also, I was told that some people were asked to go, but didn't want to. From this I infer that the conditions of the US, were so based as to make it an easy decision as whether to stay or leave. (JENN NOTE: This last sentence doesn't make sense. Are we missing a word here?)

Anyway, after a while, we all gathered together in a central area and were welcomed by President Monson and not President Hinckley there, remember this dream occurred in approximately the year 2000. (JENN NOTE: Is this part of the quote? Which is direct, which is commentary?)

(p. 130) We were told in church to go to a meeting at the Stake House that afternoon if we had our food storage. I remember more about the meeting and packing than any other part of the dream. There was turmoil in the world, but life was still pretty normal, though prices were high and there was a fear of the future. Some of the members with food storage thought it was about putting our things in a common pot. Some of them chose not to go to the meeting because they didn't feel they should have to share what they had accumulated. Other people were teasing them about having to give all of it up and share it with those who hadn't prepared.

At the meeting, I remember being concerned about my kids on missions. At the time we had

two missionaries out, and were told they would come to the place we were going, so not to worry about them.
A semi truck came late that night, at an appointed hour. They backed up and the door of it was a as close as it could get. It was so close you couldn't see from the road that things were being loaded into the truck. There were quite a few men, none of whom I recognized, who loaded the food storage up (the hour was in the wee hours of the morning, so people around us would not see a semi was taking things from our house). Somehow the food and other items were known that it was ours. I don't know how, but when we arrived at the place we got it back.

Patriarch Charles D. Evans, LDS Church Archives

My vision now became extended in a marvelous manner, and the import of the past labors of the Elders was made plain to me. I saw multitudes fleeing to the place of safety in our mountain heights. The church was established in the wilderness.

Additional Commentary

***The Spirit and Purpose of Gathering*, by Lorrie Lou Anderson**

http://www.nofearpreps.com/booksvideosvisions-list.html

The Doctrinal Significance of a Call Out

http://doctrinalessays.blogspot.com/2015/05/the-doctrinal-significance-of-callout.html?spref=fb

Call Out Summary (From multiple visions and books)

- You are "invited" by the prophet through satellite at a special meeting called by the Stake President if you have food stored.
- **90%** don't go for various reasons: They don't have food storage, they couldn't let go of their possessions, they weren't free to walk away due to debt, they didn't want to share their food, they were not spiritually prepared to heed the call when it came, etc. Some mock those who are going and even try to talk them out of it.
- There are gas/trucks/time to get resources to the places of refuge. There is a sense of calm. Most places are church owned properties. After this initial "call out" people trying to reach the places of refuge later are on foot, and the collapse of society prevents most from ever reaching them.
- The tent cities are organized by stakes, but families are kept together. Missionaries are called home for a season and delivered to the families.
- The camps last about 18 months. They set up camp in the spring before the "poison that falls from the skies" begins mid-summer. The camps are to survive the devastating plague, but they also survive the great earthquake, the nuclear attacks and troop invasion. Our men, using the priesthood (and the lost tribes) drive the troops out.

After the saints leave the camps, there are five more years of the tribulation. Millions of refugees come to Utah for peace, food and safety. We are given assignments to help gather to Missouri, or to care for those who reach Utah.

Why a Call-Out Protects the Saints, by Mechelle McDermott

The visions give us more insight to the concept of the Saints being called out. The more we study the mechanics of a Call-Out during the cleansing period or tribulation, the more it becomes apparent that it is a divine plan to protect the Saints. Here are some advantages:

- It separates the wheat from the tares, for the Lord's purposes.
- It removes the obedient from the general populous thus preserving resources (food).
- It provides an atmosphere that will be conducive to the multitude of miracles promised.
- It begins the sanctification process for those who will be prepared to build New Jerusalem.
- It rewards the obedient with protection from the calamities.
- It is the Lord's escape plan.

> **Jeffrey R. Holland**, Devotional Broadcast, 2012
>
> You see, one of the truly exciting things about this dispensation is that it is a time of mighty, accelerated change. And on thing that has changed is that the Church of God will never again flee...
>
> Of course, that statement wasn't a comment about the Salt Lake Valley only or even the Wasatch Front generally; it became a statement for members of the Church all over the world. In these last days, in this our dispensation, we would become mature enough to stop running. We would become mature enough to plant our feet and our families and our foundations in every nation, kindred, tongue, and people permanently.

Why LDS Leaders are Quiet About The End Times, by Richard Draper, BYU Professor

http://ldsemailforwards.blogspot.com/2015/03/why-lds-leaders-are-quiet-about-end.html

Between now and the time we build Zion – we are vulnerable.
Why don't church leaders speak out more and warn about the last days and what's coming?
Why is there no show of strength by the Church?
Why is there so much evil?
Why is there no parting of the Red Sea, as it were, or the ten plagues?
Why is there no drying up of the heavens, or plagues under the administration of the prophet?
Why is it that the church leaders do not march forth in strong defensive, rising up to condemn the nation like the prophets of old?
Where is the equivalent of the burden of Babylon, or the burden of Assyria, or the burden of Moab? We are just not hearing about these things!

Why do the leaders sit quietly, doing the inner work of the kingdom – rather than battling for righteousness by buying prime time slots on TV, holding huge rallies, or shouting hell fire against the sin centers of the world? Even the missionaries are encouraged not to contend, but to preach with love.

Could it be that we are now in the one thousand two hundred and sixty days when the beast walks the land? Are we now in the time, times and half-time when the three and ½ years commence? Are we in the midst of the forty-two months? Could it be that evil really is supposed to have the upper hand, to do its work ... almost unhindered (at least for the time being)? Is it really possible?

The Book of Revelation in the New Testament provides an answer. It shows us that the path of the church is not to actively fight against Babylon, or to put her down. She is to grow fat and sassy and to grow ever more arrogant and strong; and to remain ignorant that the day of her destruction is not far distant.

Our job is to flee Babylon (repent), gather Israel through the preaching of the gospel; perfect the Saints, redeem the dead, and build Zion.

The church does not have the resources to fight against principles, institutions or people. Every ounce of energy (financial and human) must be used for people, for morality, for goodness – not for actively opposing Babylon. In the Book of Revelation, the 144,000 nor the Saints, take part in any opposition against Babylon, the dragon, the beast, or false prophets. The Saints are absent from all battlefields. The 144,000 are engaged only in the gathering of those of Israel who will come to the church of the firstborn. The only task that The Book of Revelation assigns to the Saints is to worship God and not the beast; to endure in faith, maintain virtue, to withstand persecution, and to preach the gospel of God.

Evil really has to have its day! Therefore, the church, for the present, is in a kind of isolation mode – concerned mostly with itself and internal affairs, strengthening its doctrinal and theological foundation – adding to its membership all who will come, and leaving the rest of the world to build that part of hell in which they will soon fall. Yes, evil really has to have its day. This world is in the kind of stage on which the cosmos will be able to see the self-destructive nature of unrighteousness. Wickedness is going to come down! It is wickedness that is going to bring wickedness down. (The prophet won't need to do it – the wicked will bring it on themselves.) And the cosmos is going to be able to see that. And just at the point where everyone has learned this lesson… then God is going to step in and save the world."

God laid out the plan for this world before it was created, and Jesus Christ is carrying out that plan in flawless detail. The Prophet and Apostles today are doing their part in carrying out that plan, just as it was designed by God. We have been warned – and now we are being tested to see if we will be obedient to the prophet.

God's plan is working. The question is – are we?

***Clues from the Cardston Prophecy as to how the Saints will hear about preparing for a Call Out,* by Mechelle McDermott**

Excerpt from the Cardston Prophecy:

My intensified thought was "What of the Church," if such is to become of the Kingdoms of the earth? Was immediately answered by a subconscious statement. "As it is in the church today," and I saw these **higher spiritual beings** throughout the length and breadth of the air, marshalling their spiritual forces, and concentrating them upon the high officials of your church upon earth.

I saw the spiritual **forces working upon those officers**, impressing and moving them, influencing and warning them. I saw **the spiritual forces begin to unfold these things into the minds of your elders** and other high officials, especially during their spiritual devotions and official duties, and those activities which exalt the mind of the individual or groups. I saw the impressions take hold and inspire the more desired.

Again I seemed to hear the words, "As it will be." I saw the high officials in council, and **under inspired guidance** issue instructions to your people to re-consecrate their lives and energies to their faith, to voluntarily discipline themselves, by abstaining from all those forms of indulgence which weaken the body, sap the mentality and deaden the spirit, or waste the income.

I saw further on, **instructions given whereby places of refuge were prepared quietly** but efficiently by inspired elders. I saw Cardston and the surrounding foothills, especially north and west, for miles, being prepared as a refuge for your people quietly but quickly.

Notice how many times she says "higher spiritual beings" or spiritual forces.

Here we see "inspired" guidance.

Here we are told it is done "quietly". It is not in the best interest of the church to broadcast this from the pulpit.

I saw elders still under **divine guidance**, counseling and encouraging the planting of every available acre of soil in this district, so that large supplies would be near the refuge. I saw the church property under cultivation of an intensified character, not for sale or profit, but for the use of the people. I saw artesian wells and other wells dug all over that territory so that when the open waters were polluted and poisoned that the people of the church and their cattle should be provided for.

I saw the fuel resources of the district develop in many places and vast piles of coal and timber stored for future use and building. I saw the territory carefully surveyed and mapped out, for the camping of a great body of the people of the church. I saw provision also made for a big influx of people who will not at first belong to the church, but who will gather in their tribulation.

I saw vast quantities of surgical appliances, medicines, disinfectants, etc., stored in the temple basement. I saw inspiration given the elders whereby the quantity, quality and kind of things to be stored were judged, which might not be attainable in this territory in time of chaos. I saw defensive preparations working out the organizations of the camps on maps.

There are several references to divine guidance.

Here we see that the places of safety are church owned properties.

I saw elders **still under divine guidance**, counseling and encouraging the planting of every available acre of soil in this district, so that large supplies would be near the refuge. I saw **the church property** under cultivation of an intensified character, not for sale or profit, but for the use of the people. I saw artesian wells and other wells dug all over that territory so that when the open waters were polluted and poisoned that the people of the church and their cattle should be provided for.

I saw the fuel resources of the district develop in many places and vast piles of coal and timber stored for future use and building. I saw the territory carefully surveyed and mapped out, for the camping of a great body of the people of the church. I saw provision also made for a big influx of people *who will not at first belong to the church*, but who will gather in their tribulation.

I saw vast quantities of surgical appliances, medicines, disinfectants, etc., stored in the temple basement. I saw **inspiration** given the elders whereby the quantity, quality and kind of things to be stored were judged, which might not be attainable in this territory in time of chaos. I saw defensive preparations working out the organizations of the camps on maps.

I saw the mining corridors used as places of storage underground: I saw the hills surveyed and corrals built in sequestered places for cattle, sheep, etc., quietly and quickly. I saw the plans for the organization of the single men and their duties, the scouts, the guards, the nurses, the cooks, the messengers, the children, the herders, the temple guards, etc.. **I saw these things going on practically unknown to the Gentile world, except the Great Apostasy**, whose knowledge and hatred is far reaching, in this day of its temporary power. This was going on piece by piece as the Elders were instructed so to do.

I saw the other officials obeying the **inspired instructions**, carrying their message and exhorting the people to carry out, from time to time the **revelation given them**, whilst all around throughout the Gentile world the chaos developed in its varying stages, faction against faction, nation against nation, but all in open or secret hostility to your people and their faith. I saw your people draw closer and closer together, as this became more tense and as the **spiritual forces warned them through the mouth of your elders and your other officers**. I saw the **spiritual forces** influencing those members who had drifted away, to re-enter the fold. I saw a greater tithing than ever before. **I saw vast quantities of necessaries supplied by members whose spiritual eyes had been opened. I saw a liquidation of properties and effects disposed of quietly but quickly by members of the church, as the spiritual influences directed them.**

I saw the inspired call sent forth to all the church, to gather to the refuges of Zion. I saw the stream of your people quietly moving in the direction of their refuge. I saw your people moving more quickly and in larger numbers until all the stragglers were housed. I saw the wireless message flashed from Zion's refuge to Zion's refuge in their several **places that all was well with them**, and then the darkness of chaos closed around the boundaries of your people, and the last days of tribulation had begun.

Notice the preparations are going on "unknown" to the world. It must be kept quiet! The Great Apostasy is referring to the apostates within the church who can't wait to mock, hurt or destroy the members.

This is one of my favori passages in all of the visions! This is you!

Notice, we are safe and nothing bad is happenin when we are leaving to the places of refuge.

Additional Sources & Notes

Plagues

"A long time ago the Lord raised the curtain on the scene of destruction awaiting the inhabitants of the earth if they followed to the end the course they were then pursuing.
More than a hundred years ago, he said that a desolating scourge should go forth among the inhabitants of the earth, and if they repented not,
it should continue from time to time until the earth was empty and the inhabitants thereof utterly destroyed."

Marion G. Romney,
General Conference, April 1951

Scriptures

D&C 45:31-32

31 And there shall be men standing in that generation, that shall not pass until they shall see an overflowing scourge; for a desolating sickness shall cover the land.

32 But my disciples shall stand in holy places, and shall not be moved; but among the wicked, men shall lift up their voices and curse God and die.

D&C 97:23-26

23 The Lord's scourge shall pass over by night and by day, and the report thereof shall vex all people; yea, it shall not be stayed until the Lord come;

24 For the indignation of the Lord is kindled against their abominations and all their wicked works.

25 Nevertheless, Zion shall escape if she observe to do all things whatsoever I have commanded her.

26 But if she observe not to do whatsoever I have commanded her, I will visit her according to all her works, with sore affliction, with pestilence, with plague, with sword, with vengeance, with devouring fire.

D&C 5:18-19

18 And their testimony shall also go forth unto the condemnation of this generation if they harden their hearts against them;

19 For a desolating scourge shall go forth among the inhabitants of the earth, and shall continue to be poured out from time to time, if they repent not, until the earth is empty, and the inhabitants thereof are consumed away and utterly destroyed by the brightness of my coming.

Revelation 16:2

2 And the first went, and poured out his vial upon the earth; and there fell a noisome and grievous sore upon the men which had the mark of the beast, and upon them which worshipped his image.

Revelation 16:21

21And there fell upon men a great hail out of heaven, every stone about the weight of a talent: and men blasphemed God because of the plague of the hail; for the plague thereof was exceeding great.

Revelation 16:8-9

8 And the fourth angel poured out his vial upon the sun; and
power was given unto him to scorch men with fire.
9 And men were scorched with great heat, and blasphemed the name of God, which hath power over these plagues: and they repented not to give him glory.

Revelation 16:10-11

10 And the fifth angel poured out his vial upon the seat of the beast; and his kingdom was full of darkness; and they gnawed their tongues for pain,
11 And blasphemed the God of heaven because of their pains and their sores, and repented not of their deeds.

Revelation 8:7

7 The first angel sounded, and there followed hail and fire mingled with blood, and they were cast upon the earth: and the third part of trees was burnt up, and all green grass was burnt up.

Revelation 8:10-12

10 And the third angel sounded, and there fell a great star from heaven, burning as it were a lamp, and it fell upon the third part of the rivers, and upon the fountains of waters;
11 And the name of the star is called Wormwood (bitterness):
and the third part of the waters became wormwood; and many men died of the waters, because they were made bitter.

The Book of Revelation tells of Seal Judgments, 7 Trumpet Judgments, and 7 Vial Judgments.

These judgments devastate the earth. During the Tribulation the oceans become blood and most of the sea life dies, plagues and hailstones are released, and a supernatural darkness covers the earth.

Here's a brief summary…

SEALS

Rev. 6:2 1st seal conquers with a peace plan.

Rev.6:3 2nd Seal: Wars on earth.

Rev.6:5 3rd Seal: Worldwide economic trouble.

Rev.6:7 4th Seal: Death released. 1/4 of the world's population to die by plagues, disease, and beasts of the earth.

Rev.6:9 5th Seal: Persecution and mass killing of God's people worldwide.

Rev.6:12 6th Seal: Massive earthquake wrath of God. 144,000 are anointed.

Rev.8:1 7th Seal: Fire and desolation

TRUMPETS

Rev.8:7 1st Trumpet: Hail, fire, and blood. 1/3 all grass and trees burned up

Rev.8:8 2nd Trumpet: Great mountain hits sea. 1/3 all ocean becomes blood. 1/3 all sea life dies and 1/3 all ships destroyed.

Rev.8:10 3rd Trumpet: Wormwood star hits earth. 1/3 all freshwater poisoned.

Rev.8:12 4th Trumpet: 1/3 of sun and moon darkened.

Rev.9:1 5th Trumpet: locust beasts that sting and torment men are loosed from the pit.

Rev.9:13 6th Trumpet: demons released and 200 million army kills 1/3 of the world's population.

VIALS

Rev.16:2 1st Vial: Terrible and painful sores break out on all who worship beast.

Rev.16:3 2nd Vial: Entire oceans becomes blood, the sea life dies.

Rev.16:4 3rd Vial: Fresh water becomes blood, no more fresh drinking water.

Rev.16:8 4th Vial: Sun increased in heat and scorches and burns people.

Rev.16:10 5th Vial: a Supernatural darkness covers the earth

Rev.16:12 6th Vial: Armies head toward in the Middle East for the final battle –Armageddon.

Rev.16:17 7th Vial: Babylon destroyed, massive earthquakes, hundred pound hailstones

Quotes About Future Plagues, by Church Leaders

Orson Pratt, Journal of Discourses, Vol 15

This will prepare them for further ministrations among the nations of the earth, it will prepare them to go forth in the days of tribulation and vengeance upon the nations of the wicked, when God will smite them with pestilence, plague and earthquake, such as former generations never knew. Then the servants of God will need to be armed with the power of God, they will need to have that sealing blessing pronounced upon their foreheads that they can stand forth in the midst of these desolations and plagues and not be overcome by them. When John the Revelator describes this scene he says he saw four angels sent forth, ready to hold the four winds that should blow from the four quarters of heaven. Another angel ascended from the east and cried to the four angels, and said, "Smite not the earth now, but wait a little while." "How long?" "Until the servants of our God are sealed in their foreheads." What for? To prepare them to stand forth in the midst of these desolations and plagues, and not be overcome. When they are prepared, when they have received a renewal of their bodies in the Lord's Temple, and have been filled with the Holy Ghost and purified as gold and silver in a furnace of fire, then they will be prepared to stand before the nations of the earth and preach glad tidings of salvation in the midst of judgments that are to come like a whirlwind upon the wicked.

Orson Pratt, Journal of Discourses, Vol. 18

These plagues named in John's revelations, will take place literally—"The Lord God will curse the waters of the great deep, and they shall be turned into blood." "The sea shall become as the blood of a dead man, and every living thing in the sea shall be destroyed." And the time will come, when the seven angels
having the seven last trumps will sound their trumps literally, and the sound thereof will be heard among the nations, just preparatory to the coming of the Son of man; and all the judgments foretold by John, which are to succeed the sound of each of the seven trumpets, will be fulfilled literally upon the earth in their times and seasons.

Marion G. Romney, General Conference, April 1951

A long time ago the Lord raised the curtain on the scene of destruction awaiting the inhabitants of the earth if they followed to the end the course they were then pursuing. More than a hundred years ago, he said that a desolating scourge should go forth among the inhabitants of the earth, and if they repented not, it should continue from time to time until the earth was empty and the inhabitants thereof utterly destroyed.

Joseph B. Wirthlin, General Conference, October 2005

Prosperity often leads to pride, which leads to sin. Sin leads to wickedness and to hearts that become hardened to things of the Spirit. Eventually, the end of this road leads to heartbreak and sorrow.

This pattern is repeated not only in the lives of individual people but by cities, nations, and even the world. The consequences of ignoring the Lord and His prophets are certain and often accompanied by great sorrow and regret. In our day the Lord has warned that wickedness will ultimately lead to "famine, and plague, and earthquake, and the thunder of heaven" until "the inhabitants of the earth be made to feel the wrath, and indignation, and chastening hand of an Almighty God."

Dreams & Visions of Plagues & Pestilence

Spencer, *Visions of Glory*

(p. 128) About this time, a devastating plague swept across the nation. It came in three waves. Each wave was more virulent, killing healthier people, and killing them quicker. It swept across North and South America and around the world, killing billions. But the troops who arrived seemed to be mostly immune to it, though a few of them died as well… the plagues had been man-made, and the troops were inoculated against it, but it took many months before the survivors of the plague realized the true source of it.

(p.131) About this time, the same plague that had devastated so much of the east coast arrived in Utah as it spread across the nation… we found out later that the plague was man-made, and the troops had been inoculated against the pathogen that caused the plague.

(p. 132) When a person contracted the plague, they got many small pox marks on their skin, similar to pimples. These grew in size and quantity until nearly their whole body was covered by them. They grew very sick quickly. The itching and pain was severe. Shortly before death, the pox erupted and oozed. This fluid was extremely contagious. Everyone who touched it got sick… The very young and very old died first. Those who were trying to help others got contaminated by touching the fluid and died next. …The plague ultimately killed more than half of those who were exposed to it… Once symptoms appeared, a person would die about twelve hours later.

Sarah Menet, *There is No Death*

I then saw a man walk into the middle of a crowd of people and drop what seemed like a quart full of liquid. The jar broke and the liquid spread. I understand that people nearby had become infected with a disease from the liquid, and they didn't even know it. A day or two later people became sick and started dying. I saw that this would happen in at least four particular cities: New York, Los Angeles, San Francisco, and Salt Lake City. This disease started with white blisters, some the size of a dime, appearing on the hands, arms and faces of the victims. The blisters quickly developed into white puffy sores. Those with the disease would stumble around and fall over dead.

I also saw other people with a flu-like virus that spread more quickly than the first disease. The victims had blood coming from their nose, mouth, eyes, and ears. These people died even faster of this disease than the ones who had the first sickness. These diseases became widespread across the US with hundreds of thousands infected. Many died within a short time, perhaps 24 hours.

Charles Evans, LDS Church Patriarch, as published in LDS Church publication The Contributor, 1893

Again the light shone, revealing an atmosphere tinged with a leaden hue which was the precursor of an unparalleled plague whose first symptoms were recognized by a purple spot which appeared on the cheek or on the back of the hand and which invariably enlarged until it spread over the entire surface of the body, producing certain death.

The Dream of the Plagues, The Contributor, August 1884, 5:411

On the first page was a picture of a feast in progress, with the long table set upon a beautiful lawn, over which were interspersed with clumps of fine shrubs and towering trees. The landscape presented the appearance of midsummer. The sky, and indeed the whole atmosphere appeared of a peculiar sickly brassy hue, similar to that which may be observed when the sun is wholly eclipsed and the disc is just beginning again to give its light. Throughout the atmosphere small white specks were represented, similar to a scattering fall of minute snowflakes in winter.

About the table a party of richly dressed ladies and gentlemen were seated in the act of partaking of the rich repast with which the table was laden. The minute specks falling from above were dropping into the food apparently unheeded by all, for a sudden destruction had come upon them.

Below this picture was the description: "A camp of the Saints who have gathered together and are living under the daily revelations of God, and thus preserved from the plague." I understood from this that each family was in its tent during the hours of the day that the poison falls, and thus were preserved from breathing the deadly particles.

President John Taylor Wilford Woodruff's Journal, June 15, 1878, "A Vision, Salt Lake City, Night of Dec 16, 1877"

I was then in a dream, immediately in the city of Salt Lake, and wandering around in the streets and in all parts of the city, and on the doors of the houses I found badges of mourning and I could not find a house but was in mourning. I passed my own house and found the same sign there, and I asked the question, "Is that me that is dead?" Someone gave me the answer, "No, you will get through it all."

It seemed strange to me that I saw no person in the streets in all my wandering around the country. I seemed to be in their houses with the sick, but saw no funeral procession, nor anything of the kind, but the city looking still and as though the people were praying. And it seemed that they had controlled the disease, but what the disease was I did not learn; it was not made known to me. I then looked over the country, north, east, south, and west, and the same mourning was in every land and in every place.

Additional Commentary & Resources:

Legionnaires Disease strikes New York

http://www.healthmap.org/site/diseasedaily/article/legionnaires%E2%80%99-strikes-new-york-city-8915

Black Plague in Colorado

http://www.healthmap.org/site/diseasedaily/article/black-death-back-second-plague-death-reported-colorado-81615

Hantavirus found in Mumbai

http://www.healthmap.org/site/diseasedaily/article/hantavirus-reported-mumbai-india-82215

Ebola in West Africa

http://www.psmag.com/health-and-behavior/scariest-virus-ebola-back-worse-ever-87348

Basic Preparedness Tips for Plague:

http://www.theorganicprepper.ca/prepping-for-an-ebola-lockdown-no-one-goes-out-no-one-comes-in-08052014

http://www.areyouprepared.com/How-to-prepare-for-Plagues-s/773.htm

http://www.healthypreparedness.blogspot.com/p/food-storage-remedies.html

http://thepatriotnurse.com/pages/survival-supply-stash

Additional Sources & Notes

Second Civil War

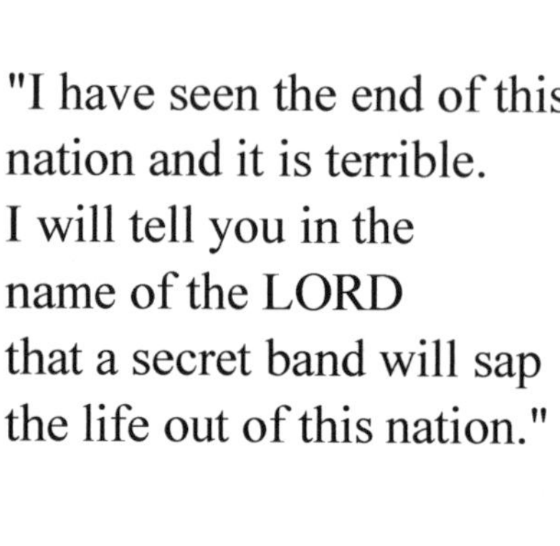

"I have seen the end of this
nation and it is terrible.
I will tell you in the
name of the LORD
that a secret band will sap
the life out of this nation."

Elder Moses Thatcher,
June 16, 1882

Scriptures

D&C 45: 68-69

68 And it shall come to pass among the wicked, that every man that will not take his sword against his neighbor must needs flee unto Zion for safety.

69 And there shall be gathered unto it out of every nation under heaven; and it shall be the only people that shall not be at war one with another.

1Nephi 22:13-14

13 And the blood of that great and abominable church, which is the whore of all the earth, shall turn upon their own heads; for they shall war among themselves, and the sword of their own hands shall fall upon their own heads, and they shall be drunken with their own blood.

14 And every nation which shall war against thee, O house of Israel, shall be turned one against another, and they shall fall into the pit which they digged to ensnare the people of the Lord. And all that fight against Zion shall be destroyed, and that great whore, who hath perverted the right ways of the Lord, yea, that great and abominable church, shall tumble to the dust and great shall be the fall of it.

D&C 87:5-8

5 And it shall come to pass also that the remnants who are left of the land will marshal themselves, and shall become exceedingly angry, and shall vex the Gentiles with a sore vexation.

6 And thus, with the sword and by bloodshed the inhabitants of the earth shall mourn; and with famine, and plague, and earthquake, and the thunder of heaven, and the fierce and vivid lightning also, shall the inhabitants of the earth be made to feel the wrath, and indignation and chastening hand of an Almighty God, until the consumption decreed hath made a full end of all nations.

7 Wherefore, stand ye in holy places, and be not moved, until the day of the Lord come; for behold, it cometh quickly, saith the Lord. Amen.

Alma 50: 21

21 And we see that these promises have been verified to the people of Nephi; for it has been their quarrelings and their contentions, yea, their murderings, and their plunderings, their idolatry, their whoredoms, and their abominations, which were among themselves, which brought upon them their wars and their destructions.

Quotes About Another Civil War by Church Leaders

***Civil War Starts in Chicago*, A. Milton Musser**

"My brother, Noah Packard, says that he heard the Prophet Joseph say that the next great (U.S. civil) war after the war of the rebellion (the Civil War of the 1860s between the North and the South) would commence in a little town now called Chicago but at that time it would have grown to be a very large city. And another brother told me that the Prophet said that the cause of the next great trouble of the United States would be the depreciation of the currency of the United States. I believe I have given you all the facts in as short and concise manner as possible."

A. Milton Musser papers, LDS Church Archives, letter from Nephi Packard to A. Milton Musser, July 24, 1896.

***Civil War more bloody than the first one,* David Whitmer**

Question: When will the temple be built in Independence?
Answer: Right after the great tribulation is over.
Question: What do you mean by that?
Answer: A civil war more bloody and cruel than the rebellion. It will be the smashing up of this nation, about which time the second great work has to be done, a work like Joseph did and the translation of the sealed plates and peace all over.

Interview by Dr. Poulson with David Whitmer, Deseret News, Friday, August 16, 1878

***The whole republic will be in general commotion and warfare*, Elder Orson Pratt**

That war, we must remember, was only one solitary judgment, compared with what will come, and that, too, in the near future. It has been revealed that the time will come in the history of our nation, that one State will rise against another, one city against another, even every man's hand shall be against his neighbor, until the whole Republic will be in general commotion and warfare. How and when this will take place, the Lord, in his wisdom, has not told us; but it is sufficient for us to say, that he has told us of the facts that such and such will be the case.

For aught we know, the fulfillment of this prophecy may grow out of politics. If the people are very nearly equally divided in politics, this feeling may run so high, in years to come, as to be the direct cause of war. And if this should be the case, it would very naturally spread to every neighborhood in the Union. One class of political opponents would rise up against the other class in the same city and country, and thus would arise a war of mobocracy.

Discourse by Elder Orson Pratt, delivered in the Eighteenth Ward Meetinghouse, Salt Lake City, Sunday Afternoon, Feb. 25, 1877.

***More ruin, more devastation than ever they have seen before*, President John Taylor**.

Need we be surprised that they should trample underfoot the Constitution of the United States? No; Joseph Smith told us that they would do it. Many around me here knew long ago that they would do this thing and further knew that the last people that should be found to rally around that sacred instrument and save it from the grasp of unrighteous men would be the Elders of Israel!

...Were we surprised when the last terrible war took place here in the United States? No; good Latter-day Saints were not, for they had been told about it. Joseph Smith had told them where it would start, that it should be a terrible time of bloodshed and that it should start in South Carolina. But I tell you today the end is not yet. You will see worse things than that, for God will lay his hand upon this nation, and they will feel it more terribly than ever they have done before; there will be more bloodshed, more ruin, more devastation than ever they have seen before.

Discourse by President John Taylor, delivered at General Conference, Salt Lake City, October 6, 1879.

***Civil War*, President Brigham Young**

When the testimony of the Elders ceases to be given, and the Lord says to them, "Come home; I will now preach my own sermons to the nations of the earth," all you now know can scarcely be called a preface to the sermon that will be preached with fire and sword, tempests, earthquakes, hail, rain, thunders and lightnings, and fearful destruction. What matters the destruction of a few railway cars? You will hear of magnificent cities, now idolized by the people, sinking in the earth, entombing the inhabitants. The sea will heave itself beyond its bounds, engulfing mighty cities. Famine will spread over the nations, and nation will rise up against nation, kingdom against kingdom, and states against states, in our own country and in foreign lands; and they will destroy each other, caring not for the blood and lives of their neighbors, of their families, or for their own lives. They will be like the Jaredites who preceded the Nephites upon this continent, and will destroy each other to the last man, through the anger that the Devil will place in their hearts, because they have rejected the words of life and are given over to Satan to do whatever he listeth to do with them. You may think that the little you hear of now is grievous; yet the faithful of God's people will see days that will cause them to close their eyes because of the sorrow that will come upon the wicked nations. The hearts of the faithful will be filled with pain and anguish for them.

Remarks by President Brigham Young, made in the Bowery, Salt Lake City, July 15, 1860.

***Neighborhood against neighborhood*, Elder Orson Pratt.**

What then will be the condition of the people when the great and dreadful war will come? It will be very different from the war between the North and South. It will be neighborhood against neighborhood, city against city, town against town, state against state, and they will go forth destroying and being destroyed. Manufacturing will almost cease, great cities will be left desolate. The time will come when the great city of New York will be left without inhabitants..."

Elder Orson Pratt, Journal of Discourses 20:150

***Can America escape destruction*? Wilford Woodruff**

When I contemplate the condition of our nation, and see that wickedness and abominations are increasing, so much so that the whole heavens groan and weep over the abominations of this nation and the nations of the earth, I ask myself the question, can the American nation escape? The answer comes, No; its destruction, as well as the destruction of the world, is sure; just as sure as the Lord cut off and destroyed the two great nations that once inhabited this continent of North and South America because of their sin, so will he them destroy, and sooner or later they will reap the fruits of their own wicked acts, and be numbered among the past. I cannot help it; I would to God they would repent, that their eyes might be opened to see their condition; but the devil has power over them; he rules the children of men, he holds Babylon in his own hand, and leads the people withersoever he will. There are changes awaiting us, they are even nigh at our very doors, and I know it by the revelations of Jesus Christ; I know it by the visions of heaven, I know it by the administrations of angels, and I know it by the inspiration of heaven, that is given to all men who seek the Lord; and the hand of God will not stay these things. We have no time to lose.

Wilford Woodruff, Journal of Discourses, Vol. 21:301

***No more stores*, Spencer W. Kimball.**

The little gardens and a few trees are very valuable. I remember when the sisters used to say, `well, but we could buy it at the store a lot cheaper than we could put it up.' But that isn't quite the answer, is it, Sister Spafford? Because there will become a time when there isn't a store.

(Spencer W. Kimball, General Conference, April 1974)

***Family against Family* Joseph Smith, Address in Illinois, June 2, 1839**

I saw men hunting the lives of their own sons, and brother murdering brother, women killing their own daughters, and daughters seeking the lives of their mothers. I saw armies arrayed against armies. I saw blood, desolation, fires. The son of man has said that the mother shall be against the daughter, and the daughter against the mother. These things are at our doors. They will follow the Saints of God from city to city. Satan will rage, and the spirit of the devil is now enraged. I know not how soon these things will take place; but with a view of them, shall I cry peace? No; I will lift up my voice and testify of them. How long you will have good crops, and the famine be kept off, I do not know; when the fig tree leaves, know then that the summer is nigh at hand.

Joseph Smith, The Prophet Joseph Smith :161

And now I am prepared to say by the authority of Jesus Christ, that not many years shall pass away before the United States shall present such a scene of bloodshed as has not a parallel in the history of our nation; pestilence, hail, famine, and earthquake will sweep the wicked of this generation from off the face of the land, to open and prepare the way for the return of the lost tribes of Israel from the north country. Joseph Smith

Duane Crowther, Duane S. (2013-08-07). Prophecy, Key to the Future

Saints prevented from holding meetings, Heber C. Kimball,.*Life of Heber C. Kimball, p. 452*

"...this government would dissolve pretty much all the laws passed by our legislature, and that the time would come when the government would stop the Saints from holding meetings. When this was done the Lord would pour out His judgments."

Dreams & Visions of Civil War

Excerpts from ***John Taylor's*** *second vision (Horseshoe Vision):*
http://www.josephsmithforum.org/doc/the-horseshoe-prophecy-john-taylor/

He said, "I saw Salt Lake City become a great and beautiful city, cement sidewalks and streets, wealthy people, beautiful homes, extending almost to the top of the mountain south of the state prison. People became indifferent. War began among the people. I saw blood running down the gutters of Salt Lake City as if it were water. People fighting so much among themselves until it became so serious that the entire church records were taken across the Colorado River.

... Not only Salt Lake City, but other adjoining cities will be destroyed, and in the East, in Jackson county, Missouri, civilization will become entirely extinct. All means of transportation such as railroads and highways will be destroyed. The only means of travel will be on foot. And manufacturing of all kinds will be destroyed. Be sure when you see these things come that you will have buttons, needles, and things to work with in order to make clothing, thread and cloth as much as possible because all tools and things to work with will be destroyed such as machinery.

It will become such a destructive war that the sufferings and drivings of the people from Nauvoo will only be as a drip in the bucket compared with the sufferings that will take place at that time. Until half the people will not follow the church leaders at that time and half the others will die or turn away because of the sufferings that they will have to go through.
But the Lord will bless those who stay with the authorities and they shall not be destroyed.

...The vision was so terrible that he asked the Lord to close it up. But he said that those who would keep the commandments and adhere to the authorities of the church would survive; and the Lord would protect them as he did the people of Israel.

Elder ***Moses Thatcher*** *Journal of Discourses Vol. 26:36*

Would to God we had statesmen with eyes clear enough to see!.... The day is not far distant, unless the Democratic and Republican parties open their eyes to the situation, when desolation and war will be in this government.

I will say when this nation, having sown to the wind, reaps the whirlwind; when brother takes up sword against brother; when father contends against son, and son against father; ***when he who will not take up his sword against his neighbor must needs flee to Zion for safety—then I would say to my friends come to Utah; for the judgments of God, commencing at the house of the Lord, will have passed away, and Utah, undisturbed, will be the most delightful place in all the Union. When war and desolation and bloodshed, and the ripping up of society come upon the nation, I have said to such, "Come to Utah and we will divide our morsel of food with you, we will divide our clothing with you, and we will offer you***

protection." I will tell you, my brethren and sisters, the day will come, and it is not far distant, when he who will not take up his sword against his neighbor, will have to flee to Zion for safety; and it is presupposed in this prediction that Zion will have power to give them protection. We are not going to do it outside of the government, either; we are going to do it inside the government. There is no power in this land to turn this people against the government of the United States. They will maintain the Constitution of this country inviolate, and although it may have been torn to shreds they will tie it together again, and maintain every principle of it, holding it up to the downtrodden of every nation, kindred, tongue and people, and they will do it, too, under the Stars and Stripes. They will stand with their feet firmly upon the backbone of the American continent and maintain the principles which cost their fathers so much, and those principles cannot be taken away by men who violate their oath of office, and betray their trust.

I tell you that there are boys growing up in these mountains who have the principles of human liberty grounded deep in their hearts, and they will maintain them, not only for themselves, but for others. God speed the day I say—if the nation pursues its downward course and tears up these fundamental principles of government which have made them strong—when the Constitution may be rescued and all men and women shall be free again."

George Washington *saw a civil war and then an invasion by foreign troops.*

..."And this time the dark shadowy angel turned his face southward. From Africa I saw an ill-omened spectre approach our land. It flitted slowly and heavily over every town and city of the latter. The inhabitants presently <u>set themselves in battle array against each other</u>. As I continued looking, I saw a bright angel on whose brow rested a crown of light on which was traced the word 'Union.' He was bearing the American flag. He placed the flag between the divided nation and said, 'Remember, ye are brethren.'

(This vision was received by George Washington in the winter of 1777. Washington told his vision to Anthony Sherman, who recounted it to Wesley Bradshaw, publisher of the National Stripes.)

LDS Bishop & Patriarch Charles D. Evans, 1894

Confidence is lost. Wealth is arrayed against labor, labor against wealth....together with the policy of many wealthy ones, has produced distress and do presage further sorrow. Mad with rage men and women rushed upon each other. Blood flowed down the streets of cities like water.

Sols Caurdisto (excerpt from what is sometimes called The Cardston Temple Prophecy), 1923

I saw the international world war automatically break down, and national revolution occur in every country and complete the work of chaos and desolation. ...I saw the international boundary line disappear (Cananda/US) and these two governments broke up and dissolved into chaos. I saw race rioting upon the American continent on a vast scale.

Commentary

Signs That 'The Elites' Are Feverishly Preparing For Something Big

Submitted by Michael Snyder via The End of The American Dream blog, April 2015

What in the world are the elite up to? In recent days, we have learned that the New York Fed is moving a lot of operations to Chicago because of concerns about what a "natural disaster" could do, the federal government is buying 62 million rounds of ammunition commonly used in AR-15 semi-automatic rifles for "training" purposes, and NORAD is moving back into Cheyenne Mountain because it is "EMP-hardened". In addition, government authorities have scheduled a whole host of unusual "training exercises" all over the nation. **So are the elite doing all of this in order to prepare for something really BIG, or should we just chalk up all of this strange activity to rampant government paranoia?**

First, let's talk about what the New York Fed has been doing. What kind of natural disaster would be bad enough to completely shut down the operations of the New York Federal Reserve Bank? It would have to be something very unusual, and apparently the New York Fed is very concerned that such an event could happen. According to Reuters, the New York Fed has been transferring personnel to Chicago and building up its satellite office there just in case a "natural disaster" makes it impossible for normal operations to continue in New York...

The New York branch of the U.S. Federal Reserve, wary that a natural disaster or other eventuality could shut down its market operations as it approaches an interest rate hike, has added staff and bulked up its satellite office in Chicago.

Some market technicians have transferred from New York and others were hired at the office housed in the Chicago Fed, according to several people familiar with the build-out that began about two years ago, after Hurricane Sandy struck Manhattan.

Officials believe the Chicago staffers can now handle all of the market operations that are done daily out of the New York Fed, which is the U.S. central bank's main conduit to Wall Street.

This seems very odd.

In all of U.S. history, there has never been a natural disaster in New York City that would have been bad enough to totally shut down the operations of the New York Fed for an extended period of time.

So why are they so concerned? Well, I can think of one event that could cause such a disruption... An east coast tsunami.

But other than that, it is hard to imagine a natural disaster which could shut down the New York Fed for an extended period of time.

Another very odd thing that we learned about this week is an absolutely massive purchase by the government of ammunition that is commonly used in AR-15 semi-automatic rifles. The following comes from an article by Paul Joseph Watson…

The Department of Homeland Security is set to purchase over 62 million rounds of ammo typically used in AR-15 semi-automatic rifles, just weeks after the ATF was forced to back down on a ban on M855 bullets.

A posting on FedBizOpps.gov this week reveals that the DHS is looking to contract with a company to provide 12.6 million rounds of .223 Remington ammunition per year for a period of five years – totaling 62.5 million bullets.

The solicitation explains that the purchase is intended, "to achieve price savings over the current .223 Rem duty ammunition." The bullets will be used by U.S. Customs and Border Protection agents nationwide for "training" purposes.

Why in the world would U.S. Customs and Border Protection agents nationwide need such a massive amount of ammunition for "training" purposes?

That seems very odd.

Something else that seems very strange is the fact that NORAD (North American Aerospace Defense Command) **is moving back into Cheyenne Mountain after all these years…**

It shut down nearly ten years ago as the threat from Russia seemed to subside, but this week the Pentagon announced that Cheyenne Mountain will once again be home to the most advanced tracking and communications equipment in the United States military.

The shift to the Cheyenne Mountain base in Colorado is designed to safeguard the command's sensitive sensors and servers from a potential electromagnetic pulse (EMP) attack, military officers said.

The Pentagon last week announced a $700 million contract with Raytheon Corporation to oversee the work for North American Aerospace Command (NORAD) and US Northern Command.

Admiral William Gortney, head of NORAD and Northern Command, said that 'because of the very nature of the way that Cheyenne Mountain's built, it's EMP-hardened.'

So the U.S. military is concerned about an EMP attack all of a sudden?

Have they been reading The Economic Collapse Blog?

Spending 700 million dollars to move back inside a mountain just because it is "EMP-hardened" is a pretty big deal.

Do they know something that we don't?

On top of everything else, we have been seeing lots of strange "training exercises" being scheduled all over the nation recently.

For example, the following is from a news story about one being held in Iowa...

This week you may notice extra emergency vehicles and public safety officers running around in tactical gear, Hazmat suits, and bomb suits. It's a part of a statewide drill Des Moines is hosting Tuesday and Wednesday to prepare emergency personnel for dealing with weapons of mass destruction.

Brian O'Keefe, with the Des Moines Fire Department, said emergency officials in Iowa need to be prepared for anything.

"You know we're number one seed producer with corn and soy, chicken embryo development, middle of the country heartland. So I'm sure all states access it. But we're a target like any other large community," said O'Keefe.

And here is an excerpt from a news story about an exercise known as "Northern Exposure" that is being held in Michigan...

The National Guard event is called Northern Exposure, which is taking place across Michigan during the month of June, he said. According to the Michigan National Guard website, Northern Exposure is "a major exercise in Michigan where the military provides defense support to civilian authorities."

In addition, the U.S. military will be conducting some "unusual" training activity out in Arizona and California...

If you see some unusual helicopters overhead in the next couple of days, there's nothing to worry about.

The I Marine Expeditionary Force G-7 will be conducting a Realistic Military Training this week, using the Prescott Municipal Airfield as a helicopter refueling point in order to facilitate a Long Range Raid at Camp Navajo, Arizona.

This Certification Exercise (CERTEX) is directed to be conducted from April 8-21, 2015 at various training locations throughout California and Arizona. The training at Prescott will take place on April 15, 16.

All of this is in addition to the exercise that people have really been buzzing about. It is called "Jade Helm", and in this particular "unconventional warfare exercise", the states of Texas and Utah will be designated as "hostile territory"...

“Jade Helm is a challenging eight-week joint military and Interagency (IA) Unconventional Warfare (UW) exercise conducted throughout Texas, New Mexico, Arizona, California, Nevada, Utah and Colorado,” according to an unclassified military document announcing the training drill, which runs from July 15 through September 15.

Multiple branches of the US military, including Green Berets, Navy Seals, and the 82nd Airborne Division, will participate in the 8-week long exercise, which may result in “increased aircraft in the area at night.”

Troops will be tasked with honing advanced skills in “large areas of undeveloped land with low population densities,” and will work alongside “civilians to gain their trust and an understanding of the issues.”

The exercise, in which some participants will be “wearing civilian clothes and driving civilian vehicles,” lists Texas and Utah as “hostile” territory.

Should we be alarmed by these exercises? Some people sure think so.

Another thing that has people scratching their heads are the weird closures of Wal-Mart stores all over the nation for supposed “plumbing problems”...

Not just one, but five Walmart stores across the U.S. are closing their doors due to plumbing problems that, in some cases, will take four to six months to repair.

Those closing include locations in Livingston and Midland, Texas; Tulsa, Oklahoma; and near Los Angeles.

For the Brandon Walmart, I talked to Hillsborough County and Walmart to get answers about why these plumbing repairs will take so long and whether the issues are connected, but local customers are already skeptical.

“Why is it just plumbing problems? It’s gonna take them six months to fix up the store?” asked customer John Mambrl.

Yes, is it really going to take them six months to fix the toilets?

Either someone at Wal-Mart is extremely incompetent, or there is something fishy going on here.

In the end, perhaps there is nothing to any of this.

Perhaps all of these examples are just unrelated coincidences. But then again, perhaps not.

The whole article can be found at: **http://tinyurl.com/m727ma8**

Fox News - America's Coming Civil War **http://tinyurl.com/na7l4mq**

Additional Sources & Notes

Earthquake

D&C 88:87-91

87 For not many days hence and the earth
shall tremble and reel to and fro as a
drunken man; and the sun shall hide his
face, and shall refuse to give light; and the
moon shall be bathed in blood; and the
stars shall become exceedingly angry, and
shall cast themselves down as a fig that
falleth from off a fig tree.

88 And after your testimony cometh
wrath and indignation upon the people.

89 For after your testimony cometh the
testimony of earthquakes, that shall cause
groanings in the midst of her, and men
shall fall upon the ground and shall not be
able to stand.

90 And also cometh the testimony of the
voice of thunderings, and the voice of
lightnings, and the voice of tempests, and
the voice of the waves of the sea heaving
themselves beyond their bounds.

Scriptures

Revelation 6:12

"And I beheld when he had opened the sixth seal, and, lo, there was a great earthquake, and the sun became black as sackcloth of hair, and the moon became as blood;"

Revelation 6:14-15

14 And the heaven departed as a scroll when it is rolled together; and every mountain and island were moved out of their places.

15 And the kings of the earth, and the great men, and the rich men, and the chief captains, and the mighty men, and every bondman, and every free man, hid themselves in the dens and in the rocks of the mountains;

Doctrine and Covenants 87:6

"And thus, with the sword and by bloodshed the inhabitants of the earth shall mourn; and with famine, and plague, and earthquake and the thunder of heaven, and the fierce and vivid lighting also, shall the inhabitants of the earth be made to feel the wrath, and indignation, and chastening hand of an Almighty God, until the consumption decreed hath made a full end of all nations."

Doctrine and Covenants 45:33

"And there shall be earthquakes also in divers places, and may desolations; yet men will harden their hearts against me, and they will take up the sword, one against another, and they will kill one another."

Leadership Quotes

Joseph Smith, *Teachings of The Prophet Joseph Smith*, p. 17

“And now I am prepared to say by the authority of Jesus Christ, that not many years shall pass away before the United States shall present such a scene of bloodshed as has not a parallel in the history of our nation; pestilence, hail, famine, and earthquake will sweep the wicked of this generation from off the face of the land, to open and prepare the way for the return of the lost tribes of Israel from the north country.”

Ezra Taft Benson, General Conference, Oct. 1980

“Too often we bask in our comfortable complacency and rationalize that the ravages of war, economic disaster, famine and earthquake cannot happen here. Those who believe this are either not acquainted with the revelations of the Lord, or they do not believe them. Those who smugly think these calamities will not happen, that they somehow will be set aside because of the righteousness of the Saints, are deceived and will rue the day they harbored such a delusion.

The Lord has warned and forewarned us against a day of great tribulation and given us counsel, through His servants, on how we can prepare for these difficult times. Have we heeded His counsel?

…I bear witness to that inspired counsel from 1936 to present day that the Saints lay up a year’s supply of food.”

Erastus Snow, September 14, 1873. Journal of Discourses, Vol. 16, No. 27

“Thus we learn, my friends that the warning voice of God will go forth among the nations, and he will warn them by his servants; and by thunder, by lightning, by earthquakes, by great hailstorms and by devouring fire; by the voice of judgment and by the voice of mercy; by the voice of angels and by the voice of his servants the Prophets; he will warn them by gathering out the righteous from among the wicked, and those who will not heed these warnings will be visited with sore judgments until the earth is swept as with the besom of destruction.”

Elder M. Russell Ballard, General Conference, Oct. 1992

"Although the prophecies tell us that these things are to take place, more and more people are expressing great alarm at what appears to be an acceleration of worldwide calamity. As members of the Church, we must not forget the Savior's admonition, "Be not troubled: for all these things must come to pass."

Dreams & Visions of Earthquakes

David Wilkerson, published 1974 www.alamongordo.com

"The United States is going to experience in the future the most tragic earthquakes in its history. One day soon this nation will be reeling under the impact of the biggest news story of modern times. It will be coverage of the biggest most disastrous earthquake in history. It will cause widespread panic and fear, Without a doubt, it will become one of the most completely reported earthquakes ever. Television networks will suspend all programming and carry all day coverage. Another earthquake, possibly in Japan may precede the one that I see coming here. There is not the slightest doubt in my mind about this forthcoming massive earthquake in our continent. I am not at all convinced that this earthquake will take place in California. In fact, I believe it is going to take place where it is least expected. This terrible earthquake may happen in an area that is not known as an earthquake belt. It will be so high on the Richter scale that it will trigger two other major earthquakes."

New Madrid Dreams www.z3news.com

There have been multiple dreams concerning the Madrid fault line. It seems that the country will have an actual divider, separating the east from the west. And that this will trigger more earthquakes in other areas.

#1 **Pastor Shane Warren**, First Assembly of God, West Monroe, LA

"Ladies and gentlemen another tragedy has hit America. Right in the heartland on the new Madrid fault line a major earthquake has just hit. Immediately pictures of devastation began to pop up all over the heartland of America along the new Madrid fault line as earthquakes caused cities to crumble. While I was sitting there, I heard a booming voice behind my ear that said, 'They have divided my land. Now I will divide their land.'

#2 **Pastor John Kilpatrick**, Pensacola, FL May 2008

"It was a very stirring dream. I never had one that real before. When I woke up, it stirred me to the point that I asked my wife to hold me and I am, you know, a grown man. I have never done that ever before with a dream of any kind. But I dreamed of an earthquake that took place and it was shown to me and several stages but I won't go into all of the details of it. The Lord showed me that an earthquake was going to hit in the middle part of the country right where the new Madrid fault line is. It was so real when the Lord showed it to me that I would walk by the television set for several days after that night and in my mind I could not understand why it was not on television. That's how real it was. But the lord was showing me, I believe, that if we continue to fool with Jerusalem and our secretary of state and our President keep putting pressure on Israel to give up land and to give up Jerusalem for peace then I believe that a major earthquake is going to strike America. If we pressure Israel to divide their land then our land will be divided. "

#3 Minister **Sadhu Sundar Selvaraj**

"Suddenly I saw an open vision right before my eyes. I saw a mighty angel with a long, drawn sword in his hand. And he stood before me speaking all of these words. Then he said, 'This is what will happen to the best friend that will betray Israel and divide Jerusalem.' When he spoke those words, I saw this map of the U.S. like in three-dimensional. It appeared right before my eyes beside the angel. And he took the sword and he pierced right into the heart of the U.S. and he cut it into two. He said 'Likewise will this nation be divided as Jerusalem will be divided.' He cut the land into two exactly in the center."

Spencer, Visions of Glory

My flight across North America began in Salt Lake City. There had been a massive earthquake in that area in the fall of the year. The fault that runs along the Wasatch front had moved dramatically, causing a great deal of damage to cities along the front.

I saw that the next spring after the destruction in Utah, there were another devastating series of earthquakes that occurred along the west coast of North and South America. The western coast of CA and Mexico and all the way to the tip of S. America was shaken so badly that much of it broke away from the mainland and formed a series of islands off the coast.

(p 121) Now, back to N. Temple, the earthquake had broken up the streets and where there were cracks in the road, water was shooting into the sky. Water was also gushing from manhole covers, storm drains and cracks in the earth. All this time I was wondering where all the water was coming from. The water was shooting up about six feet into the air. It was all astonishing.

(p. 123) All of this water drained into the Great Salt Lake, moving the salted water in a tidal wave out into the desert northwest of the lake. In some places I-15 was covered and the whole airport was flooded. It was months before military planes could land there.

(p.127) The earthquake had not been centered in downtown SLC but here where the land had dropped away (Draper). Apparently it had been overarching a massive underground lake.

Gayle Smith's Dream (online)

Within 10 days of the economic collapse we have the first earthquake affecting Utah which takes place early in the morning, about 4 or 5 am. When I first saw it I didn't think it was very hard because I saw there wasn't much damage done to my home in Utah County, but it lasts a long time. People will think this is the big one. I saw that this earthquake was much stronger somewhere else like on the west coast area of California but it also affects Nevada. There is a lot of damage done and there is some loss of life though there are a lot of people who survive. The second time my mother showed it to me I realized that it is a very significant earthquake. The second earthquake affecting Utah takes place about 15 days after the first and also takes place in the early morning. This earthquake is like the world has never seen and affects a much larger area than Utah. It's right off the Richter Scale. (All of Utah dams break.)

Sarah Menet, *There is No Death*

Now the smoke became very heavy, dark, and thick. Just as things appeared to be as bad as they could get, the earth began to quake. This occurred during a winter, seemingly the winter that followed the very long one I saw earlier.

The chaos had existed for almost a full year by this time. The earthquakes began in the West, around Idaho and Wyoming and then quickly spread in every direction. I saw a huge earthquake hit Utah and then California.

John H. Koyle, excerpt from "The Dream Mine"

I saw that during the time of great tribulation there would be a massive earthquake out in the Pacific Ocean that would bring giant tidal waves along our Pacific Coast. This would in turn bring destructive quakes along the San Andreas Fault and wreck great destruction in San Francisco and Oakland. If inspired, prophetic warnings were heeded in time, many of our people would escape these disasters.

Commentary

Bruce R. McConkie talks about pole shift, *The Millennial Messiah, p. 412*

Knowing that the earth is to reel to and fro, knowing that the mighty deep shall return to its place in the north, knowing that the continents and islands shall join again, what about the stars and their fall from heaven? Our answer is that it will seem to men on earth as though the stars -- those great suns in the sidereal heavens around which other planets revolve -- are falling because the earth reels. The great fixed stars will continue in their assigned orbits and spheres. The sun also will continue to give light, but it will appear to men to be darkened; and the moon will remain as she has been since the creation, but it will seem to mortal eyes as though she is bathed in blood.

Many scriptures speak of **earthquakes as one of the signs of the times**. We have noted this, somewhat repetitiously, as it has been associated with other matters. The clear inference is that for some reason as yet unknown to man, earthquakes have been and are destined to increase both in number and intensity in the last days. Certainly they shall increase in terror and destructive power simply because there are more people and more man-made structures on earth than at any previous time. And clearly the crowning earthquake -- the earthquake of earthquakes -- is the one that shall occur as the earth reels to and fro and the stars seem to fall from their places in the sidereal heavens.

As we consider the reeling of the earth to and fro and the total realignment of its land masses incident to the Second Coming, and as we consider the burning of the vineyard by fire to destroy the wicked, as they were once destroyed by water in the days of Noah, we are faced with a somewhat difficult problem relative to the rainbow. We say difficult because not all things relative to it have been revealed, and we have only a few slivers of divine truth upon which to build our house of understanding. In the eternal sense nothing is difficult once the whole matter has been revealed to minds prepared and qualified to receive and understand. Let us lay a foundation for the place the rainbow is destined to play in the Second Coming by recounting the circumstances under which it apparently came into being.

Seed time and harvest, in the sense of one season following another, exist because the axis of the earth is tilted twenty-three and a half degrees from the upright. This is the reason we have summer and winter, spring and fall. The first reference in the scriptures to **seasons** as we know them is in connection with the flood of Noah. There is a presumption that prior to the flood there were no **seasons** because the **axis of the earth was upright**, and a similar presumption that when **the Millennium comes and the earth returns to its original paradisiacal state, once again the seasons as we know them will cease** and that seed time and harvest will go on concurrently at all times. The whole earth at all times will be a garden as it was in the days of Eden.

Whatever the case may be with reference to these things, something apparently happened with reference to the rainbow in Noah's day, and something is certainly going to happen with reference to it in connection with the Lord's return. **We are left to speculate relative to some of these matters**, which is not all bad as long as any expressed views are clearly identified for what they are. In fact, in our present state of spiritual enlightenment the Lord deliberately leaves us to ponder and wonder about many things connected with his coming; in this way our hearts are centered upon him so that we will qualify in due course to receive absolute and clear revelation on many things.

Additional Sources & Notes

Secret Combinations

Concerning the United States, the Lord revealed to his prophets that its greatest threat would be a vast, worldwide "secret combination" which would not only threaten the United States but also seek to "overthrow the freedom of all lands, nations, and countries."

Ezra Taft Benson, Oct. 1961

Scriptures

2 NEPHI 26:14, 22

14 But behold, I prophesy unto you **concerning the last days**; concerning the days when the Lord God shall bring these things forth unto the children of men.

22 And there are also secret combinations, even as in times of old, according to the combinations of the devil, for he is the founder of all these things; yea, the founder of murder, and works of darkness; yea, and he leadeth them by the neck with a flaxen cord, until he bindeth them with his strong cords forever.

MORMON 8:26-27

26 And no one need say they shall not come, for they surely shall, for the Lord hath spoken it; for out of the earth shall they come, by the hand of the Lord, and none can stay it; and it shall come in a day when it shall be said that miracles are done away; and it shall come even as if one should speak from the dead.

27 And it shall come in a day when the blood of saints shall cry unto the Lord, because of secret combinations and the works of darkness.

MOSES 5:31

31 And Cain said: Truly I am Mahan, the master of this great secret, that I may murder and get gain. Wherefore Cain was called Master Mahan, and he gloried in his wickedness.

D&C 63: 33-34,

33 I have sworn in my wrath, and decreed wars upon the face of the earth, and the wicked shall slay the wicked, and fear shall come upon every man;

34 And the saints also shall hardly escape; nevertheless, I, the Lord, am with them, and will come down in heaven from the presence of my Father and consume the wicked with unquenchable fire.

D&C 45: 31

And there shall be men standing in that generation, that shall not pass until they shall see an overflowing scourge; for a desolating sickness shall cover the land.

2 Nephi 10:11-16

11 And this land shall be a land of liberty unto the Gentiles, and there shall be no kings upon the land, who shall raise up unto the Gentiles.

12 And I will fortify this land against all other nations.

13 And he that fighteth against Zion shall perish, saith God.

14 For he that raiseth up a king against me shall perish, for I, the Lord, the king of heaven, will be their king, and I will be a light unto them forever, that hear my words.

15 Wherefore, for this cause, that my covenants may be fulfilled which I have made unto the children of men, that I will do unto them while they are in the flesh, I must needs destroy the secret works of darkness, and of murders, and of abominations.

16 Wherefore, he that fighteth against Zion, both Jew and Gentile, both bond and free, both male and female, shall perish; for they are they who are the whore of all the earth; for they who are not for me are against me, saith our God.

Leadership Quotes

Gordon B Hinckley, General Conference, October 2001.

We of this Church know something of such (terrorist organizations) groups. The Book of Mormon speaks of the Gadianton robbers, a vicious, oath-bound, and secret organization bent on evil and destruction. In their day they did all in their power, by whatever means available, to bring down the Church, to woo the people with sophistry, and to take control of the society. We see the same thing in the present situation.

Hinckley, Ensign Aug 2005

The Book of Mormon narrative is a chronicle of nations long since gone. But in its descriptions of the problems of today's society, it is as current as the morning newspaper and much more definitive, inspired, and inspiring concerning the solutions of those problems.

I know of no other writing which sets forth with such clarity the tragic consequences to societies that follow courses contrary to the commandments of God. Its pages trace the stories of two distinct civilizations that flourished on the Western Hemisphere. Each began as a small nation, its people walking in the fear of the Lord. But with prosperity came growing evils. The people succumbed to the wiles of ambitious and scheming leaders who oppressed them with burdensome taxes, who lulled them with hollow promises, who countenanced and even encouraged loose and lascivious living. These evil schemers led the people into terrible wars that resulted in the death of millions and the final and total extinction of two great civilizations in two different eras.

Yes, there is a conspiracy of evil. The source of it all is Satan and his hosts. He has a great power over men to 'lead them captive at his will, even as many as would not hearken' to the voice of the Lord. His evil influence may be manifest through governments; through false educational, political, economic, religious, and social philosophies; through secret societies and organizations; and through myriads of other forms. His power and influence are so great that, if possible, he would deceive the very elect. As the second coming of the Lord approaches, Satan's work will intensify through numerous insidious deceptions." CR

Presiding Bishop Charles W. Nibley, General Conference, Oct 1923

Brethren and sisters, let me say in closing that we have it of record, that the prophet Joseph Smith said the time would come when, through secret organizations taking the law into their own hands, not being governed by law or by due process of law, but becoming a law unto themselves, when, by those disintegrating activities, the Constitution of the United States would be so torn and rent asunder, and life and property and peace and security would he held of so little value, that the Constitution would, as it were, hang by a thread. But he never said, so far as I have heard, that that thread would be cut. I believe, with Elder Richards, that this Constitution will be preserved, but it will be preserved very largely in consequence of what the Lord has revealed and what this people, through listening to the Lord and being obedient, will help to bring about, to stabilize and give permanency and effect to the Constitution itself. That also is our mission. That also is what we are here for. I glory in it. I praise God with all my heart and soul that I am a member of it.

Ezra Taft Benson, General Conference, Oct 1988

I testify that wickedness is rapidly expanding in every segment of our society. It is more highly organized, more cleverly disguised, and more powerfully promoted than ever before. Secret combinations lusting for power, gain, and glory are flourishing. A secret combination that seeks to overthrow the freedom of all lands, nations, and countries is increasing its evil influence and control over America and the entire world.

Ezra Taft Benson, General Conference, April 1989

Pride results in secret combinations which are built up to get power, gain, and glory of the world. This fruit of the sin of pride, namely secret combinations, brought down both the Jaredite and the Nephite civilizations and has been and will yet be the cause of the fall of many nations.

Bruce R McConkie, General Conference, Apr 1979

Bands of Gadianton robbers will infest every nation, immorality and murder and crime will increase, and it will seem as though every man's hand is against his brother.

Ezra Taft Benson, General Conference, Oct 1980

Too often we bask in our comfortable complacency and rationalize that the ravages of war, economic disaster, famine, and earthquake cannot happen here. Those who believe this are either not acquainted with the revelations of the Lord, or they do not believe them. Those who smugly think these calamities will not happen, that they somehow will be set aside because of the righteousness of the Saints, are deceived and will rue the day they harbored such a delusion. The Lord has warned and forewarned us against a day of great tribulation and given us counsel, through His servants, on how we can be prepared for these difficult times. Have we heeded His counsel?...The revelation to produce and store food may be as essential to our temporal welfare today as boarding the ark was to the people in the days of Noah."

Ezra Taft Benson. General Conference, Oct 1961

In the prophecies there is no promise except to the obedient. To a modern prophet the Lord said: "Therefore, what I say unto one, I say unto all: Watch, for the adversary spreadeth his dominions, and darkness reigneth; And the anger of God kindleth against the inhabitants of the earth."
"…I give unto you directions how you may act before me, that it may turn to you for your salvation. I, the Lord, am bound when ye do what I say; but when ye do not what I say, ye have no promise." (D&C 82:5-6, 9-10.)
May God give us the wisdom to recognize the threat to our freedom and the strength to meet this danger courageously.

Heber C Kimball *Life of Heber C. Kimball*, pp 452-453 (JN: found this online, didn't see book myself)

This government would dissolve pretty much all the laws passed by our legislature, and that the time would come when the government would stop the Saints from holding meetings. When this was done the Lord would pour out His judgments.

Gordon B. Hinckley, First Presidency Message, Ensign, Aug 2005

The Book of Mormon narrative is a chronicle of nations long since gone. But in its descriptions of the problems of today's society, it is as current as the morning newspaper and much more definitive, inspired, and inspiring concerning the solutions of those problems.

I know of no other writing which sets forth with such clarity the tragic consequences to societies that follow courses contrary to the commandments of God. Its pages trace the stories of two distinct civilizations that flourished on the Western Hemisphere. Each began as a small nation, its people walking in the fear of the Lord. But with prosperity came growing evils. The people succumbed to the wiles of ambitious and scheming leaders who oppressed them with burdensome taxes, who lulled them with hollow promises, who countenanced and even encouraged loose and lascivious living. These evil schemers led the people into terrible wars that resulted in the death of millions and the final and total extinction of two great civilizations in two different eras.

Ezra Taft Benson, General Conference, Oct 1961

Concerning the United States, the Lord revealed to his prophets that its greatest threat would be a vast, worldwide "secret combination" which would not only threaten the United States but also seek to "overthrow the freedom of all lands, nations, and countries.

Ezra Taft Benson, General Conference, Oct 1961

No true Latter-day Saint and no true American can be a socialist or a communist or support programs leading in that direction. These evil philosophies are incompatible with Mormonism, the true gospel of Jesus Christ.

John A. Widtsoe, General Conference, April 1944

The Gadianton Robbers from the Book of Mormon are loose among us. The King-men and women, are running our government. And, worst of all, we are blindly electing them or appointing them so they can continue to destroy the things we cherish most."

Gordon B. Hinckley, Ensign Magazine, June 1988

The people succumbed to the wiles of ambitious and scheming leaders who oppressed them with burdensome taxes, who lulled them with hollow promises, who countenanced and even encouraged loose and lascivious living, who led them into terrible wars that resulted in the death of millions and the final extinction of two great civilizations in two different eras.

Dreams & Visions

Patriarch Charles Evans Vision Excerpt

Thereupon addressing me, he said, "Son, I perceive thou hast grave anxieties over the perilous state of thy country, that thy soul has felt deep sorrow for its future. I have therefore come to thy relief and to tell thee of the causes that have led to this peril. Hear me attentively. Seventy-one years ago, after an awful apostasy of centuries, in which all nations were shrouded in spiritual darkness, when angels had withdrawn themselves, the voice of prophets hushed, and the light of Urim and Thummim shone not, and the vision of the seers was closed, while heaven itself shed not a ray of gladness to lighten a dark world, when Babel ruled and Satan laughed, and church and priesthood had taken their upward flight, and the voice of nations, possessing the books of the Jewish prophets, had ruled against vision and against Urim, against the further visits of angels, and against the doctrine of a church of apostles and prophets, thou knowest that then appeared a mighty angel with the solemn announcement of the hour of judgment, the burden of whose instructions pointed to dire calamities upon the present generation. This, therefore, is the cause of what thou seest and the end of the wicked hasteneth."

My vision now became extended in a marvelous manner, and the import of the past labors of the Elders was made plain to me. I saw multitudes fleeing to the place of safety in our mountain heights. The church was established in the wilderness. Simultaneously the nation had reached an unparalled prosperity, wealth unbounded, new territory was acquired, commerce extended, finance strengthened, confidence was maintained, and peoples abroad pointed to her as the model nation, the ideal of the past realized and perfected, the embodiment of the liberty sung by poets, and sought for by sages.

"But," continued the messenger, "Thou beholdest a change. Confidence is lost. Wealth is arrayed against labor, labor against wealth, yet the land abounds with plenty for food and raiment, and silver and gold are in abundance. Thou seest also that letters written by a Jew have wrought great confusion in the finances of the nation which, together with the policy of many wealthy ones, has produced distress and do presage further sorrow."

Factions now sprang up as if by magic; capital had entrenched itself against labor throughout the land; labor was organized against capital. The voice of the wise sought to tranquilize these two powerful factors in vain. Excited multitudes ran wildly about; strikes increased; lawlessness sought the place of regular government. At this juncture I saw a banner floating in air whereon was written the words Bankruptcy, Famine, Floods, Fire, Cyclones, Blood, Plague. Mad with rage men and women rushed upon each other. Blood flowed down the streets of cities like water. The demon of bloody hate had enthroned itself on the citadel of reason; the thirst for blood was intenser than that of the parched tongue for water. Thousands of bodies lay untombed in the streets. Men and women fell dead from the terror inspired from fear. Rest was but the precursor of the bloody work of the morrow. All around lay the mournfulness of a past in ruins. Monuments erected to perpetuate the names of the noble and brave were ruthlessly destroyed by combustibles. A voice now sounded aloud these words, "Yet once again I shake not the earth only, but also heaven. And this word yet once again signifies the removing of things that are shaken, as of things that are made; that those things that cannot be shaken may remain."

Gayle Smith, personal dream, 1993

My mother then started showing me a scenario of events that will take place beginning with a worldwide economic collapse that would take place in the month of October…

I was told it will actually begin in the US. The reason it happens is to bring down America. I don't think they want to destroy America, they just want to bring it under their control. My mother said I would hear rumors and they will get louder and the collapse will happen quickly. We will wake up one morning and it will have happened…

After the economy collapses I saw marauding bands or gangs running around. People just go crazy and start rioting. looting and killing because they're angry. Everything they know of value on this earth is being taken away from them within a few short days. They're angry at first and then they go crazy because they're hungry. In a very short time there will be a famine like we've never seen before.

I believe for the most part this famine is brought upon us. It's premeditated and planned out. No one works. No trucks bring food deliveries. Famine is brought on quickly and the stores are cleared out within hours… A short term after the collapse we are put under FEMA and Martial law.

Commentary

Comments from Political Leaders & Public Figures

"The drive of the Rockefellers and their allies is to create a one-world government combining supercapitalism and Communism under the same tent, all under their control. Do I mean a conspiracy? Yes, I do. I am convinced there is such a plot, international in scope, generations old in planning, incredibly evil in intent."
–Rep. Larry P. MacDonald, later killed in Korean Air Lines Flight 007, 1983

"Each of us has the hope to build a New World Order."
–President Richard Nixon, Hangzhou, China, February 1972

"We are moving toward a new world order, the world of communism. We shall never turn off that road."
—Mikhail Gorbachev, 1987

"I think that his [Obama's] task will be to develop an overall strategy for America in this period, when really a New World Order can be created."
—Henry Kissinger, CNBC 2008

"No one will enter the New World Order unless he or she will make a pledge to worship Lucifer. No one will enter the New Age unless he will take a Luciferian intiation."

David Spangler, Director of Planetary Initiative, United Nations quoted in *Unicorn in the Sanctuary* by Randy England

We are on the verge of a global transformation. All we need is the right major crisis and the nations will accept the New World Order."
—David Rockefeller, NWO Banker

One of the least understood strategies of the world revolution now moving rapidly toward its goal is the use of mind control as a major means of obtaining the consent of the people who will be subjects of the New World Order."
–K.M. Heaton, *National Educator*

"We shall have World Government, whether or not we like it. The only question is whether World Government will be achieved by consent or conquest."
–James Paul Warburg [son of Paul Warburg, the author of the Federal Reserve Act] February 7, 1950

"Today the path of total dictatorship in the United States can be laid by strictly legal means, unseen and unheard by the Congress, the President, or the people. Outwardly we have a Constitutional government. We have operating within our government and political system, another body representing another form of government – a bureaucratic elite."
–Senator William Jenner, 1954

"The real truth of the matter is, as you and I know, that a financial element in the larger centers has owned the Government ever since the days of Andrew Jackson."
–Franklin D. Roosevelt, letter to Col. House, November 21, 1933

"From the days of Spartacus-Weishaupt to those of Karl Marx, to those of Trotsky, Bela Kun, Rosa Luxembourg, and Emma Goldman, this world-wide conspiracy for the overthrow of civilization and for the reconstitution of society on the basis of arrested development, of envious malevolence and impossible equality, has been steadily growing. It played a definitely recognizable role in the tragedy of the French Revolution. It has been the mainspring of every subversive movement during the nineteenth century, and now at last this band of extraordinary personalities from the underworld of the great cities of Europe and America have gripped the Russian people by the hair of their heads, and have become practically the undisputed masters of that enormous empire."
—Winston Churchill, to the London press, 1922

"Some of the biggest men in the United States, in the field of commerce and manufacture, are afraid of something. They know that there is a power somewhere so organized, so subtle, so watchful, so interlocked, so complete, so pervasive, that they had better not speak above their breath when they speak in condemnation of it."
—Woodrow Wilson, *The New Freedom*, 1913

"All of us will ultimately be judged on the effort we have contributed to building a New World Order."
—Robert Kennedy, presidential candidate and US Attorney General, 1967

"Fundamental Bible-believing people do not have the right to indoctrinate their children in their religious beliefs because we, the state, are preparing them for the year 2000, when America will be part of a one-world global society and their children will not fit in."
–Nebraska State Sen. Peter Hoagland, radio interview, 1983.

"The renewal of the nonproliferation treaty was described as important 'for the welfare of the whole world and the new world order'."
—Hosni Mubarak, Egyptian president, New York Times, April 1995

"I would support a Presidential candidate who pledged to take the following steps: ... At the end of the war in the Persian Gulf, press for a comprehensive Middle East settlement and for a 'new world order' based not on Pax Americana but on peace through law with a stronger U.N. and

World Court."
—George McGovern, Democratic presidential candidate, New York Times, February 1991

"The one aim of these financiers is world control by the creation of inextinguishable debts."
—Henry Ford

"The governments of the present day have to deal not merely with other governments, with emperors, kings and ministers, but also with the secret societies which have everywhere their unscrupulous agents, and can at the last moment upset all the governments' plans. "
—Benjamin Disraeli, first Prime Minister of England, *Coningsby, the New Generation*

"What is important is to dwell upon the increasing evidence of the existence of a secret conspiracy, throughout the world, for the destruction of organized government and the letting loose of evil."
—*Christian Science Monitor*, editorial, June 19th, 1920

"The most powerful clique in these (Council on Foreign Relations) groups have one objective in common: they want to bring about the surrender of the sovereignty and the national independence of the U.S. They want to end national boundaries and racial and ethnic loyalties supposedly to increase business and ensure world peace. What they strive for would inevitably lead to dictatorship and loss of freedoms by the people. The CFR was founded for 'the purpose of promoting disarmament and submergence of U.S. sovereignty and national independence into an all-powerful one-world government'."
—*Harper's*, July 1958

"Three hundred men, all of-whom know one another, direct the economic destiny of Europe and choose their successors from among themselves."
—Walter Rathenau, head of German General Electric, 1909. (Rathenau was Prime Minister of Germany until he was assassinated in 1922.)

"There does exist, and has existed for a generation, an international Anglophile network which operates, to some extent, in the way the radical Right believes the Communists act. In fact, this network, which we may identify as the Round Table Groups, has no aversion to cooperating with the Communists, or any other groups, and frequently does so. I know of the operations of this network because I have studied it for twenty years and was permitted for two years, in the early 1960's, to examine its papers and secret records. I have no aversion to it or to most of its aims and have, for much of my life, been close to it and to many of its instruments...my chief difference of opinion is that it wishes to remain unknown, and I believe its role in history is significant enough to be known...because the American branch of this organization (sometimes called the "Eastern Establishment") has played a very significant role in the history of the United States in the last generation."
–Dr. Carroll Quigley, a professor of history at the Foreign Service School of Georgetown University. Dr. Quigley was Bill Clinton's mentor while he was at Georgetown University.

"If the New World Order agenda is not realized by the terrorist attacks on America and if Americans don't agree to give up their weapons and relinquish their sovereignty to the New

World Order, the next attack will be the use of chemical, biological and/or atomic warfare against the American people. The architects of the New World Order will not hesitate to use as a last resort an atomic or hydrogen bomb in a major American city."
—Reference Op Ed page of the New York Times 9/24/01

"We have undertaken a new order of things; yet we progress to it under the framework and in the spirit and intent of the American Constitution. We have proceeded throughout the Nation a measurable distance on the road toward this new order."
–Franklin D. Roosevelt, 2nd State of the Union address

"We are grateful to The Washington Post, The New York Times, Time Magazine and other great publications whose directors have attended our meetings and respected their promises of discretion for almost forty years. It would have been impossible for us to develop our plan for the world if we had been subject to the bright lights of publicity during those years. But, the world is now more sophisticated and prepared to march towards a world government. The supranational sovereignty of an intellectual elite and world bankers is surely preferable to the national autodetermination [read that "democracy"] practiced in past centuries."

-David Rockefeller, to the Trilateral Commission, June 1991

"The 'affirmative task' before us is to "create a New World Order."
–VP Joe Biden, speech to Import Export Bank, April 5, 2013

"Some even believe we (the Rockefeller family) are part of a secret cabal working against the best interests of the United States, characterizing my family and me as 'internationalists' and of conspiring with others around the world to build a more integrated global political and economic structure – one world, if you will. If that's the charge, I stand guilty, and I am proud of it."
– David Rockefeller, *Memoirs*, page 405

To achieve world government, it is necessary to remove from the minds of men their individualism, loyalty to family traditions, national patriotism, and religious dogmas."

– Brock Adams, Director UN Health Organization *"In the next century, nations as we know it will be obsolete; all states will recognize a single, global authority. National sovereignty wasn't such a great idea after all."*
–Strobe Talbot, Deputy Secretary of State, *TIME*, July 1992

How Rich Corporate Elites Are Lobbying Lawmakers to Crush Marriage Advocates

http://dailysignal.com/2015/07/29/how-rich-corporate-elites-are-lobbying-lawmakers-to-crush-marriage-advocates/

What do you do when you can't persuade the American people to embrace your values?

You use government coercion to impose those values on people. And you get rich corporate elites to lobby government on your behalf.

That's what's taking place right now in the aftermath of the Supreme Court's ruling on gay marriage.

Last week, Democrats in both houses of Congress introduced a bill they call the "Equality Act." This bill adds the phrase "sexual orientation and gender identity" to more or less every federal law that has protections on the basis of race.

If the bill ever became law, the government would treat ordinary Americans who believe we are created male and female, and that male and female are created for each other in marriage, as if they were racists.

The Human Rights Campaign, the LGBT activist group behind the bill, has been trumpeting that "Corporate Giants Announce Support" for the bill. That's right: "corporate giants" want the federal government to coerce and penalize mom-and-pop flower shops because they have a different set of cultural values.

This sort of special interest rent-seeking has a name: cultural cronyism.

In "Truth Overruled: The Future of Marriage and Religious Freedom," I explain how cultural cronyism has been the primary technique the Left has used to redefine marriage.

The basic idea is that LGBT activists couldn't persuade a majority of citizens to vote to redefine marriage, so they got five unelected judges to redefine marriage for the entire country. Now, they're using corporate giants to pressure lawmakers in D.C. to enact legislation that would eliminate any dissent.

It gets worse.

Remember the way that "corporate giants" attacked the Indiana religious freedom bill? That wasn't a fluke. It was part of a well-coordinated, well-financed campaign to eliminate religious liberty protections. CNA reports:

A leader in LGBT grant-making has told business leaders that he wants to shut down the political fight for religious freedom exemptions in the U.S. within three years.

And these words are not empty rhetoric. A CNA investigation has found that millions of dollars have been poured into efforts to combat religious freedom exemptions in the United States.

Again we see business leaders who want the freedom to run their businesses in accordance with their values using the force of government to prevent other Americans from running their businesses, and schools, and charities in accordance with their values.

Indeed, the CNA report shows that one LGBT group gave over $275,000 to defeat religious liberty protections in Oregon.

As I recount in Truth Overruled, Oregon is the state where an evangelical baker was fined $135,000 for declining to bake a cake for a same-sex wedding.

Public policy should not be the result of cultural cronyism.

Whatever you think about gay marriage, and regardless of whether you'd bake a gay wedding cake or not, all Americans should agree that the government should not be coercing bakers into violating their beliefs and fining them if they refuse.

The problem is that liberal activists have undone core elements of the American Founding.

The result is the overreach of progressive government and the administrative state, the sexual revolution's elevation of desire over reason and the whittling of religious free exercise down to the freedom to worship. We need to counter all of these developments. Policy organizations, religious and civic organizations and legal organizations will have to play their roles in empowering the citizenry to reclaim their government and culture.

I offer a roadmap for these groups to follow in Truth Overruled.

Without a return to the principles of the American Founding—ordered liberty based on faith and reason, natural rights and morality, limited government and civil society—Americans will continue to face serious and perplexing challenges. The dilemmas faced by bakers and florists and charities and schools are only the beginning.

Recommended books or articles to read on this subject:

None Dare Call It Conspiracy by Gary Allen

(Not an LDS book but recommended in Conference by Ezra Taft Benson)

The Naked Communist by W. Cleon Skousen

(Recommended in Conference by David O. McKay)

The Naked Capitalist by W. Cleon Skousen

(Important sequel to *The Naked Communist)*

The Naked Socialist *by Paul B. Skousen*

(Third book in the Naked series, written by W. Cleon Skousen's son, published 2012)

The 5000-Year Leap by W. Cleon Skousen

(A classic easy-read book on liberty)

The Elders of Israel and the Constitution by Jerome Horowitz

(Recommended in General Conference by Ezra Taft Benson)

The Book of Mormon and the Constitution by H. Verlan Andersen

(Author was an LDS General Authority and very close friend to Ezra Taft Benson)

The Moral Basis of a Free Society by H. Verlan Andersen

An Enemy Hath Done This by Ezra Taft Benson

(A compilation of political speeches)

Awakening to Our Awful Situation, Books 1 & 2 (Jack Monnett)

(Warnings From the Nephite Prophets, and Responding to Satan's War on Agency)

The Law by Frederic Bastiat

(A classic treatise on liberty by a famous French author. He was not an LDS member but was quoted frequently by Ezra Taft Benson)

http://www.breitbart.com/big-government/2014/11/22/america-has-been-warned-virgil/

http://www.breitbart.com/big-government/2014/11/24/decline-and-fall-the-grim-message-of-the-camp-of-the-saints/

Agenda: Grinding America Down

https://www.youtube.com/watch?v=6JGUT62Bhvo

Agenda 21

http://guardianlv.com/2013/09/agenda-21-revealed-you-need-to-know-this/

In September 2015, Agenda 21 Will Be Transformed Into The 2030 Agenda

http://endoftheamericandream.com/archives/in-september-2015-agenda-21-will-be-transformed-into-the-2030-agenda

Illuminati Agenda Fully Explained - 25 Goals That Destroyed The Planet

https://www.youtube.com/watch?v=ER68ywwAmz4

Additional Sources & Notes

Troop Invasion & Withdrawal

"There will be two great political parties in this country. One will be called the Republican, and the other the Democrat party. These two parties will go to war and out of these two parties will spring another party, which will be the Independent American Party. The United States will spend her strength and means warring in foreign lands until other nations will say, *"Let's divide up the lands of the United States,"* then the people of the U.S. will unite and swear by the blood of their forefathers, that the land shall not be divided. Then the country will go to war, and they will fight until one half of the U.S. army will give up, and the rest will continue to struggle. They will keep on until they are very ragged and discouraged, and almost ready to give up—when the boys from the mountains will rush forth in time to save the American Army from defeat and ruin. And they will say, "Brethren, we are glad you have come; give us men, henceforth, who can talk with God." Then you will have friends, but you will save the country when its liberty hangs by a hair, as it were."

Joseph Smith, June 19th 1844

Scriptures

Isaiah 5:-6

5 Let me now inform you what I will do to my vineyard: I will have its hedge removed and let it be burned; I will have its wall broken through and let it be trampled.

6 I will make it a desolation: it shall neither be pruned nor hoed, but briars and thorns shall overgrow it. Moreover, I will forbid the rainclouds to rain on it.

2 Nephi 20:3-7

3 And what will ye do in the day of visitation, and in the desolation which shall come from far? to whom will ye flee for help? and where will ye leave your glory?
4 Without me they shall bow down under the prisoners, and they shall fall under the slain. For all this his anger is not turned away, but his hand is stretched out still.
5 O Assyrian, the rod of mine anger, and the staff in their hand is their indignation.
6 I will send him against a hypocritical nation, and against the people of my wrath will I give him a charge to take the spoil, and to take the prey, and to tread them down like the mire of the streets.
7 Howbeit he meaneth not so, neither doth his heart think so; but in his heart it is to destroy and cut off nations not a few.

Isaiah 28:18

18 And your covenant with death shall be disannulled, and your agreement with hell shall not stand; when the overflowing scourge shall pass through, then ye shall be trodden down by it.

Leadership Quotes

***This nation will be overthrown,* John Taylor**

This nation and other nations will be overthrown, not because of their virtue, but because of their corruption and iniquity. The time will come, for the prophecies will be fulfilled, when kingdoms will be destroyed, thrones cast down and the powers of the earth shaken, and God's wrath will be kindled against the nations of the earth, and it is for us to maintain correct principles, political, religious and social, and to feel towards all men as God feels. He makes the sun to shine on the just as well as on the unjust; and if he has enlightened our minds and put us in possession of more correct principles than others have, let us be thankful and adore the God of Israel. Let us thank our heavenly Father for his goodness towards us in making us acquainted with the principles of the everlasting Gospel, and let us go on from strength to strength, from purity to purity, from virtue to virtue, from intelligence to intelligence; and when the nations shall fall and crumble, Zion shall arise and shine, and the power of God shall be manifest among his people. No man can overturn or permanently hurt those who do right. They may kill some of our bodies, but that is all they can do. We shall live and shout among the assembled throng, in the eternal heavens, "Hosanna, blessed be the God of Israel," and his kingdom shall grow and increase until the kingdoms of this world shall become the kingdoms of our God and his Christ, and he will rule and reign forever and ever.

Discourse by Elder John Taylor, delivered in the Fourteenth Ward Assembly Rooms, Salt Lake City, Sunday Afternoon, Feb. 1, 1874.

***Country will be in danger of overthrow,* Joseph Smith.**

Prophecy of Joseph Smith, (According to Orson Hyde): was that the time would come when the Constitution and the country would be in danger of an overthrow; and ... "if the Constitution be saved at all, it will be by the Elders of this Church."

Journal of Discourses, Vo1.6, p 152, January 3, 1850

***Becoming a law unto themselves,* Charles W. Nibley, October 1923**

Brethren and sisters, let me say in closing that we have it of record, that the prophet Joseph Smith said the time would come when, through secret organizations taking the law into their own hands, not being governed by law or by due process of law, but becoming a law unto themselves, when, by those disintegrating activities, the Constitution of the United States would be so torn and rent asunder, and life and property and peace and security would he held of so little value, that the Constitution would, as it were, hang by a thread. But he never said, so far as I have heard, that that thread would be cut. I believe, with Elder Richards, that this Constitution will be preserved, but it will be preserved very largely in consequence of what the Lord has revealed and what this people, through listening to the Lord and being obedient, will help to bring about, to stabilize and give permanency and effect to the Constitution itself. That also is our mission. That also is what we are here for. I glory in it. I praise God with all my heart and soul that I am a member of it.

***Secret Combination seeks to overthrow the freedom of all nations,* Ezra T. Benson**

I testify that wickedness is rapidly expanding in every segment of our society. It is more highly organized, more cleverly disguised, and more powerfully promoted than ever before. Secret combinations lusting for power, gain, and glory are flourishing. A secret combination that seeks to overthrow the freedom of all lands, nations, and countries is increasing its evil influence and control over America and the entire world.

***Nation will be on the verge of crumbling,* Joseph Smith**

Even this nation will be on the verge of crumbling to pieces and tumbling to the ground and when the Constitution is on the brink of ruin this people will be the staff upon which the nation shall lean and they shall bear the Constitution away from the very verge of destruction.

Joseph Smith Papers, LDS Church Historical Archives, Box 1, March 10, 1844; D. Michael Stewart, Ensign, Vol. 6, No.6, June 1976, pp. 64-65

***We may stand alone,* Boyd K. Packer**

Will the Constitution be destroyed? No. It will be held inviolate by this people; and as Joseph Smith said 'the time will come when the destiny of this nation will hang upon a single thread, and at this critical juncture, this people will step forth and save it from the threatened destruction.' It will be so. I do not know when that day will come or how it will come to pass. I feel sure that when it does come to pass, among those who will step forward from among this people will be men who hold the Holy Priesthood and who carry as credentials a bachelor or doctor of law degree. And women also, of honor. And there will be judges as well. Others from the world outside the Church will come, as Colonel Thomas Kane did, and bring with them their knowledge of the law to protect this people. We may one day stand alone, but we will not change or lower our standards, or change our course.

BYU J. Reuben Clark Law Society Devotional, Feb 28, 2004.

***Kingdom will be given to the Saints*, John Taylor**

We will now notice those men who are contending for it without any authority, and make a contrast between the two. We see them gathering their forces, and using their influence to destroy the poor among men. How long will the kings and rulers of the earth do this? Until they are dead and damned. And what then? They will be cast down into a pit. Isaiah saw them there, along with many other scoundrels, murderers, and scamps. After many days they will be visited, but they have got to lie in prison a long time for their transgressions. The one is legitimacy, and the other is illegitimacy; the one is the order of God, and the other is the order of the devil.

Such is the position of things in relation to the world, to legitimacy and illegitimacy, in regard to things that are right and things that are wrong. Jesus Christ created all things, and for him were they made, whether it be principalities, powers, thrones, or dominions. Now the question is, is he going to be dispossessed of his right because scoundrels exist in the world, and stand in power and dominion; because his subjects have rebelled against him from time to time, and usurpers have taken his place, and the dominion is given to another? Verily, no. But the time will come when the kingdom and the greatness of the kingdom under the whole heaven will be given to the Saints of the Most High, and they will possess it forever and ever.

A Sermon by Elder John Taylor, Delivered at the General Conference, in the Tabernacle, Great Salt Lake City, April 8, 1853.

***The government is fallen and needs redeeming,* George A. Smith**

Parley P. Pratt wrote in 1841 that the prophet said, 'The government is fallen and needs redeeming. It is guilty of Blood and cannot stand as it now is but will come so near desolation as to hang as it were by a single hair. Then the servants goes [sic] to the nations of the earth, and gathers the strength of the Lord's house! A mighty army! And this is the redemption of Zion when the saints shall have redeemed that government and reinstated it in all its purity and glory.

George A. Smith Papers, Church Archives, Box 7, Folder 5, January 21, 1841. Also: D. Michael Stewart, "I Have a Question," Ensign, June 1976

Uphold and defend the Constitution, **David O. McKay**.

Next to being one in worshiping God, there is nothing in this world in which this Church should be more united than in upholding and defending the Constitution of the United States. If members of the Melchizedek Priesthood allow the U.S. Constitution to be destroyed. they not only forfeit their rights to the Priesthood, but to a place in this highest degree of glory as well.

David O. McKay, *The Instructor,* Feb. 1956, p.34

Elders of Israel will step forward, **Ezra Taft Benson**

The Prophet Joseph Smith declared it will be the elders of Israel who will step forward to help save the Constitution, and not the church. Brethren, if we had done our homework and were faithful, we could step forward at this time and help save this country. The fact that most of us are unprepared to do it is an indictment we will have to bear. The longer we wait, the heavier the chains, the deeper the blood, the more the persecution, and the less we can carry out our God-given mandate and world-wide mission. The war in heaven is raging on earth today. Are you being neutralized in the battle?

Ezra Taft Benson, General Conference, Apr 1965

Undermine one principle after another, **Erastus Snow**.

We were told by the prophet Joseph Smith, that the United States Government and people would undermine one principle of the Constitution after another, until its whole fabric would be torn away, and that it would become the duty of the Latter-day Saints and those in sympathy with them to rescue it from destruction, and to maintain and sustain the principles of human freedom for which our fathers fought and bled. We look for these things to come in quick succession.

Statement of Apostle Erastus Snow, 1885. Journal of Discourses, vol. 26, p. 226, May 31, 1885

After the troops are driven out, people will come to live in Zion**, Ezra Taft Benson**

When the standard of freedom is raised, we shall bid all classes welcome to the rights and privileges of liberty. When that day comes, people can come with all creeds and enjoy their liberties, providing they will acknowledge the laws of God; and I can tell you they will come by hundreds, by thousands, and by tens of thousands. Yes, they will flock to the standard of liberty.

Journal of Discourses, Vo1.6, p.182, January 24, 1858

Dreams & Visions

Spencer, *Visions of Glory*, p.119

I saw foreign troops landing on the east and west coasts of America. There were tens of thousands of them. They came in large ships, some of them former cruise ships and naval escorts. They landed with thousands of vehicles, most of them laden with relief supplies, but also with large tanks and missile launchers.

In California, some Americans tried to fight the troops because they saw them as invaders. There were a few battles where the local people lost. The foreign troops did not punish the survivors; they just asked them to cooperate, fed them and released them.

George Washington

And this time the dark shadowy angel turned his face southward. From Africa I saw an ill-omened spectre approach our land. It flitted slowly and heavily over every town and city of the latter. The inhabitants presently set themselves in battle array against each other. As I continued looking, I saw a bright angel on whose brow rested a crown of light on which was traced the word 'Union.' He was bearing the American flag. He placed the flag between the divided nation and said, 'Remember, ye are brethren.'

...And again I heard the mysterious voice saying, 'Son of the Republic, look and learn.' At this, the dark, shadowy angel placed a trumpet to his mouth and blew three distinct blasts; and taking water from the ocean, he sprinkled it upon Europe, Asia, and Africa. Then my eyes beheld a fearful scene. From each of these countries arose thick, black clouds that were soon joined into one. And throughout this mass, there gleamed a dark red light by which I saw hordes of armed men, who, moving with the cloud, marched by land and sailed by sea to America, which country was enveloped in the volume of cloud. And I dimly saw these vast armies devastate the whole country, and burn the villages, towns and cities that I beheld springing up."

-This vision was received by George Washington in the winter of 1777. Washington told his vision to Anthony Sherman, who recounted it to Wesley Bradshaw, publisher of the National Stripes.

Gayle Smith's Dream, 1993

I also saw an invasion of the country. I saw millions of Chinese coming in along the west coast and down towards the Mexican border. I also saw Russians invading the east coast at the same time. Additionally I saw an army coming down from the north, but they didn't get close enough for me to see who they were. I saw thousands of parachutes until they just darkened the sky. I saw individuals coming down on ropes out of the helicopters all over. I saw the beginning of this invasion that there are nuclear explosions on both coasts. I also saw a nuclear explosion north toward SLC which could be Hill Air Force Base but I really don't know for sure. When I was shown these things I went to the Lord and asked how we could possibly survive all this. I saw that this invasion takes place on a holiday when families get together and eat which I believe could be either Thanksgiving or Christmas.

Sarah Menet, *There is No Death*

While viewing the cities of light (tent cities), my focus changed again and I became aware of missiles being launched and hitting US cities. I watched as mushroom clouds started forming over many areas of the states. Some of the clouds came from missiles that I knew were fired from Russia and others were not from missiles at all but from bombs that were already within the US. These latter bombs had been hidden in trucks and cars and were driven to certain locations and then detonated.

I specifically saw Los Angeles, Las Vegas, and NYC hit with bombs. NYC was hit with a missile, but I think Los Angeles was hit by at least one truck bomb, it not several, because I did not see any missile. I also saw a small mushroom cloud form north of SLC without the aid of a missile.

At almost the same time and in the same locations as the mushroom clouds I saw Russian and Chinese troops invading the US. The Russians were parachuting into many spots along the eastern coast. I also saw them parachuting in Utah. Chinese troops were invading from the west coast near LA. The Chinese and Russians were met with resistance from those who had survived the disease and bombs. I did not see any US military there at that time. I did not see much of this war, but was impressed that it was short in duration and that the troops lost and left.

Additional Visions: President George Albert Smith and Patriarch Lohani Wolfgramm

Note: The full context of these visions can be found at www.nofearpreps.com. The search box feature there can help you locate a particular vision.

Commentary

Why China warned the US to stay away

http://www.bbc.com/news/magazine-33205815

Speech By Comrade Chi Haotia, Vice-Chairman Of China's Military Commission

http://www.rense.com/general85/China%27sPlanToConquer.htm

Obama unveils plans for pared-down military

http://www.cnn.com/2012/01/05/politics/pentagon-strategy-shift/

Why has Obama fired 167 Military Commanders?

http://tinyurl.com/p54zma8

Obama revamps nuclear codes.

http://www.cnn.com/2014/11/14/us/hagel-nuclear/

Barack Obama's Muslim Appointees in High Security Positions

http://tinyurl.com/q6hbttc

Additional Sources & Notes

Persecution & Apostasy

> But make no mistake about it, brothers and sisters; in the months and years ahead, events will require of each member that he or she decide whether or not he or she will follow the First Presidency. Members will find it more difficult to halt longer between two opinions (see 1 Kings 18:21).
>
> **Elder Neal A. Maxwell**
> BYU Speeches, October 10, 1978

Scriptures

Matthew 24:7-12

7 For nation shall rise against nation, and kingdom against kingdom: and there shall be famines, and pestilences, and earthquakes, in divers places.

8 All these are the beginning of sorrows.

9 Then shall they deliver you up to be afflicted, and shall kill you: and ye shall be hated of all nations for my name's sake.

10 And then shall many be offended, and shall betray one another, and shall hate one another.

11 And many false prophets shall rise, and shall deceive many.

Luke 6:22-23

22 Blessed are ye, when men shall hate you, and when they shall separate you from their company, and shall reproach you, and cast out your name as evil, for the Son of man's sake.

23 Rejoice ye in that day, and leap for joy: for, behold, your reward is great in heaven: for in the like manner did their fathers unto the prophets.

2 Timothy 3:12

12 Yea, and all that will live godly in Christ Jesus shall suffer

1 Nephi 8:26-28

26 And I also cast my eyes round about, and beheld, on the other side of the river of water, a great and spacious building; and it stood as it were in the air, high above the earth.

27 And it was filled with people, both old and young, both male and female; and their manner of dress was exceedingly fine; and they were in the attitude of mocking and pointing their fingers towards those who had come at and were partaking of the fruit.

28 And after they had tasted of the fruit they were ashamed, because of those that were scoffing at them; and they fell away into forbidden paths and were lost.

2 Corinthians 12:10

10 Therefore I take pleasure in infirmities, in reproaches, in necessities, in persecutions, in distresses for Christ's sake: for when I am weak, then am I strong.

Luke 21:12-13

12 But before all these, they shall lay their hands on you, and persecute you, delivering you up to the synagogues, and into prisons, being brought before kings and rulers for my name's sake.

13 And it shall turn to you for a testimony.

3 Nephi 12:10

10 And blessed are all they who are persecuted for my name's sake, for theirs is the kingdom of heaven.

D&C 101:35

35 And all they who suffer persecution for my name, and endure in faith, though they are called to lay down their lives for my sake yet shall they partake of all this glory.

3 Nephi 18:15

15 Verily, verily, I say unto you, ye must watch and pray always, lest ye be tempted by the devil, and ye be led away captive by him.

D&C 112:24-26

24 Behold, vengeance cometh speedily upon the inhabitants of the earth, a day of wrath, a day of burning, a day of desolation, of weeping, of mourning, and of lamentation; and as a whirlwind it shall come upon all the face of the earth, saith the Lord.

25 And upon my house shall it begin, and from my house shall it go forth, saith the Lord;

26 First among those among you, saith the Lord, who have professed to know my name and have not known me, and have blasphemed against me in the midst of my house, saith the Lord.

2 Nephi 30: 8-10

8 And it shall come to pass that the Lord God shall commence his work among all nations, kindreds, tongues, and people, to bring about the restoration of his people upon the earth.

9 And with righteousness shall the Lord God judge the poor, and reprove with equity for the meek of the earth. And he shall smite the earth with the rod of his mouth; and with the breath of his lips shall he slay the wicked.

10 For the time speedily cometh that the Lord God shall cause a great division among the people, and the wicked will he destroy; and he will spare his people, yea, even if it so be that he must destroy the wicked by fire.

D&C 122:7-8

7 And if thou shouldst be cast into the pit, or into the hands of murderers, and the sentence of death passed upon thee; if thou be cast into the deep; if the billowing surge conspire against thee; if fierce winds become thine enemy; if the heavens gather blackness, and all the elements combine to hedge up the way; and above all, if the very jaws of hell shall gape open the mouth wide after thee, know thou, my son, that all these things shall give thee experience, and shall be for thy good.

8 The Son of Man hath descended below them all. Art thou greater than he?

Quotes About Persecution & Apostasy, by Church Leaders

Heber C. Kimball, Deseret News, May 23, 1931

An army of Elders will be sent to the four quarters of the earth to search out the righteous and warn the wicked of what is coming. All kinds of religions will be started and miracles performed that will deceive the very elect if that were possible. Our sons and daughters must live pure lives so as to be prepared for what is coming. After a while the gentiles will gather by the thousands to this place, and Salt Lake City will be classed among the wicked cities of the world. A spirit of speculation and extravagance will take possession of the Saints, and the results will be financial bondage. Persecution comes next and all true Latter-day Saints will be tested to the limit. Many will apostatize and others will be still, not knowing what to do. Darkness will cover the earth and gross darkness the minds of the people. The judgments of God will be poured out on the wicked to the extent that our Elders from far and near will be called home, or in other words the gospel will be taken from the Gentiles and later on carried to the Jews. The western boundary of the State of Missouri will be swept so clean of its inhabitants that as President Young tells us, when you return to that place, there will not be left so much as a yellow dog to wag his tail. Before that day comes, however, the Saints will be put to tests that will try the integrity of the best of them. The pressure will become so great that the more righteous among them will cry unto the Lord day and night until deliverance comes. Then the prophet and others will make their appearance and those who have remained faithful will be selected to return to Jackson County, Missouri, and take part in the up-building of that beautiful city, the New Jerusalem."

Heber C. Kimball, Dec 13, 1857, Journal of Discourses, 6:126

The world is ripe, and there are no saving principles within them, with a very few exceptions; and they [the righteous] will gather out, and the rest of mankind are ready for destruction, for they will have no salt to save them. I know the day is right at hand when men will forfeit their priesthood and turn against us and against the covenants they have made, and they will be destroyed as Judas was.

Ezra Taft Benson, *The Teachings of Ezra Taft Benson*, p. 107

There is a real sifting going on in the Church, and it is going to become more pronounced with the passing of time. It will sift the wheat from the tares, because we face some difficult days, the like of which we have never experienced in our lives. And those days are going to require faith and testimony and family unity, the like of which we have never had.

Ezra Taft Benson, General Conference, April 1969

Sometimes we hear someone refer to a division in the Church. In reality, the Church is not divided. It simply means that there are some who, for the time being at least, are members of the Church but not in harmony with it. These people have a temporary membership and influence in the Church; but unless they repent, they will be missing when the final membership records are recorded.

It is well that our people understand this principle, so they will not be misled by those apostates within the Church who have not yet repented or been cut off. But there is a cleansing coming. The Lord says that his vengeance shall be poured out "upon the inhabitants of the earth. . . . And upon my house shall it begin, and from my house shall it go forth, saith the Lord; First among those among you, saith the Lord, who have professed to know my name and have not known me. . . . (D&C 112:24-26.)

J. Reuben Clark, General Conference, April 1949

The ravening wolves are amongst us, from our own membership, and they, more than any others, are clothed in sheep's clothing because they wear the habiliments of the priesthood. . . . We should be careful of them. . . .

Neal A. Maxwell , *All These Things Shall Give Thee Experience,*)

President Marion G. Romney said, many years ago, that he had "never hesitated to follow the counsel of the Authorities of the Church even though it crossed my social, professional or political life" (in Conference Report, Apr. 1941, p. 123). This is a hard doctrine, but it is a particularly vital doctrine in a society which is becoming more wicked. In short, brothers and sisters, not being ashamed of the gospel of Jesus Christ includes not being ashamed of the prophets of Jesus Christ! ...

Your discipleship may see the time when such religious convictions are discounted... This new irreligious imperialism seeks to disallow certain opinions simply because those opinions grow out of religious convictions. Resistance to abortion will be seen as primitive. Concern over the institution of the family will be viewed as untrendy and unenlightened...

If people, however, are not permitted to advocate, to assert, and to bring to bear, in every legitimate way, the opinions and views they hold which grow out of their religious convictions, what manner of men and women would we be? Our founding fathers did not wish to have a state church established nor to have a particular religion favored by government. They wanted religion to be free to make its own way. But neither did they intend to have irreligion made into a favored state church...

Before the ultimate victory of the forces of righteousness, some skirmishes will be lost. Even in these, however, let us leave a record so that the choices are clear, letting others do as they will in the face of prophetic counsel.

There will also be times, happily, when a minor defeat seems probable, but others will step forward, having been rallied to rightness by what we do. We will know the joy, on occasion, of having awakened a slumbering majority of the decent people of all races and creeds which was, till then, unconscious of itself. Jesus said that when the fig trees put forth their leaves, "summer is nigh" (Matt. 24:32). Thus warned that summer is upon us, let us not then complain of the heat!

Neal A. Maxwell, BYU Speech, Oct 10, 1978

But make no mistake about it, brothers and sisters; in the months and years ahead, events will require of each member that he or she decide whether or not he or she will follow the First Presidency. Members will find it more difficult to halt longer between two opinions (see 1 Kings 18:21).

Neal A. Maxwell, General Conference, Oct 1982

Alas, brothers and sisters, we likewise live in a time when the love of many will wax cold. (See D&C 45:27; Matt. 24:12.) Fear will therefore increase. Why? Because when men fear, it is because we are not perfect in love. (See 1 Jn. 4:18; Moro. 8:16.) The less love, the more fear—as well as the more war!

As with Paul, however, we may be perplexed, but we are not in despair. (See 2 Cor. 4:8.) For if we are prepared spiritually, we need not fear. (See D&C 38:30.)

Even so, the Lord has made no secret of the fact that He intends to try the faith and the patience of His Saints. (See Mosiah 23:21.) We mortals are so quick to forget the Lord: "And thus we see that except the Lord doth chasten his people with many afflictions … they will not remember him." (Hel. 12:3.)

However, the Lord knows our bearing capacity, both as to coping and to comprehending, and He will not give us more to bear than we can manage at the moment, though to us it may seem otherwise. (See D&C 50:40; D&C 78:18.) Just as no temptations will come to us from which we cannot escape or which we cannot bear, we will not be given more trials than we can sustain. (See 1 Cor. 10:13.)

Dreams & Visions of Coming Persecution

White Horse Prophecy, attributed to Joseph Smith, 1843

The sometimes disputed White Horse Prophecy states "a man who had heard the Prophet give the toast returned to visit the mansion of the Prophet, and so abused him with bad language, that the man was ordered out by the Prophet. It was while the two were out that my attention was attracted to them and hearing the man speaking in a loud tone of voice, I went toward them; the man finally leaving. There were present the Prophet Joseph Smith, Theodore Turley and myself. The prophet began talking to us of the mobbings and drivings and persecutions we as a people have endured, but, said he, "We will have worse things to see; our persecutors will have all the mobbings they want. Don't wish them any harm, for when you see their sufferings you will shed bitter tears for them."

Vision of Heber Kimball, told by Amanda Wilcox, 1868

After a while the Gentiles will gather to this place by the thousands, and Salt Lake will be classed among the wicked cities of the world. A spirit of speculation and extravagance will take possession of the Saints, and the result will be financial bondage.

Persecution comes next, and all true Latter-day Saints will be tested to the limit. Many will apostatize, and others will stand still, not knowing what to do. Darkness will cover the earth and gross darkness the minds of the people.

Cardston Temple Vision, Sols Caurdisto

I saw that the opposing forces were roughly divided by so-called Christianity on the one side, and by the so-called followers of Mohammed and Buddha on the other. I saw that the great driving power within these so-called Christian nations, was the Great Apostasy of Rome, in all its political, social and religious aspects. I saw the worldwide dislocation and devastation of production and slaughter of people occur more swiftly and upon a larger scale than ever before. <u>I saw an antagonism begin to express itself from those so-called Christian nations against your people.</u> I saw those with a similar faith to yours in the far east begin to look toward Palestine for safety....

I saw the other officials obeying the inspired instructions, carrying their message and exhorting the people to carry out, from time to time the revelation given them, <u>whilst all around throughout</u>

the Gentile world the chaos developed in its varying stages, faction against faction, nation against nation, but all in open or secret hostility to your people and their faith. I saw your people draw closer and closer together, as this became more tense and as the spiritual forces warned them through the mouth of your elders and your other officers. I saw the spiritual forces influencing those members who had drifted away, to re-enter the fold. I saw a greater tithing than ever before.

Vision of Alma D. Erickson (1930s)

I see our church represented by a high building, and we are in the top thereof, or the most recently constructed portion, which is very shaky; and I perceive that this last constructed portion is going to fall, and we must get down to the lower part of this great structure, which rests solidly upon its foundations. And while I am thus viewing it, the top, or last part built, does crash with a loud and fearful crash.

Additional Commentary & Resources:

In ***His Return: Prophecy, Destiny & Hope*** **by Richard N. Skousen**, the author has a chapter called Gathering the Wheat and Removing the Tares. Much of the apostasy in the church will come about when the church is greatly persecuted. We're beginning to see this today but in the future we can expect a great increase. The author refers to this: "As the tares reject the light of the gospel and leave the Church, they will join with the wicked, where they will be bound tighter and tighter in darkness." (P. 68)

"Heber C. Kimball prophesied that these fallen members would leave the Church, attack it and be destroyed in the same manner that Judas Iscariot was: "Judas was like salt that had lost its saving principles-- good for nothing but to be cast out and trodden under foot of men. It is just so with you men and women, if you do not honor your callings and cultivate the principles you have received. It is so with you, ye elders of Israel, when you forfeit your covenants. ...

Behold, vengeance cometh speedily upon the inhabitants of the earth, a day of wrath, a day of burning, a day of desolation, of weeping, of mourning, and of lamentation; and as a whirlwind it shall come upon all the face of the earth, saith the Lord. ...

And upon my house shall it begin, and from my house shall it go forth, saith the Lord;

First among those among you, saith the Lord, who have professed to know my name and have not known me, and have blasphemed against me in the midst of my house, saith the Lord. D&C 112:23-26"

The Apostasy of the Latter Days**, by H. Verlan Andersen** (of the First Quorum of the Seventy of the LDS Church) – Excerpts from Chapter 18 "The Great and Abominable Church of the Devil":

HISTORY WARNS THAT APOSTASY MUST BE EXPECTED

Religious history testifies that, with the single exception of the inhabitants of the City of Enoch, no people to whom the gospel has been given have remained faithful to their covenants for more than a few generations. Time after time the Lord has established his church among a group who have lived his commandments for a few years and then fallen away thus bringing upon themselves his judgments. This cycle of human folly which so many prophets have noted, has repeated itself with such consistent regularity that any group which finds itself to be the favored recipients of the gospel would do well to assume that their own apostasy is certain and the only question about it is how long it will take.

Christ, who as governor of the world, has the painful duty of punishing transgression, has spoken of the infidelity of the House of Israel and the frequency with which they have rejected him. Just before he made his appearance to those righteous Nephites who survived the terrible disaster inflicted upon their nation, he uttered these words of anguish:

"O ye people of these great cities which have fallen, who are descendants of Jacob, yea who are of the house of Israel, how oft have I gathered you as a hen gathereth her chickens under her wings, and have nourished you. And again, how oft would I have gathered you as a hen gathereth her chickens under her wings, yea, O ye people of the house of Israel, who have fallen; ... how oft would I have gathered you as a hen gathereth her chickens, and ye would not." (3 Nephi 10:4-5)

To the Jews the Lord said:

"O Jerusalem, Jerusalem, thou that killest the prophets, and stonest them which are sent unto thee, how oft would I have gathered thy children together, even as a hen gathereth her chickens under her wings, and ye would not!" (Matt. 23:37)

The fact that the Lord has found it necessary to restore his gospel so many times is in itself evidence of the regularity with which apostasy has occurred because the only thing which will cause the destruction of His Church is the wickedness of its members. As the angel told Alma who had been trying to destroy the Lord's work among the Nephites:

"Alma, arise and stand forth, for why persecutest thou the church of God? For the Lord has said: 'This is my church, and I will establish it; and nothing shall overthrow it, save it is the transgression of my people.'" (Messiah 27:13)

The prophet, Mormon, whose labor as an historian gave him the opportunity to observe the frequency of the righteousness - wickedness - punishment cycle, spoke of it as though it were a law of life which operates as a certain consequence of a universal human weakness. His analysis of apostasy and its causes should interest us deeply:

"And thus we can behold how false, and also the unsteadiness of the hearts of the children of men; yea, we can see that the Lord in his great infinite goodness doth bless and prosper those who put their trust in him. Yea, and we may see at the very time when he doth prosper his people, yea, in the increase of their fields, their flocks and their herds, and in gold and silver, and in all manner of precious things of every kind and art; sparing their lives, and delivering them out of the hands of their enemies ... yea, and in fine, doing all things for the welfare and happiness of his people; yea, then is the time that they do harden their hearts, and do forget the Lord their God, .. and this because of their ease and exceedingly great prosperity. And thus we see that except the Lord doth chasten his people with afflictions, yea, except he doth visit them with death and with terror, and with famine and with all manner of pestilence, they will not remember him. O how foolish, and how vain, and how evil and devilish and how quick to do iniquity and how slow to do good, are the children of men..." (Helaman. 12:1-4)

ARE THE CONDITIONS WHICH ORDINARILY ACCOMPANY APOSTASY PRESENT TODAY?

Do the words of Mormon quoted above have application today? If "ease" and "exceedingly great prosperity" are certain to cause people to "forget the Lord their God," then the Church is in deep trouble because seldom, if ever, has any group been as prosperous as it is today. Its beginnings were humble enough. Starting in 1830 with an initial membership of six, the Church was persecuted, its property destroyed and confiscated, its leaders slain, and the people finally driven into a forbidding wilderness before they could find a measure of peace. But all that has now changed. After 140 years of growth, membership numbers in the millions, persecution has long vanished, and instead of ostracism, members are, for the most part accepted and respected.

These conditions in prior dispensations have been sure signs of weakened faith. To fail to consider the possibility that the members of the Church are again "falling away" would be to ignore one of the most thoroughly documented lessons of history. Especially is this true in light of the fact that the cultural, political, and educational life of Church members has become so deeply and thoroughly involved with that of non-members that they are being overwhelmingly influenced by the "ways of the world." Through newspapers and magazines, motion pictures and television, schools and lecture halls, and a thoroughly integrated economic system, Church members come into close and continuous contact with those not of their faith.

Some may assume that a "Gentile apostasy" in the latter days cannot occur because Christ's Church is here to stay this time. They may assume that widespread departure from the gospel principles by Church members is contrary to prophecy. While the scriptures do assure us that the Church will continue to exist and be divinely led by prophets of the Lord right up until his Second Coming, they do not state that all, or even a majority of its members will follow those prophets. On the contrary they foretell extensive, and in some cases, almost total defection from true principles. For example, we noted in the Lord's prophecy that only one-half of the small group he calls "virgins" will avoid being deceived and destroyed. Let us consider other scriptures which discuss this problem.

THE FAILURE OF PEOPLE TO RECOGNIZE THE SIGNS OF APOSTASY

In the great majority of cases where apostasy has occurred, it appears that people become wicked while believing themselves righteous. This happened time and again to the Children of Israel and the Nephites, and was plainly evident in the case of the Jews at the time of Christ. There are recorded exceptions to this rule. For example, when the Nephites apostatized immediately prior to Christ's visit, we are told:

"Now they did not sin ignorantly, for they knew the will of God concerning them, for it had been taught unto them; therefore they did willingly rebel against God." (3 Nephi 6:18)

But the typical situation is described thus by Mormon as he commented on the frequency and rapidity with which a people who have been blessed forsake their Lord:

"...they do harden their hearts, and do forget the Lord their God, and do trample under their feet the Holy One-- yea, and this because of their ease, and their exceedingly great prosperity." (Helaman 12:2)

Prophecies regarding the Gentile apostasy of the latter days indicate that it will be the typical one wherein Church members will be led away by false beliefs into evil practices. Nephi had much to say regarding the event. Among other things he predicted that:

(1) "Because of pride, and because of false teachers, and false doctrine, their churches have become corrupted...." (Nephi 28:12)

(2) "The humble followers of Christ" will err in many instances because of being taught by the precepts of men. (2 Nephi 28:14)

(3) Some will be lulled away "into carnal security, that they will say: All is well in Zion; Zion prospereth, all is well--and thus the devil cheateth their souls, and leadeth them away carefully down to hell." (2 Nephi 28:21)

(4) Others will be deceived into believing that there is no devil and no hell. (2 Nephi 28:22)

(5) There will be many who will say:

"Eat, drink and be merry; nevertheless, fear God--he will justify in committing a little sin; yea, lie a little, take the advantage of one because of his words, dig a pit for thy neighbor; there is no harm in this; and do all these things, for tomorrow we die; and if it so be that we are guilty, God will beat us with a few stripes, and at last we shall be saved in the kingdom of God. Yea, and there shall be many which shall teach after this manner, false and vain and foolish doctrines..." (Nephi 28:8-9)

TO EXERCISE UNRIGHTEOUS DOMINION

Each man desires to be free to spend his own money, manage his own home, operate his own farm or business, and otherwise conduct the affairs of his life which are personal to him. Usually he doesn't want others knowing about his personal affairs, much less does he want them using force and the threat thereof to dictate how he shall handle them. Therefore people are not inclined to intrude into one another's concerns-- at least on a private level. It would not only be in poor taste, but criminal as well. But that which is seen so clearly when done by any individual becomes hidden when done as a group. When men act in the name of government, no person's property or business is sacred. No longer do they hesitate to deny others the privacy and freedom they desire for themselves. No longer is there any fear of retaliation or public condemnation to restrain them from exhibiting that disposition common to almost all men-- the tendency to exercise unrighteous dominion.

Additional Sources & Notes

Additional Dreams & Visions

"Now there's one more way by
which revelations may come,
and that is by dreams.
Oh, I'm not going to tell you that every dream you have is a direct revelation from the Lord. But I fear that in this age of sophistication there are those of us who are prone to rule out all dreams as of no purpose, and of no moment. And yet all through the scriptures there were recorded incidents where the Lord, by dreams, has directed His people."

President Harold B. Lee
Teachings of Presidents of the Church: Harold B. Lee,,pg. 48

Scriptures & Quotes

Joel 2:28

28 And it shall come to pass afterward, that I will pour out my spirit upon all flesh; and your sons and your daughters shall prophesy, your old men shall dream dreams, your young men shall see visions:

Acts 2:18

18 And on my servants and on my handmaidens I will pour out in those days of my Spirit; and they shall prophesy:

Joseph Smith

"We believe that we have a right to revelations, visions, and dreams from God, our heavenly Father; and light and intelligence, through the gift of the Holy Ghost, in the name of Jesus Christ, on all subjects pertaining to our spiritual welfare; if it so be that we keep his commandments, so as to render ourselves worthy in his sight."

-The Prophet Joseph Smith, Times and Seasons, Feb 1840

Volume One The Great Gathering has a trove of dreams and visions from LDS members. The following pages are dreams mostly from nonmembers. It is amazing to see the commonality and patterns found within the dreams of so many different people, regardless of their religious affiliation.

Dr. Patricia Green, highlights:

http://www.prophecyclub.com/latest-prophecies/prophecies-from-dr-patricia-green, https://www.youtube.com/user/joyministries777/videos

1. Obama wins 2008
2. U.S. culture and government pushes for abortion/homosexuality
3. God gave a president who would further the abortion and homosexuality agenda.
4. Forked Tongue Devil
5. 1st Tsunami wave washes to North Carolina
6. 2nd Tsunami, East Coast, 10 days later, taller than hotels
7. 3rd Tsunami devastates coastal cities
8. Florida Decimated
9. Washington D.C. under water
10. New York Harbor flooded
11. Flooding up to Appalachian Mountains
12. Millions perish in waves
13. New pattern to the seasons
14. Prosperous times short in length
15. Series of devastations cripple the U.S.
16. Hoover Dam breaks
17. Power supplies cut off
18. Ash clouds and debris falling
19. Tall buildings crumble
20. Heap of rubble similar to Twin Towers'
21. Deep Fissures, causeways, bridges to islands collapse
22. All schools and universities shut down
23. Medicine scarce
24. Martial Law instituted
25. Curfews and roadblocks
26. Civil War
27. Military authority over civilians
28. Executive Order by Obama
29. U.S. collapses due to wickedness
30. Abortion after sinful sexual bondage is cause
31. Loss of utilities like electricity
32. Modern day Jeremiah
33. Sword=Nuclear War
34. Black Plague
35. Famine like Egypt experienced with Joseph of Egypt
36. Waterways poisoned
37. Weather pattern and climate changes: North becomes warm, South is flooded, West experiences earthquakes East seas roar, Central Plains suffers great hurricanes
38. Cities of refuge/safety
39. Wicked in high places
40. State secrets are given to Russia, in order to destroy U.S. infrastructure
41. Banks line their pockets with gold
42. The Lord will save his righteous children

Pastor T.D. Hale, highlights of Dreams from December 28 and 29, 2011

http://tinyurl.com/nndkgb7, http://tinyurl.com/ooxcug7

http://tinyurl.com/on99rxl, http://tinyurl.com/q2akaqj

http://z3news.com/w/td-hale-prophetic-dreams-tell-the-future-of-america/

1. America Bombed 2. Families Weep
3. Riots, plundering
4. Citizens killing each other
6. Obama standing on Truman Balcony, shoots American Eagle (symbolic)
7. Cities of Refuge
8. Righteous people protected
9. Final Call by the Lord
10. Obama wins 2008 election
11. America punished
12. Concentration Camps
13. Federal Government arrests resistors
14. Citizens are segregated and loaded into railroad cars
15. Romney blocked ascending staircase inside Kirtland Temple by Egyptian Falcon
16. Obama seen with a dark, evil mist around heart
17. Constitution removed
18. Flooding covers much of U.S.
19. Persecution of religious people
20. The judgments of God begin after Obama is sworn in
22. Prepare should prepare spiritually

T.D. Hale Dream #1 (December 28, 2011) Excerpts:

"In a dream I began to see myself going across America. I was floating. All of a sudden I began to see bombs had landed everywhere. The land was totally destroyed.

It looked like things were totally just wiped off: grass, trees, everything. Everything was gone, burned. I don't know if it was everywhere but it was everywhere that I could see, from the point I was at.

When I saw this I saw people standing around their homes and things that were left, holding onto each other. I saw people that lay dead, and heard the cries of the people saying 'This should never have happened, oh Lord, this should never have happened.'

You could tell that life had changed. There was no food. There was no water. I could see babies crying, grownups, men all crying, holding onto their families. They were begging God for mercy. As I moved along I saw people running, looking for their loved ones who were missing and they were completely, completely out of their minds. Insanity had taken over.

Then I came over a big city that looked like Columbus, Ohio. That is when all of a sudden I saw mass hysteria, riots and all kinds of things breaking out in the streets of the city. There were people just grabbing things left and right. But when I saw it, I did not see them grabbing things like TVs and Electronics. They were grabbing food. They were grabbing chips. They were grabbing water. I could tell that this was different from riots that we have seen in the past. They were seeking everything they could get for survival. The rioters were fighting among themselves. …

The next part of the dream was most startling for me. I found myself standing on the backside of the White House. I heard a voice say, 'Look up to the Truman Balcony.' I knew what a balcony was, but I did not know the balcony had a name. I did not know that there was a Truman Balcony until I later shared this with a friend who told me there is a balcony by that name at the White House.

I saw all of a sudden the President of United States, President Obama, standing on the balcony and I saw in his hands a shotgun. All of a sudden I heard a loud scream, real loud. When I turned my head to see where the scream was coming from I saw flying high in the air a majestic eagle flying in the air around Washington DC. I knew that scream. I knew it was an eagle.

I saw all of a sudden the President of United States point that shotgun and shot that eagle dead and it fell to the ground. When it did I looked back at him and he just had a smile on his face like a smirk. And these were the words I heard in the dream, 'I've done it and I won't have to deal with this in my administration.'

Then there was dead silence. Then I heard a voice day 'Tell the people that this is my will, that this is the hand of the Almighty both upon the generation of the righteous and the cursed. The righteous will find their way and will know what to do. The cursed will wander around with no compass because the cup is full.' …

At that point in the dream I know we were coming to a showdown between good versus evil. I saw people gathering in their homes and there were prayer meetings. People were praying in the spirit. Then I heard the Lord say 'Tell my servants and my handmaidens a special anointing will reside on you in the last days. Hold not back your voices but speak your hearts for out of them come the issues of life. Pick up the mantle of prayer and cover yourselves in a secret place of prayer. Your eyes will be anointed with special anointing. There will be others who will be blinded to my word. All things will be revealed in their due course. There will be a supernatural wave of the spirit that will come over this generation very soon.' …

All of a sudden, things changed in the dream and I began to hear a voice, the voice of God. I saw in front of me a very old antique table… I am hesitant to say this but I saw a voting ballot laying there on the table. As I looked at the ballot I saw two names on it. I saw the President's name and I saw mitt Romney's name on it. Then all of a sudden I looked and I saw the President of United States name check marked. I knew then what that meant. I looked at the ballot and I saw written on the ballot, 'This is the will of the Lord.' Then I woke up."

T.D. Hale. Dream #2 (December 29, 2011) Excerpts:

"In this dream I came upon a wooded area where I saw some people that were camping. They were not camping like we normally think. They were hiding. They were all standing by their tents. The people looked tattered, they were trying to light a fire but they didn't want to bring attention to themselves. But they had already been found out.

I saw some federal official coming up around and they took these families. They handcuffed the adults and took them to the cars, and they took their children with them. I also saw two elderly people and they took them and put them in the car. I saw federal agents and they said 'We are from the United States government and you are under arrest.'

I knew that these people had been running to get away from being arrested. They took these people to some king of a processing place. I was standing in front of this building where I watched them being taken in and processed… I knew they were old military bases that had been shut down. I even saw them being fingerprinted.

I saw rail cars that came up beside this place… I knew America was in trouble when I saw that. I knew we were headed down a path that was not going to be turned around.

I felt like I had entered into a death camp. What I saw literally sickened me. I knew that America was about to change."

T.D. Hale. Dream #3 (November 24, 2012) Excerpts:

"In this dream I was immediately taken into the oval office. I was standing in the oval office looking at the President of United States. When I stood in front of him all of a sudden I heard a voice and I knew it was the voice of God. 'Weep and howl for the misery that shall come shortly.'…

As I began to look at him (the President) again he was dressed in all black. All of a sudden his chest cavity around his heart began to open up. His heart was exposed and as I was looking at his heart, thick, black, dark mist was swirling around his heart and I knew that God was letting me see the evil that is really in that man.

Now at this point he walked over to the desk and he picked up a gavel in his hand. The gavel was part wood and part stone. On the desk of the President of United States there is a document with these words written on it: The Final Abomination. He then hit the document on his desk with the gavel and when he hit this document on the desk then all of a sudden I felt a shaking. I shot up into the air and I was standing up above the White House.

Then an earthquake hit Washington DC. I saw the earth open up and it went towards the Washington monument then towards the Jefferson Memorial. At that point I began to see and odd colored rain falling. It was the color of fire or something. It started slowly coming down then it intensified little by little. It was coming down faster and faster until the waters started rising. I saw a map of the United States. I could see the outline. The waters left Washington and began to flood across the whole United States. I saw them hit Maryland, West Virginia, Ohio, Michigan, Kentucky, Indiana, South Carolina, until it completely went all across the United States

People began to scream across the nation and all I could hear was a mournful sound. It was as if something had happened, a great loss.

As I was in the air I saw America in this state being covered with these flood waters. Then all of a sudden as I was suspended in the air I could see these beams of light quickly coming up out of the flood waters. Like at the speed of light they were quickly going up into the air. There were millions it looked like. Then at that moment I was taken higher above the earth and I could see the round earth and all over the earth I started seeing those lights shooting up all over the world. Then I heard a voice say, 'The shifting has begun.'

At this point I was looking over the top. I was going across the top of several churches in America. These were the mega-churches. I heard a voice say. 'A breeding ground for sin for the people know not Me but they play around their golden calf.'

I knew that we had entered into the time of the end. It will not be these large churches but will be home prayer meetings where the saints will be gathering in secret and praying. This is going to get to the point where we are going to have to meet in secret. The days of persecution had come upon this generation.

The Lord let me know a long time ago that there would be a remnant that would be called out. There would be a little here and a little there. God is going to have some people here and there who are going to be praying in secret.

At this point I was looking again at the homes. I knew that these people loved and served God with all of their hearts. I saw the homes of men and women that were gathered together in deep intercessory prayer across the nation and then I heard a voice say. 'The season is upon this nation because you have set abomination before my eyes, I will set judgment before yours.'

Then I asked the Lord, 'When will this happen?'

I heard the voice answer. 'After he is sworn in.'"

Pastor Ken Peters

http://tinyurl.com/p37fh95, http://www.heavenvisit.com/Ken_Peters.php

Dream in 1980, summary of things he saw:

- People being raised from the graves wearing robes that glimmer. Their countenance was brighter than the sun, they radiated.
- Older people came out looked mature but not aged. Young people resurrected were young, but there was a maturity about them.
- All of the globe experienced,mass pandemonium, hopelessness, and fear. Lawlessness permeated society. No one was safe from the turmoil on every continent, it was as if the entire world had become a third world continent but didn't have resources or skills to deal with it emotionally. It was as if every person on earth had just left their mother's funeral. People were despondent and full of despair.
- Two weeks of no electricity..
- Once television became available again a man who was smooth and convincing, with a demonic charisma, was able to rally the globe. He began to communicate about new order, world order, new times. Never heard the term "New World Order". People at staggering rates were buying into what this man was saying. This anti-Christ was the most handsome man ever seen, he has a very chiseled look about his face.
- Freedom and patriotism were being eroded.
- Babies from infancy to 18 months were abandoned in baby carriers everywhere.
- There was a group of people who were able to meet the needs of the people. They prayed for people and those people would be healed. Their supplies multiplied.
- Earthquake was massive, worldwide. There were millions of lives lost. The loss could not be measured. It was global destruction.
- The massive earthquake changed the weather patterns. Predicting weather became totally impossible. Weather seemed to have its own mind. It was manipulated by the Earth being shifted on its axis.

- Fertile farming areas were totally destroyed with drought and famine. Places that were once fertile became an arid desert.
- At the time of the earthquake, law began to change. Military police drove unusual looking vehicles. Soldiers wore blue helmets, holding big guns in the back of vehicles with flags flying. The soldiers seemed to be peaceful. You had to have current papers to cross state lines.
- Cameras on the traffic lights, whereabouts of vehicles monitored.
- People were being monitored in their homes through their televisions sets.
- Told if we aligned ourselves with the new order all our problems would go away.
- Certain regions of the earth had light rays that would shoot out into the atmosphere; they were very brilliant and almost supernatural. They were beams of light coming from camps of the children of God. People were praying for sick people and they would be healed instantly. The dead would be resurrected. These regions were totally one, for Jesus Christ.
- There were Cities of Light next to cities of blackness.
- Those running the world order were very angry about the Cities of Light. Persecution began, to an extent not seen before.
- Many penitentiaries/prisons were used as detention centers for Christians – concentration camps.
- RFID Chips in the right hand. Everyone had to have one in order to conduct business.
- People felt prompted to flee.
- People were beheaded for not denying Christ.
- There was a clear line between who was on God's side and who was not.

Warnings & Counsel:

1) All countries the U.S. entered outside of God's will, God has considered encroachment and will allow these nations to afflict the US.
2) The U.S. has until the end of 2003 to change its course back to God; if it fails to do so God will judge the U.S. as a "goat" nation.

3) Judgment will begin soon on cities, which will qualify for a regional blessing or punishment. There will be giant fire hail stones projected from the heavens upon the unrepentant areas. Blessings of revival and increased harvest will come to the areas where people were responsive to the direction of the Holy Spirit..
4) America's regions of sin and debauchery will face harsher judgment. The homosexual agenda will launch an all-out attack against Christianity.
5) America will adopt "new laws and times". We must pray to stop this!
6) The wickedness of religious leaders will come to light as God brings forth a more righteous church, clean and without spot or blemish.
7) Churches will lose their tax-exempt status.
8) The true character of governmental leaders will continue to be exposed, revealing our need for elected officials with higher moral character and personal righteousness.
9) Judgment is coming to the mortgage business.
10) Bombings will increase on unrepentant U.S. cities.
11) Earthquakes will increase in frequency and intensity of destruction and loss of life in America; this will take thousands of lives.
12) This decade will see more famine, pestilence, floods, and disasters than ever before in the history of man. These events will continue with increased intensity and will not slow down.
13) We will see superstorms and extreme weather (like El Nino) on a regular basis.
14) Riots and violence will be unleashed upon lawless regions, especially those regions scorning God and His laws.
15) Mainline churches will wither and die due to extreme compromise.
16) Judgment will come to America's farmers because they have failed to enthrone the God of the harvest.
17) Debtor's prisons will return. Get out and stay out of consumer debt!
18) Get out of the system of Babylon and turn to God. Gad and Meni,are false gods of prosperity and destiny. (Isaiah 65:8-15)
19) Return to your first love: Jesus. Not His word, prophecy or gifts – but Him. (Rev. 2:2-5)

20) Love your neighbor, avoid the spirit of intolerance and hatred.

21) Don't run after signs or you will be deceived. Tear down idolatry. NOW!

22) Begin to fast and pray, sanctify yourselves now. Don't be foolish virgins.

23) Change your assets into more stable wealth like gold and silver.

24) Avoid slick technology that gives away your personal power.

25) Don't fail to study God's word. Keep your path lit. (2 Timothy 2:15)

26) Continually stand in the gap (Ezekiel 22:30). Repent as did Daniel and God will hear (2 Chr. 7:14)

RaNelle Wallace

http://tinyurl.com/qeloyo3 , http://ww3.ranellewallace.com/

http://www.near-death.com/experiences/notable/ranelle-wallace.html

RaNelle and her husband were in a dramatic single-engine airplane crash in October 1985. 75% of her body was burned, and after climbing down a mountainside to find help she died. She tells about her experience in the next world in her book *The Burning Within.* Some of the highlights are:

1. She saw her entire earth life in review.
2. Events that seemed important to her when she was alive were of little value there,
3. but she had many regrets about lost opportunities to serve others, etc, when she was allowed to clearly see what they had truly meant.
4. There were mistakes she had made in life that she dreading seeing come up in the life review, but which were not traumatic because she had repented of them while alive. The Atonement had taken the weight and healed her.
5. She spent time with her own grandmother, learning about the preexistence, the purpose of life, and her own personal life mission.
6. She was told that uncompleted life missions can be worked on further in the next life.
7. She learned that we chose our challenges and knew something of the experiences we would have before we came here.

"The powers we are given," she explained, "are self-given. We grow by the force of our desires to learn, to love, to accept things by faith that we cannot prove. Our ability to accept truth, to live by it, governs our progress in the spirit, and it determines the degree of light we possess. Nobody forces light and truth upon us, and nobody takes it away unless we let them. We are self-governed and self-judged. We have total agency.

"The Lord never gives more challenges in life than can be handled," she continued, "Rather than jeopardize someone's spiritual progression or cause more suffering than can be endured, he will bring that spirit home, where he or she can continue progressing."

"All this comes from God, and the power to sustain it comes from him. It is the power of his love. Just as the plant life on Earth needs soil, water, and light for nourishment, spiritual life needs love. All creation springs from God's love, and everything he creates has the capacity to love in turn. Light, truth, and life are all created in love and are sustained by love.

It is within the simple principles of the gospel that the mysteries of heaven are found."

5. Dreaded scenes were erased that she repented of
6. Saw People she failed as part of her mission and their pain she caused
7. Founded her charity on conditions of repayment, selfish
8. Spirit world
9. Spent time leading from her Grandma about purpose of life, pre-existence, mission
10. Un-completed missions on earth can be in progress in heaven

11. We chose our challenges, experiences
12. We have total agency
13. Heavenly Garden
14. Garden endless vista of grass Illini into shining radiant hills
15. Every blade of grass a brilliant shade of green
16. Flowers have no stems
17. Flowers grow their own spiritual potential so they float
18. Plants communicate with us
19. Plants essence is power of love from God who sustains all living
20. We need to learn to have faith
21. Grandmother teaches RaNelle
22. Simple principles of the gospel, mysteries of Heaven are found in our scriptures we must learn
23. Love is a power that gives action to all around it
24. Love is the power of life
25. Fear limits progress, enjoyment of life
26. We chose to come to earth to face trials and gain experience
27. We elected to follow a savior
28. We made a sacred covenant with God to do all in our power to accomplish our missions here on earth
29. We promised to use our time, energies, and talents to help bring about the Saviors full purposes
30. We promised to bring our brothers and sisters back to Him and our heavenly Father
31. We are loved unconditionally
32. We need each other
33. Saw millions waiting for their work to be done in this huge organized family puzzle
34. Ranelle Didn't want to go back till she met her future son Nathaniel
35. Nathaniel showed his future mother Ranelle his mission on earth and he needed her to go back
36. The key is love
37. 7 years later, Nathaniel was born

Mena Lee Grebin, highlights:

http://tinyurl.com/qap9uev, http://tinyurl.com/puhgtsw

- Started having dreams and visions at seven years old.
- Saw a headline that read "America's Freedom is Over".
- Saw current president from Chicago and he would be the last president and would lead the people into the tribulations.

- Arabic nations were cheering when Obama won the elections. He is responsible for taking peace from the earth and causing war.
- Was shown ISIS.
- Saw plagues.
- Churches will be punished for speaking out against the gay marriage agenda.
- We are living in an era where there is much false prophesy.
- There will be an end to secure finances, a recession within a recession is coming.
- Everything that needs to be done, needs to be done before the end of summer, 2015.
- Stock-up on food and supplies, time is running out.
- We must prepare now.
- Jade Helm is a preparation for martial law, and part of disarming America.
- Many believe they will be shielded from the tribulations, but in reality they will go through it, or perish.
- For every 10 people who claim to know the Lord, only one truly knows Him.

Maurice Sklar, highlights:

http://tinyurl.com/pmgnydd

- Darkness covers the land.
- Heard screaming of lost souls.
- Saw the tree of Good and Evil.
- Felt an urgency to work while it is still day.
- Knowledge will increase exponentially.
- Saw fires hit different cities, all over the country.
- Saw mushroom clouds exploding all over North America in nuclear explosions.
- Saw a lot of smoke' after smoke clears U.S.A. is in total devastation.
- The U.S. is Babylon – symbol of man saying, "I did it my way" while shaking fist at God.
- Global economic system that will ensnare man, put in place by the enemy.
- Time is running out.
- The day will come as a 'thief in the night', sudden destruction will come.
- America ceases to be a world leader.
- The spirit is our antidote for deception.
- The Islands of the Sea is where the rich have hidden their wealth.
- The time will come when God must judge the nations.
- There are those who only pretend to know Him.
- Those who are His shall burn with the brightness of His glory.
- Christ warned over and over to "be ready".
- The United States of America is being devoured from the inside out by demonic creatures, its days are numbered.
- The dollar will collapse and all of America's wealth will be devoured.
- The days of America's beauty and glory will never been seen again.
- The darkness and tribulations are soon coming.
- The protection over the nations will be removed because of the wickedness of Babylon.
- Jerusalem will become the focal point of the world.
- Every single nation will come to attack Israel.
- The mighty U.S.A. will fall.
- God is not happy because we have been given so much, and much is expected.
- Many souls perish in the earthquake. It will be so terrible it will be felt in many states.

Rebecca Sterling: http://tinyurl.com/ntutugk

- (Sept 1999) Saw mixed-race U.S. President.
- PassPort Secret Agent (IDK what this means)
- Islamic Flag
- Abnormally Tall Wife dripping in Diamonds
- Chicken Blood VooDoo Dance in Whitehouse
- Sanctuary FEMA Camps
- 2015 Beginning Of The End
- Elites Orchestrating Things
- Meteor Shower
- Racial Riots
- Set-Up Financial Collapse
- Bankrupt Russia
- Martial Law
- No Election
- No electronics, no gas
- 89% Population Drop
- Nuclear Bomb
- Guillotine by Thousands
- No Rapture
- Obama lied to, he won't be the Anti-Christ
- Anti-Christ

Temple Dreamer, ldsfreedomforum.com

1. There is a small exodus of prepared saints who leave their homes.
2. The LDS Church leadership planned for the exodus years before it was made known.
3. Plans were confidential and similar to when saints moved to the valley of the Great Basin.
4. The endeavor is well organized, with assigned leaders (captains over 20, and 100, etc).
5. Telephone calling trees, couriers, etc are all pre-arranged.
6. There is a special meeting only for those who have their stored supply of food.
7. Trucks are sent to the homes to haul food storage.
8. Members are told to prepare for a long journey to places of safety.
9. Some people bring RVs to be used for specific purposes or for those with special needs like pregnant women, babies, the elderly or ill.
10. Most families stay in tents.
11. Most members will be asked to leave with only clothes they are wearing and limited necessities.
12. People leave in haste, but without fear.
13. Members meet at Stake Centers in early morning of late winter.
14. They are grouped by families, transported by buses.
15. Some people are asked to stay behind, for reasons not yet known.

16. There is a worldwide economic collapse.
17. Americas military power is eroded, soldiers fight with limited resources and support..
18. Gasoline is too expensive for people, cars are mostly abandoned on streets.
19. Homes are cold and dark, only a few hours of power per day and limited natural gas.
20. No civilian travel, times harder than pioneer days.
21. Food is in short supply, due to the cost of fuel to produce and transport it.
22. Europe is mostly in the dark, Israel is hanging on by her fingernails.
23. The alliance between China and Russia is strong, and they are preparing for war.
25. Starvation and disease are commonplace.
26. Lawlessness is rampant, propaganda is deliberately created and spread
27. There is an invasion by foreign troops.

28. Tent cities look similar to pioneer times.
29. Church headquarters communicates with the groups of saints via courier.
30. Everyone who is healthy must work in tent cities, some who won't are banished .
31. Green houses are built and agriculture is developed there..
32. Some tent cities are hidden in plain sight.
33. Camps were seen in northern Idaho, southern Utah, northern Arizona, Nevada, New Mexico..Virginia.
34. Underground camps in Maryland from the 1950s.
35. Bartering of services in camps.
36. Many great cities in ruin London and Tel Aviv are battlegrounds, Paris has been taken over, Berlin is uninhabitable..L.A. and San Francisco frantic, Boston in ruin except for LDS temple, which still stands..Chicago a battleground, Denver only city hit by

atomic attack.
37. SLC is dangerous even in daylight due to roving gangs, but Temple square remains pristine.
38. Church government continues to function and all tunnels in SLC area are heavily guarded.
39. Diesel fuel used for temple generators, no other power, temple dreaded by outsiders.
40. "2 legged unclean predators" try to enter temple but die or run in fear.
41. Thousands die within few hours to a few days ,from incurable virus type disease. The disease kills only a few in the tent cities.

Additional dreams, including many listed below, can be found in *Volume One:* ***The Great Gathering.***

Sarah Menet: http://www.nofearpreps.com/sarah-menet.html

Julie Rowe: http://julieroweprepare.com/

Gayle Smith: http://www.nofearpreps.com/gayle-smith-vision.html

Dream of Plagues: http://visionsandtribulation.blogspot.com/2013/12/the-dream-of-plagues.html

Cardston Prophecy: http://www.reliefmine.com/articles/prophecy/93-the-cardston-temple-vision-world-war-iii

John Taylor 1 & 2: http://www.nofearpreps.com/john-taylors-dream.html and http://www.nofearpreps.com/2nd-john-taylor-dream.html

Moses Thatcher: http://www.nofearpreps.com/elder-moses---people-coming-to-utah.html

Alma Erickson: http://www.reliefmine.com/articles/prophecy/96-vision-of-alma-d-erickson-early-1930s

John Koyle: http://woodyoubelieveit.blogspot.com/2009/08/john-koyle-prophecies-dream-mine.html

GA Smith: http://www.nofearpreps.com/ga-smith-vision-horne-version.html

Suzanne Freeman: https://latterdaycommentary.wordpress.com/tag/suzanne-freeman/

Temple Dreamer: http://www.ldsfreedomforum.com/viewtopic.php?t=4076

David Wilkerson: https://www.youtube.com/watch?v=bRn3UznKjAE

Renae Lee: http://www.greaterthings.com/Visions/Herendair_Sept08.htm

Man From Modesto: http://tinyurl.com/md3e9tq (Obama is the last president.)

Additional Sources & Notes

Iniquity

Talk to them; hear what they have to say—these learned men of the world. 'We have had worse times,' they say. 'You are wrong in thinking there are more calamities now than in earlier times. There are not more earthquakes, the earth has always been quaking, but now we have facilities for gathering the news which our fathers did not have. These are not signs of the times; things are not different from former times.' And so the people refuse to heed the warnings the Lord so kindly gives to them, and thus they fulfill the scriptures. Peter said such sayings would be uttered, and he warned the people. ...

Joseph Fielding Smith, April 1966

Scriptures

D&C 101:11

11 Mine indignation is soon to be poured out without measure upon all nations; and this will I do when the cup of their iniquity is full.

Mormon 8: 31,35-36

31 Yea, it shall come in a day when there shall be great pollutions upon the face of the earth; there shall be murders, and robbing, and lying, and deceivings, and whoredoms, and all manner of abominations; when there shall be many who will say, Do this, or do that, and it mattereth not, for the Lord will uphold such at the last day. But wo unto such, for they are in the gall of bitterness and in the bonds of iniquity.
35 Behold, I speak unto you as if ye were present, and yet ye are not. But behold, Jesus Christ hath shown you unto me, and I know your doing.
36 And I know that ye do walk in the pride of your hearts; and there are none save a few only who do not lift themselves up in the pride of their hearts, unto the wearing of very fine apparel, unto envying, and strifes, and malice, and persecutions, and all manner of iniquities; and your churches, yea, even every one, have become polluted because of the pride of your hearts.

Matt 24:12 / D&C 45:27

And the love of men shall wax cold, and iniquity shall abound.

2 Timothy 3:1-7, 13

1 This know also, that in the last days perilous times shall come.
2 For men shall be lovers of their own selves, covetous, boasters, proud, blasphemers, disobedient to parents, unthankful, unholy,
3 Without natural affection, trucebreakers, false accusers, incontinent, fierce, despisers of those that are good,
4 Traitors, heady, highminded, lovers of pleasures more than lovers of God;
5 Having a form of godliness, but denying the power thereof: from such turn away.
6 For of this sort are they which creep into houses, and lead captive silly women laden with sins, led away with divers lusts,
7 Ever learning, and never able to come to the knowledge of the truth.
13 But evil men and seducers shall wax worse and worse, deceiving, and being deceived.

D&C 123:7

7 It is an imperative duty that we owe to God, to angels, with whom we shall be brought to stand, and also to ourselves, to our wives and children, who have been made to bow down with grief, sorrow, and care, under the most damning hand of murder, tyranny, and oppression, supported and urged on and upheld by the influence of that spirit which hath so strongly riveted the creeds (apostate doctrines) of the fathers, who have inherited lies, upon the hearts of the children, and filled the world with confusion, and has been growing stronger and stronger, and is now the very mainspring of all corruption, and the whole earth groans under the weight of its iniquity.

D&C 1:11-16

11 Wherefore the voice of the Lord is unto the
ends of the earth, that all that will hear may
hear:
12 Prepare ye, prepare ye for that which is to
come, for the Lord is nigh;
13 And the anger of the Lord is kindled, and his
sword is bathed in heaven, and it shall fall upon
the inhabitants of the earth.
14 And the arm of the Lord shall be revealed;
and the day cometh that they who will not hear
the voice of the Lord, neither the voice of his
servants, neither give heed to the words of the
prophets and apostles, shall be cut off from
among the people;
15 For they have strayed from mine ordinances,
and have broken mine everlasting covenant;
16 They seek not the Lord to establish his
righteousness, but every man walketh in his own
way, and after the image of his own god, whose
image is in the likeness of the world, and whose
substance is that of an idol, which waxeth old
and shall perish in Babylon, even Babylon the
great, which shall fall.

Alma 37:22,25-26

22 For behold, the Lord saw that his people
began to work in darkness, yea, work secret
murders and abominations; therefore the
Lord said, if they did not repent they should
be destroyed from off the face of the earth.
25 I will bring forth out of darkness unto
light all their secret works and their
abominations; and except they repent I will
destroy them from off the face of the earth;
and I will bring to light all their secrets and
abominations, unto every nation that shall
hereafter possess the land.
26 And now, my son, we see that they did
not repent; therefore they have been
destroyed, and thus far the word of God has
been fulfilled; yea, their secret abominations
have been brought out of darkness and made
known unto us.

Isaiah 5:21-24

20 Wo unto them that call evil good, and good
evil, that put darkness for light, and light for
darkness, that put bitter for sweet, and sweet for
bitter!
21 Woe unto them that are wise in their own
eyes, and prudent in their own sight!
22 Woe unto them that are mighty to drink wine,
and men of strength to mingle strong drink:
23 Which justify the wicked for reward, and take
away the righteousness of the righteous from
him!
24 Therefore as the fire devoureth the stubble,
and the flame consumeth the chaff, so their root
shall be as rottenness, and their blossom shall go
up as dust: because they have cast away the law
of the Lord of hosts, and despised the word of
the Holy One of Israel.

Isaiah 24:5-6

5 The earth also is defiled under the inhabitants
thereof; because they have transgressed the laws,
changed the ordinance, broken the everlasting
covenant.
6 Therefore hath the curse devoured the earth,
and they that dwell therein are desolate:
therefore the inhabitants of the earth are burned,
and few men left.

1 Nephi 22:23

3 For the time speedily shall come that all churches which are built up to get gain, and all those who are built up to get power over the flesh, and those who are built up to become popular in the eyes of the world, and those who seek the lusts of the flesh and the things of the world, and to do all manner of iniquity; yea, in fine, all those who belong to the kingdom of the devil are they who need fear, and tremble, and quake; they are those who must be brought low in the dust; they are those who must be consumed as stubble; and this is according to the words of the prophet.

Quotes About Iniquity, by Church Leaders

The Family: A Proclamation to the World, The First Presidency and Council of the Twelve Apostles of The Church of Jesus Christ of Latter-Day Saints

We warn that individuals who violate covenants of chastity, who abuse spouse or offspring, or who fail to fulfill family responsibilities will one day stand accountable before God. **Further, we warn that the disintegration of the family will bring upon individuals, communities, and nations the calamities foretold by ancient and modern prophets.**

President Ezra Taft Benson, "Beware of Pride", General Conference, April 1989

The central feature of pride is enmity—enmity toward God and enmity toward our fellowmen. Enmity means "hatred toward, hostility to, or a state of opposition." It is the power by which Satan wishes to reign over us.

Pride is essentially competitive in nature. We pit our will against God's. When we direct our pride toward God, it is in the spirit of "my will and not thine be done." As Paul said, they "seek their own, not the things which are Jesus Christ's." (Philip. 2:21)

Our will in competition to God's will allows desires, appetites, and passions to go unbridled. (See Alma 38:12; 3 Ne. 12:30)

The proud cannot accept the authority of God giving direction to their lives. (See Hel. 12:6) They pit their perceptions of truth against God's great knowledge, their abilities versus God's priesthood power, their accomplishments against His mighty works."

President Thomas S. Monson, "Priesthood Power", General Conference, April 2011

We have come to the earth in troubled times. The moral compass of the masses has gradually shifted to an "almost anything goes" position. I've lived long enough to have witnessed much of the metamorphosis of society's morals. Where **once the standards of the Church and the standards of society were mostly compatible, now there is a wide chasm between us, and it's growing ever wider.**"

President Thomas S. Monson, "Looking Back and Moving Forward", General Conference, April 2008

The world can at times be a frightening place in which to live. The moral fabric of society seems to be unraveling at an alarming speed. None—whether young or old or in-between—is exempt from exposure to those things which have the potential to drag us down and destroy us. Our youth, our precious youth, in particular, face temptations we can scarcely comprehend. The adversary and his hosts seem to be working nonstop to cause our downfall.

President Gordon B. Hinckley, "Bring up a Child in the Way He Should Go", October 1993 General Conference

Some few months ago there appeared in the Wall Street Journal what was spoken of as an index of what is happening to our culture. I read from this statement:

"Since 1960, the U.S. population has increased 41%; the gross domestic product has nearly tripled; and total social spending by all levels of government [has experienced] more than a fivefold increase. … But during the same … period there has been a 560% increase in violent crime; a 419% increase in illegitimate births; a quadrupling in divorce rates; a tripling of the percentage of children living in single-parent homes; more than a 200% increase in the teenage suicide rate" (William J. Bennett, "Quantifying America's Decline," Wall Street Journal, 15 Mar. 1993).

The article concludes with a statement from Alexander Solzhenitsyn:
"The West … has been undergoing an erosion and [an] obscuring of high moral and ethical ideals. The spiritual axis of life has grown dim."

One need not, of course, read statistics to recognize a moral decay that seems to be going on all about us….

What is happening is simply an ugly expression of the declining values of our society…

When all is said and done, the primary place in building a value system is in the homes of the people.

Elder D. Todd Christofferson, "Why Marriage, Why Family" General Conference, April 2015

In the premortal world, **Lucifer** rebelled against God and His plan, and his opposition only grows in intensity. **He fights to discourage marriage and the formation of families, and where marriages and families are formed, he does what he can to disrupt them.** He seeks to convince men and women that marriage and family priority can be ignored or abandoned, or at least made subservient to careers, other achievements, and the quest for self-fulfillment and individual autonomy.

Elder Neil L. Andersen, BYU Education Week, 2015

As we find our way in a world less attentive to the commandments of God, we will certainly be prayerful, but we need not be overly alarmed, The Lord will bless His Saints with the added spiritual power necessary to meet the challenges of our day. …

"As the world slides from its spiritual moorings, the Lord prepares the way for those who seek Him, offering them greater assurance, greater confirmation, and greater confidence in the spiritual direction they are traveling. The gift of the Holy Ghost becomes a brighter light in the emerging twilight."

As evil increases in the world, there is a compensatory power, an additional spiritual endowment, a revelatory gift for the righteous. This added blessing of spiritual power does not settle upon us just because we are part of this generation. It is willingly offered to us; it is eagerly put before us. But as with all spiritual gifts, it requires our desiring it, pursuing it, and living worthy of receiving it.

I promise you that as you embrace the spiritual gifts prepared for the righteous, He will steady you, strengthen you, shape you, and secure you. You will be His.

Elder Robert D. Hales "General Conference: Strengthening Faith & Testimony"
General Conference October 2013

In recent decades the Church has largely been spared the terrible misunderstandings and persecutions experienced by the early Saints. It will not always be so. The world is moving away from the Lord faster and farther than ever before. The adversary has been loosed upon the earth. We watch, hear, read, study, and share the words of prophets to be forewarned and protected. For example, "The Family: A Proclamation to the World" was given long before we experienced the challenges now facing the family. "The Living Christ: The Testimony of the Apostles" was prepared in advance of when we will need it most.

We may not know all the reasons why the prophets and conference speakers address us with certain topics in conference, but the Lord does. President Harold B. Lee taught: "The only safety we have as members of this church is to … give heed to the words and commandments that the Lord shall give through His prophet. There will be some things that take patience and faith. You may not like what comes from the authority of the Church. It may contradict your [personal] views. It may contradict your social views. It may interfere with some of your social life. But if you listen to these things, as if from the mouth of the Lord Himself, with patience and faith, the promise is that 'the gates of hell shall not prevail against you; … and the Lord God will disperse the powers of darkness from before you, and cause the heavens to shake for your good, and his name's glory (D&C 21:6)."

Elder David A. Bednar, "We believe in being Chaste", General Conference, April 2013

The precise nature of the test of mortality, then, can be summarized in the following question: Will I respond to the inclinations of the natural man, or will I yield to the enticings of the Holy Spirit and put off the natural man and become a saint through the Atonement of Christ the Lord (see Mosiah 3:19)? That is the test. Every appetite, desire, propensity, and impulse of the natural man may be overcome by and through the Atonement of Jesus Christ. We are here on the earth to develop godlike qualities and to bridle all of the passions of the flesh.

Elder Dallin H. Oaks, "The Great Plan of Happiness," General Conference. October 1993

The power to create mortal life is the most exalted power God has given his children. Its use was mandated in the first commandment, but another important commandment was given to forbid its misuse. The emphasis we place on the law of chastity is explained by our understanding of the purpose of our procreative powers in the accomplishment of God's plan. ... Outside the bonds of marriage, all uses of the procreative power are to one degree or another a sinful degrading and perversion of the most divine attribute of men and women.

Dallin H. Oaks "Preparation For the Second Coming", General Conference, April 2004

Marriage and family responsibilities are discarded as impediments to personal indulgence. The movies and magazines and television that shape our attitudes are filled with stories or images that portray the children of God as predatory beasts or, at best, as trivial creations pursuing little more than personal pleasure. And too many of us accept this as entertainment.

The men and women who made epic sacrifices to combat evil regimes in the past were shaped by values that are disappearing from our public teaching. The good, the true, and the beautiful are being replaced by the no-good, the "whatever," and the valueless fodder of personal whim. Not surprisingly, many of our youth and adults are caught up in pornography, pagan piercing of body parts, self-serving pleasure pursuits, dishonest behavior, revealing attire, foul language, and degrading sexual indulgence.

An increasing number of opinion leaders and followers deny the existence of the God of Abraham, Isaac, and Jacob and revere only the gods of secularism. Many in positions of power and influence deny the right and wrong defined by divine decree. Even among those who profess to believe in right and wrong, there are "them that call evil good, and good evil" (Isa. 5:20; 2 Ne. 15:20). Many also deny individual responsibility and practice dependence on others, seeking, like the foolish virgins, to live on borrowed substance and borrowed light.

All of this is grievous in the sight of our Heavenly Father, who loves all of His children and forbids every practice that keeps any from returning to His presence.

Elder Neal A. Maxwell, "For I Will Lead You Along", General Conference, April 1988

We are told, by way of example, that some conditions preceding the second coming of the Savior will be as in the days of Noah (see Matthew 24:37–39) and "also as it was in the days of Lot" (Luke 17:28). Noah's time was one of disobedience and wickedness. People were uncomprehending and "knew not until the flood came" (Matthew 24:39; see also Genesis 6:5, 1 Peter 3:20). The choking cares and pleasures of this life led to the general rejection of Noah's prophetic message. Two especially interesting words are used in the Bible to describe Noah's time: violence and corruption (see Genesis 6:11). Violence and corruption, seldom strangers to the human scene, appear to be increasing today.

Elder Richard G Scott, "How to Live Well Amid Increasing Evil", General Conference, April 2004

Much of the world is being engulfed in a rising river of degenerate filth, with the abandonment of virtue, righteousness, personal integrity, traditional marriage, and family life. Sodom and Gomorrah was the epitome of unholy life in the Old Testament. It was isolated then; now that condition is spread over the world. Satan skillfully manipulates the power of all types of media and communication. His success has greatly increased the extent and availability of such degrading and destructive influences worldwide. In the past some effort was required to seek out such evil. Now it saturates significant portions of virtually every corner of the world. We cannot dry up the mounting river of evil influences, for they result from the exercise of moral agency divinely granted by our Father. But we can and must, with clarity, warn of the consequences of getting close to its enticing, destructive current.

Dreams & Visions of Iniquity

Spencer, ***Visions of Glory***

(p. 134-135) "In all of my visions I never saw a mark upon people, or heard people talking of being forced to receive a mark or microchip in order to buy and sell. It is already true that we each have a number of our name, and that number is required for any large transaction, such as buying a home or obtaining credit. That may have been part of the mark.

But, what I did see was that we had spiritually marked ourselves. This marking began perhaps thirty years before the tribulations, when the counterculture of political correctness began, and the assault on Christian values and traditions began. At first it seemed so ridiculous that it was harmless, kind of like a disease to which we were immune. Soon, however, it was recolored to equal compassion, acceptance, tolerance and equality. From there it evolved into a power with the ability to take any truth and repaint it as a lie, to take any lie and relabel it as truth. Subscribing to this thinking and tuning out the Holy Spirit marked us with darkness. It was a mark we placed upon our own soul. It was not visible to another human, but those who had marked themselves in this way could not discern the Holy Spirit, and they found themselves completely reliant upon the foreign troops, who in truth had no long-term interest in their survival, and who had many demands and rules to qualify one for assistance.

When the tribulations began it was nearly impossible for those who had received the mark of the beast to see God's hand reaching out to lead them to safety. They were blinded to the only thing that could redeem them, and many were eventually lost. "
Hector Sosa, Jr. , ***A Change is Coming***

(p. 17) Another dream I had was about the ocean. I was standing at night, with a full moon, on a road that had a guardrail. On the other side of the guardrail was a beach. I could hear the surf breaking against the sand and rocks. It was swishing back and forth. The water then started swishing harder and harder as if the ocean was angry. The water receded back into the ocean. I then heard a very angry feminine voice. The earth itself was crying out in frustration.

"Another dream I had was about the ocean. I was standing at night, with a full moon, on a road that had a guardrail. On the other side self again with water. I wait for the time when my righteous anger will be released. I will cleanse myself of this pollution. I will rid myself of the wicked sons of man. They are wicked as the sons of Adam of old."

Additional Commentary & Resources:

Top 10 Similarities between the fall of Rome and the fall of America

- **Over-Extended Military**
- **Government Corruption**
- **Immigration**
- **Birth Control**
- **Elimination of the Middle Class**
- **Obsession with Sports and Entertainment**
- **Redistribution of Wealth**
- **Exporting "Culture"**
- **Morality**
- **Inflation**

To read more:

www. http://www.moneycrashers.com/united-states-america-roman-empire/

America in Decline:

http://www.case-studies.com/nation-in-decline

Additional Sources & Notes

Famine

"We urge all Latter-day Saints to be prudent in their planning, to be conservative in their living, and to avoid excessive or unnecessary debt. Many more people could ride out the storm-tossed waves in their economic lives if they had a supply of food and clothing and were debt-free. Today we find that many have followed this counsel in reverse: they have a supply of debt and are food-free… We live in turbulent times. Often the future is unknown; therefore, it behooves us to prepare for uncertainties. When the time for decision arrives, the time for preparation is past.

President Thomas S Monson
"Are We Prepared?" Ensign Magazine, Sept. 2014

Scriptures

D&C 45:31-32

31 And there shall be men standing in that generation, that shall not pass until they shall see an overflowing scourge; for a desolating sickness shall cover the land.

32 But my disciples shall stand in holy places, and shall not be moved; but among the wicked, men shall lift up their voices and curse God and die.

D&C 97:23-26

23 The Lord's scourge shall pass over by night and by day, and the report thereof shall vex all people; yea, it shall not be stayed until the Lord come;

24 For the indignation of the Lord is kindled against their abominations and all their wicked works.

25 Nevertheless, Zion shall escape if she observe to do all things whatsoever I have commanded her.

26 But if she observe not to do whatsoever I have commanded her, I will visit her according to all her works, with sore affliction, with pestilence, with plague, with sword, with vengeance, with devouring fire.

D&C 5:18-19

18 And their testimony shall also go forth unto the condemnation of this generation if they harden their hearts against them;

19 For a desolating scourge shall go forth among the inhabitants of the earth, and shall continue to be poured out from time to time, if they repent not, until the earth is empty, and the inhabitants thereof are consumed away and utterly destroyed by the brightness of my coming.

Revelation 16:2

2 And the first went, and poured out his vial upon the earth; and there fell a noisome and grievous sore upon the men which had the mark of the beast, and upon them which worshipped his image.

Revelation 16: 21

21And there fell upon men a great hail out of heaven, every stone about the weight of a talent: and men blasphemed God because of the plague of the hail; for the plague thereof was exceeding great.

Revelation 16:8-9

8 And the fourth angel poured out his vial upon the
sun; and power was given unto him to scorch men with
fire.
9 And men were scorched with great heat, and
blasphemed the name of God, which hath power over
these plagues: and they repented not to give him glory.

Revelation 16:10-11

10 And the fifth angel poured
out his vial upon the seat of the
beast; and his kingdom was full
of darkness; and they gnawed
their tongues for pain,
11 And blasphemed the God of
heaven because of their pains
and their sores, and repented
not of their deeds.

Revelation 8:7

7 The first angel sounded, and there followed hail and fire mingled with blood, and they were cast upon the earth: and the third part of trees was burnt up, and all green grass was burnt up.

Revelation 8:10-12

10 And the third angel
sounded, and there fell
a great star from
heaven, burning as it
were a lamp, and it fell
upon the third part
of the rivers, and upon
the fountains of waters;
11 And the name of the
star is called
Wormwood
(bitterness):
and the third part of the
waters became
wormwood; and many
men died of the waters,
because they were
made bitter.

Quotes About Famine, by Church Leaders

I have asked of the Lord concerning His coming; and while asking the Lord, He gave a sign and said, "In the days of Noah I set a bow in the heavens as a sign and token that in any year that the bow should be seen the Lord would not come; but there should be seed time and harvest during that year: but whenever you see the bow withdrawn, it shall be a token that there shall be famine, pestilence, and great distress among the nations, and that the coming of the Messiah is not far distant."

Ezra Taft Benson, "Prepare for the Days of Tribulation", General Conference, Oct. 1980

Too often we bask in our comfortable complacency and rationalize that the ravages of war, economic disaster, famine, and earthquake cannot happen here. Those who believe this are either not acquainted with the revelations of the Lord, or they do not believe them. Those who smugly think these calamities will not happen, that they somehow will be set aside because of the righteousness of the Saints, are deceived and will rue the day they harbored such a delusion.

Ezra Taft Benson, "Not Commanded in All Things", General Conference, April 1965

Should the Lord decide at this time to cleanse the Church—and the need for that cleansing seems to be increasing—a famine in this land of one year's duration could wipe out a large percentage of slothful members, including some ward and stake officers. Yet we cannot say we have not been warned.

President Gordon B. Hinckley, "If Ye Are Prepared Ye Shall Not Fear", General Conference, Oct 2005

If anyone has any doubt concerning the terrible things that can and will afflict mankind, let him read the 24th chapter of Matthew… The church has built grain storage and storehouses and stocked them with the necessities of life in the event of a disaster, but the best storehouse is the family storeroom… Our people for three-quarters of a century have been counseled and encouraged to make such preparation as will assure survival should a calamity come.

President Gordon B. Hinckley, "The Times in Which We Live", General Conference, Oct. 2001

As we have been continuously counseled for more than 60 years, let us have some food set aside that would sustain us for a time of need…I do not wish to sound negative, but I wish to remind you of the warnings of scripture and the teachings of the prophets which we have had constantly before us. I cannot forget the great lesson of Pharaoh's dream of the fat and lean kine and of the full and withered stalks of corn.

Boyd K. Packer, "Solving Emotional Problems in the Lord's Own Way", April 1978

When people are *able* but *unwilling* to take care of themselves, we are responsible to employ the dictum of the Lord that the idler shall not eat the bread of the laborer (see D&C 42:42).

Elder Dallin H. Oaks, "Preparation for the Second Coming", General Conference, April 2004

What if the day of His coming were tomorrow? If we knew that we would meet the Lord tomorrow—through our premature death or through His unexpected coming—what would we do today? What confessions would we make? What practices would we discontinue? What accounts would we settle? What forgiveness would we extend? What testimonies would we bear? If we would do those things then, why not now? Why not seek peace while peace can be obtained? If our lamps of preparation are drawn down, let us start immediately to replenish them.

Dreams & Visions

Patriarch Wolfgramm (p. 41 D&VII) 1989

Big financial collapse last two years of a sitting president. There will be a great drought about the same time all over the country.

Anonymous (D&VII, p. 81) 2008

Complete breakdown in civil society. I understood that the beginning of this event was a result of the collapse of the food delivery supply chain. In my dream I did not see what precipitated this event, but it was starvation and famine that drove society over the edge.

Gayle Smith (personal dream/story on internet) 1993

After the collapse I saw marauding bands or gangs running around. People just go crazy and start rioting. They are killing because they are angry and hungry. Everything they know of value on this on this earth is being taken away from them within a few days. In a very short time there will be a famine.

I believe for the most part this famine is brought upon us. It's premeditated and planned out. No trucks bring food deliveries. Famine is brought on quickly and the stores are cleared out within hours. A short term after the collapse we are put under FEMA and Martial law.

Bishop John Koyle Vision

The messenger told him the purpose of the mine would be to bring relief to the Lord's faithful people at a time when great tribulation and distress would be in the land. The mine was to be called the "Relief Mine." He told him of a period of four years of famine and explained that the first two years the Saints would be able to get by, but the third and fourth years they would have nothing to eat unless it was prepared and stored up against that time. Then there would be two more years which would be a recovery period. The messenger explained that there would be winters of heavy snow and big snow drifts after which there would be a mild open winter, but whether that winter was to follow immediately or whether some other winters would be in between, he never explained.

However, immediately following the mild open winter, there would be a hot, dry summer. The crops would come up in the spring, and there would be considerable moisture, and the crops would be glorious (that is the word Bishop used to use.) He saw the wheat would grow up and head out beautifully, and the irrigated wheat would mature, but the dry land wheat would not have enough moisture to fill out. By harvest time the heads would curl over in a sort of crescent shape. This was shown to him in another dream wherein he saw he went into the wheat fields when they were binding the grain which looked like it would be a splendid crop. He picked up a bundle of wheat by the binding twine, and the head's end of the bundle came up with the butt end of the bundle hanging down because it was heavier. Realizing that the head end should have gone down if there had been good wheat in it, he examined the heads of wheat by crushing them in his hands to bring out the kernels. He found that the wheat was terribly shrunken and not fit for food. He was told by the messenger that this condition would bring about a shortage of food during the first year of harvest.

The second year he was shown would be the same only much less food raised. Still, the irrigated grain would be good. He was told we would need to store up the first and second years grain to supply food for the third and fourth years. The third year the shortage would be so great that there would hardly be anything raised for food. The fourth year they would not be able to raise anything for food.

He was shown in another dream that during the fourth year there would be plenty of money to buy food and he with others went up and down throughout the country seeking to buy food and they could not buy any. Any people who had a little food would not sell it at any price. During this time of famine there would be no rain to do any good. He saw the clouds would come up, and it would look like it was going to rain, but a wind would come up and blow the clouds away; and if there was any rain at all, it was just a few drops which were not sufficient to do any good.

The purpose of the mine was to build store bins and store up wheat and other foods like Joseph of old who was sold into Egypt. He saw the rains would come in the fifth year, and they would be forced to spare a little wheat for seed but would be sorely pressed to raise enough to eat during the fifth year and save enough for seed for the sixth year. The rains continued to come, the crops grew, and at the harvest time of the sixth year they would have enough food to carry on.

He was told by the messenger that there would be a great crash in the land before the period of famine began. This crash would be brought about by prices going up, which condition was illustrated to him as being like a person on high stilts. When prices became extremely high, something happened in the land like knocking the stilts from under the person and down came everything. Businesses closed down, labor was thrown out of work, people were hungry, and great tribulations were in the land. He saw that the best place to live and to work would be at the mine. Those who worked there would be the best off. He was told by the messenger that the Church program to care for the poor would all be used up during the first and second years of famine, that the mine would bring relief during the third year and would carry on the relief from the third year on.

Commentary

Have you Ever Been Hungry? by Brent Halls

Have you ever been hungry, really hungry? --two or more days without food and not knowing when you will eat again?

Most of us have not, nor do we know anyone who has been. I asked myself this question: How can we really understand how terrible severe hunger would be?

Perhaps if we had even a glimpse o f this condition we would better comprehend how important it is to have food set aside for ourselves and our family against a day of want.

Here are some books that give us a glimpse into this situation:

by Ezra Taft Benson

- Immediately following World War II, Apostle Ezra Taft Benson was called to Europe to organize the distribution of welfare supplies to the members of the church who were suffering greatly as a result of the war

- In this book Frederick W. Babbel, Elder Benson's secretary, described their experiences and the situations they encountered: encountered:

- "In a letter to my wife I reported the conditions we had faced: It is a shame to see people— members of our Church —in the last stages of starvation, eyes bulging out, legs and ankles swelling, and becoming so listless that it is a major effort to speak. So far we haven't lost too many members as a result of starvation. Unofficially, we have had less than 100 so far, but unless something is done very soon, diseases and permanent maladjustments due to faulty nutrition, etc., are sure to take a terrible toll.

- Some families of three and four are living on what one person in the United States throws away. If a person hasn't enough money to pay fantastic prices illegally on the "black market" he must face starvation. If he deals on the "black market" he is not a loyal citizen and is liable to face fines or imprisonment, if caught.

- The pace we are keeping is terrific. I hope we are able to slow down eventually. When one sees all the starving and suffering of these people, he is driven to work day and night."

by Sidney Iwens

- One man's story of the holocaust, told in his day-by-day account of hardship and miraculous survival.

- Towards the war's end, imprisoned in Dachau concentration camp, with artillery guns booming in the distance offering a hope of liberation, he describes his fortunate encounter with "food".

- "How long could I go on without food? How long had it been since I last ate bread? Five days? I didn't have much strength, but after a while I could no longer sit in the barracks. I tramped around outside— searching, looking. I moved away from the milling crowds toward the fence. No people there. At the hospital building, I stopped abruptly. On the ground, next to a trashcan, were a few chicken bones. The source of the bones was apparent: An overflowing garbage can. The lid could not quite conceal a bundle loosely wrapped with newspaper, partly open; it was crammed with chicken bones. It was hard to believe but shreds of chicken had been left on them. They must have been discarded only minutes ago; otherwise someone else would have discovered them by now. What luck! I crammed them into my pockets and slunk away from there fast.

- Careful not to be noticed by anyone, I chewed on the soft bone of a wing. I was in seventh heaven!

- Shells had been exploding since before noon. In the evening the explosions sounded closer, but I was beyond fear, absorbed in grinding and chewing my bones. I did it deliberately and with relish. During the day I ate stealthily, concerned that my windfall might be noticed. But now, enveloped by the protective darkness, I felt contented and relaxed, chewing away. A few explosions sounded so loud I felt certain that the shells had landed in the next barracks. Sometime in the night the shelling quieted down, and I fell asleep."

by John Noble

- John Noble was an American whose family owned a camera factory in Dresden, Germany at the beginning of World War II.

- Caught in Germany at the beginning of the war, the family survived the bombings and wartime conditions there.

- When the war finally ended, they were within the Soviet Zone, the area occupied by the Russian Army. Unexpectedly, John and his father were arrested by the Soviets and imprisoned. John eventually spent 9 ½ years in a Soviet labor camp in Siberia.

- In this and his companion book, I found God in Soviet Russia, John describes how, early in his imprisonment, the Russian guards tried to starve him and the other prisoners to death…

- "Each day my strength diminished. After an entire week without a morsel of food to eat, I found myself too weak to walk. . . . By this time my weakness was so great that I could no longer sleep at night. I did not feel any pain but felt dizzy and giddy, as if I were intoxicated. It was difficult to keep my thoughts collected. At times, I became delirious . . .

- On the ninth day of the fast, both my bodily strength and my mental processes had sunk to such a level that, in one of the few lucid moments I had in my delirium, I realized death could not be far away. . .

- The starvation regime continued four or five days longer. During the time, more and more prisoners died, until over half our number had gone. The rest were at death's door . . .

- The period of systematic starvation did finally come to an end after twelve hideous days. On Tuesday morning, August 14, without explanation, the 'liquid diet' order [consisting of a daily cup of warm water] was suddenly lifted and we received bread. It was not a full slice but some stale crumbs on a piece of paper, amounting in all to perhaps two ounces. However, it was our first nourishment of any kind and when I received these crumbs in my hand, I must have sat transfixed for at least a quarter of an hour, trying to comprehend that it was real and that the Lord had seen fit to save my life. Tears ran from my eyes and I offered a prayer of gratitude to God. Then I ate each crumb slowly, as though I were partaking of a communion wafer."

by Laura Hillenbrand

- Three men are on a raft in the Pacific, struggling to survive in the endless sea, after their bomber had crashed while on a rescue mission to find other downed airmen.

- They spent 47 days at sea before they were rescued… by the enemy.

- "As hunger bleated inside them, the men experienced a classic symptom of starvation, starvation, the inability to direct their thoughts away from food. The men studied their shoes and wondered if they could eat the leather. They decided they couldn't.

- The men's bodies slowly wasted away. Each day, Louie noticed incremental differences in his weight and the weight of his raft mates, the pants looser, the faces narrower,… they began to look grotesque. Their flesh had evaporated. Their cheeks, now bearded, had sunken into concavity. Their bodies were digesting themselves.

- They were reaching a stage of their ordeal that for other castaways had been a gruesome turning point. In 1820, after the whale ship Essex was sunk by an enraged while, the lifeboat-bound survivors, on the brink of death, resorted to cannibalism."

by Nathaniel Philbrick

- The story of the whale ship Essex, the real-life story that was the inspiration for Herman Melville's classic book, Moby Dick.

- In 1820 the Essex was sunk by an enraged whale leaving 20 men in 3 whaleboats 3 thousand miles from the South American coast.

- As their meager supplies ran out, they resorted to cannibalism, first eating those who died naturally, but finally drawing lots to determine who would be the one sacrificed for food.

- One boat was lost and never heard of again.

- Those remaining on the other two boats were finally rescued…

- "It had been twelve days since the death of Barzillai Ray. They had long since eaten the last scrap of his flesh. The two famished men now cracked open the bones of their shipmates—beating them against the stone on the bottom of the boat and smashing them with the boat's hatchet—and ate the marrow, which contained the fat their bodies so desperately needed. Both of them were so weak that they could barely lift their lands. They were drifting in and out of consciousness.

- For Pollard and Ramsdell, it was the bones—gifts from the men they had known and loved—that became their obsession. They stuffed their pockets with finger bones; they sucked the sweet marrow from the splintered ribs and thighs.

- The men were not much more than skeletons themselves, and the story that would be passed from ship to ship in the months ahead was that they were "found sucking the bones of their dead mess mates, which they were loath to part with."

by Miron Dolot

- In 1929, Joseph Stalin ordered the "collectivization" of all Ukrainian farms in order to destroy the well-to-do peasant farmers.

- The farms and their produce were confiscated by the state. The farmers were left destitute. Their livestock and most of the tools and implements needed to produce food were also taken. The result was a widespread famine in which millions died.

- This had previously been a happy and prosperous community; families, friends and neighbors living and working together.

- The following pages tell of the suffering of the people and the deterioration of their community as the result of the famine, as witnessed by the author, then a 16 year-old boy, who, along with his mother and younger brother, struggled each day to survive...

- "Around this time the plight of the villagers became desperate. This was the memorable spring of 1932 when the famine broke out, and the first deaths from hunger began to occur. I remember the endless procession of beggars on roads and paths, going from house to house. They were in different stages of starvation, dirty and ragged. With outstretched hands, they begged for food, any food: a potato, a beet, or at least a kernel of corn. Those were the first victims of starvation: destitute men and women; poor widows and orphaned children who had no chance of surviving the terrible ordeal."

- "Faced with starvation, the villagers tried everything possible to save themselves and their families. Some of them started eating dogs and cats. Others went hunting for birds: crows, magpies, swallows, sparrows, storks, and even nightingales. Driven by hunger, people ate everything and anything: even food that had already rotted—potatoes, beets, and other root vegetables that pigs normally refused to eat. They even ate weeds, the leaves and bark of trees, insects, frogs, and snails. Nor did they shy away from eating the meat of diseased horses and cattle. Often that meat was already decaying and those who ate it died of food poisoning."

- "We finally left our village behind and stepped onto the open road which led to the county seat. However, another ghostly panorama now opened in front of us. Everywhere we looked dead and frozen bodies lay by the sides of the road. To our right were bodies of those villagers who apparently had tried to reach the town in search of work and food. Weakened by starvation, they were unable to make it and ended up lying or falling down by the roadside, never to rise again. The gentle snow mercifully covered their bodies with its white blanket.

- A few steps further, we saw another frozen body. It was the corpse of a woman. As I brushed away the snow, horror made my blood turn cold: under her ragged coat, clutched tightly to her bosom with her stiff hands, was the frozen little body of her baby."

- "Thefts, burglaries, and robberies that were seldom heard of in our region became common occurrences now. A murder or suicide ceased to be a sensational event. Lawlessness was the result of the complete reorganization of communal life and the dissolution of human relationships. For instance, we heard that two brothers, Fedir and Vasil, good friends of mine, were beaten to death and thrown into an abandoned well. It was rumored that they were killed by their neighbor for stealing a cooked meal from his house. Another boy was beaten to death for stealing strawberries from someone's garden. A young woman met with the same fate for stealing vegetables."

- Upon entering the house of a neighbor, and finding her and her daughter dead…

- "In my imagination I was recreating the agony of their dying: the child's hunger cries, and then the death convulsions of its exhausted little body.

- How great must have been the sufferings of the mother. She had to listen helplessly to the pleas of her child for food, while she herself was near starvation. She must have felt great relief, I thought, when she saw her little daughter breathing for the last time. Then, in my imagination, I saw the mother attending to her lifeless child: dressing her in the best and cleanest clothing she had, praying on her knees near the body, and finally kissing her for the last time before her own suicide."

- "Toward the end of March, the famine struck us with full force. Life in the village had sunk to its lowest level, an almost animal-like struggle for survival of the fittest. The village ceased to exist as a coherent community. The inhabitants who still managed to stay alive shut themselves within the walls of their houses. People became too weak even to step outside their doors. Each house became an entity in itself. Visits became a rarity. All doors were bolted and barred against any possible intruders. Even between immediate neighbors, there was little, if any, communication, and people ceased caring about one another. In fact, they avoided each other. Friends and even relatives became strangers. Mothers abandoned their children, and brother turned away from brother."

- "The plight of the children was one of the most heartbreaking experiences for me during that time, and their pathetic faces, parched or swollen, and streaked with tears, will remain in my memory forever. They could not understand why they couldn't get a piece of bread or something else to eat. They were not able to comprehend what was going on in their own small world. Thinking of them still makes me tremble with horror. God is my witness that as I write these words the paper is wet with my tears."

Wheat Shortage in America and the World by Kellene Bishop

www.preparednesspro.com/wheat-shortage-in-america-and-the-world

http://www.cbsnews.com/pictures/californias-drought/

http://www.cadrought.com/

https://stateimpact.npr.org/texas/tag/drought/

http://droughtmonitor.unl.edu/

http://www.ers.usda.gov/topics/in-the-news/california-drought-farm-and-food-impacts/california-drought-food-prices-and-consumers.aspx

Additional Sources & Notes

Appendix

This section is a collection of articles written and submitted by individuals who were a part of a Face Book preparedness group. Used with permission.

Page Title

How To Make Your Own Family Emergency Binder

First, I found a sturdy 2" binder, and I already had heavy weight sheet protectors. I wanted my divider tabs to stick out beyond those sheet protectors, so I cut a thick cardstock (almost cardboard) paper the same width as my sheet protectors and I bought the divider tabs that are self-sticking to adhere to your own page. That way, my tabs stuck out to where I could see them.

The categories I did for my family binder are: Finance, Taxes, Legal, Medical, Household, Vehicles, and Church. Below I will share what basic kinds of things I put into each category.

1. Finance

- List of each Checking & Savings account of everyone in the family with the Bank name/address/contact numbers, Account Number. Also online username and passwords for each account.
- List of all investments: retirement accounts, stocks/bonds, whole life insurance, etc. with the Institutions name/address/contact numbers, Account number, interest, and any rules regarding each account. Also online username and passwords for each account.
- List of all debts (Mortgage, car loans, student loans, credit cards, etc.) Including each Bank name/address/contact number, Account number, interest rate, monthly payment, & due date. Also online username and password for each account.
- List of your monthly bills, Name/Address/ Phone/ Account numbers and when each are due
- List of all your sources of income, with contact information for each
- Any accidental death insurance policies offered by my bank

2. Taxes

- Make a copy of the last 5 years of state and federal tax returns - just the main pages not the whole return.
- Any other vital information related to taxes

3. Legal

- Originals of all Birth Certificates and Social Security Cards of each member of your family
- Copies of State ID or Drivers Licenses for each member who has one
- Original Marriage Certificate
- Life Insurance Policies with the Company's name, address, phone number, and Policy number

4. Medical

- Medical records or notes for each member of your family (including blood type, allergies, major concerns or sicknesses, past surgeries/injuries)
- List of medications and dosages for each member of your family
- List of all family Doctors and medical professionals including addresses and phone numbers
- Dental records or notes for each member of your family
- List of family dentist(s) with address and contact information
- Immunization record for each member of your family applicable

5. Household

- Password Keeper - a list of ALL online accounts with user names and passwords
- Copies or Originals of school credits or degrees
- Mortgage packet documents - just put the whole pack in there (or rental agreement if renting)
- Latest appraisal and any other official information about your home
- List of your all your belongings, including serial numbers and pictures if you can
- Homeowners or Renters Insurance Information - Company, address, contact information
- Up to date pictures of each member of your family, and of you all together. If you get separated, having pictures to identify and help find your loved ones may be crucial and pictures to "prove" you are a family in certain situations might be needed.
- List of all important family and friends with their contact information

6. Vehicles

- List of all your vehicles with License plate, VIN number, date you got it, If it's paid for yet, and description with pictures
- Original title of any vehicle you own
- Basic records of upkeep, repairs and maintenance for each vehicle
- Copy of your Auto Insurance Policy with the Company's name, address, phone number, and Policy number
- List of your Auto Mechanics with their address and contact information

7. Church

- Church marriage certificate, certificates of ordinations (baptism, priesthood, etc.) and special achievements
- Copies of personal blessings
- Church record numbers and dates of ordinances for each member of the family
- List of church leaders and contact information

BONUS:

- Keep extra keys to your home, garage and vehicles in a zipper pouch in the front of your binder so if you lose your other keys, you'd have your emergency backup.

Remember after you get your binder together, to go through it at least once a year and UPDATE the information so it can be as current as possible. Bonus if you go through it every 6 months.

You don't have to put pictures on the front or be that fancy.

Just looking over this, you may be thinking "That's crazy to have all that vital information in the same binder where a burglar can just take it." In some sense, that seems true. But in another sense, how many burglars go looking around through binders when they rob a home? Is that even on their stealing agenda? You could name your binder something that a thief wouldn't even be looking for like "Uncle Ted's Journals" or "Grandma's Stories".

Also, it's recommended storing your emergency binder in a fire proof safe. A large enough safe may also be a deterrent for any thief who wants a quick get-a-way. If getting a safe isn't in the cards right now, you could opt for a safety deposit box at the bank. Or find a secure location in your home where it would least likely be discovered by an intruder. For me, I think the benefits far outweigh the risks.

Also, just thinking about a situation where my home might be destroyed and I need documentation that I owned the home, or of my belongings, I would have it right there. Emergency situations are already traumatic and can leave you in a panic, but having all your most important documents and information right with you can certainly ease a bad situation and help give you peace of mind. Especially when it comes to being separated from loved ones.

Original Post: http://www.diypreparedness.net/how-to-make-your-own-family-emergency-binder/

How to Recognize and Overcome The Normalcy Bias in These Last Days

The Normalcy Bias is a state of mind where a person is in DENIAL when faced with pending danger.

Having Normalcy Bias allows an individual to minimize and even underestimate the possibility of a disaster even happening (sometimes even while it is happening), thus not acting in a way to protect ones safety and health. Being subject to the Normalcy Bias causes individuals and families to fail to prepare for likely impending calamities.

The Normalcy Bias is related to prophecy in the scriptures. Since we haven't experienced a real famine, nuclear attack, major earthquake, and a massive volcano erupting; folks presume these calamities won't happen in their lifetime. Most of the same individuals believe that there is a God, yet they don't truly believe the ominous prophecies made by Him.

2nd Peter 3:3-4: "Knowing this first, that there shall come in the last days scoffers, walking after their own lusts. And saying, Where is the promise of his coming? For since the fathers fell asleep, all things continue as they were from the beginning of the creation"

EXAMPLES of NORMALCY BIAS:

1) One story was shared where a plane had problems that required an emergency landing. After a jolted landing, no announcement was made or flight attendants seen. One man jumped up and headed to the emergency exit, opened it, pulled the zip for the blow up slide, went down and waited for everyone else. No one else came. He saw the tail of the plane was on fire. So he climbed back up into the plane and yelled for everyone to get out. They looked at him and made comments like "Who are you to tell us what to do?" "You aren't in charge!" They all just stayed in their seats, waiting for the pilot or authority figure to tell them what to do. The exasperated man went to the exit and just then the plan blew up and he was blown out of the plane through the exit. He was the only survivor.

2) Folks in New Orleans had never witnessed a levee collapse. So when it became obvious during Hurricane Katrina that their levee system would fail, thousands of people in the direct line of the coming flood still remained in their houses. Thousands of them perished in the waves.

3) Probably the best example and the one most applicable to what seems to be repeating itself in America is the Nazi Holocaust. Why would so many Jews underestimate and ignore the ever present signs of uncertainty and peril even after they were compelled to wear yellow stars of identification and had unfair laws passed that targeted them and their businesses? Why would many of these

wealthy Jews not move out and leave the country? It was the Normalcy Bias that kept them there and lead to their eventual exterminated. They didn't see the danger in front of them.

WHY the NORMALCY BIAS is so DANGEROUS For us NOW:

Here are some reasons as to why it's alarming to be stuck in a Normalcy Bias.

- It hinders our ability to cope with disaster.
- Makes it difficult to react to things we have not experienced before.
- It can lead us to misinterpret warnings, or even not recognize them as warnings.
- Makes us take a disaster or emergency lightly and leads us to not prepare accordingly.
- Lulls us into distraction, even when events and signs (nationally and globally) are all around us.
- Makes us question if there really is any danger – or that we would "know" if there was.

10 STEPS to TAKE NOW:

- **Prepare 72 hour kits** (If you haven't already) for each member of your family. Something you can grab and take if you need to leave quickly. Be sure it has water, water filter, good shoes, change of clothes, flashlight w/ extra batteries, list of contacts and phone numbers, food for 3 days, jacket/coat, first aid kits, and other survival items needed. Keep kits easy to access and let everyone in the family know where they are and what is in them.
- **Obtain 3 months of food and water storage**. Start with water first, then move on to food. Plan on how you would do a home quarantine if a pandemic situation presented itself. Be prepared with food and water you would need if you had to isolate your family for an extended amount of time.
- **Build a comprehensive First Aid Kit** for your family. Consider what would be needed if there was no option to go to the doctor or hospital during a pandemic, or after a calamity. Start with basics like bandages, wraps, pain killers, fever reducers, antiseptics, anti-bacterials, and medicines; then move on to things like tourniquet, brace, Israeli bandage, blood clotters, skin stapler, and so forth.
- **Make the Unknown Familiar by PRACTICING.** Do family drills and scenarios to get your brain thinking of emergency situations and how you would best ACT. Practicing can also help you RECOGNIZE danger beforehand, so you don't get trapped in the Normalcy Bias. Play the "What would we do if…" game as a family and go over the different situations that might happen. Thinking about that now will bring a sense of familiarity when it does happen. And actually practicing a drill can develop muscle memory for those traumatic situations.
- **Learn Situational Awareness.** The complete OPPOSITE of the Normalcy Bias is Situational Awareness! It includes having a full perception of your surroundings and a comprehension of what might occur in the near future. Because other people may attempt to give you false information, situational awareness obligates you to be the guardian of your own life.
- **Work on Preparing Every Needful Thing.** This includes a means of power, fuel, communications, medical needs, spare parts, personal hygiene, cleaning items, shelter, and

a means to protect yourself and your family – plus the myriad other items that make up a complete preparedness package. This should be carefully thought out with the needs of your family, home, resources and types of calamities most at risk in your area.

- **Do not go into Debt to prepare.** It can feel overwhelming, but do what you can. Make a list of what you need so the angels can see it. Pray about what you need and allow God to open doors for you. Be sure to budget your money, consider skipping a trip or newer car purchase. Sacrificing is so worth it for the peace of mind of being prepared.
- **Continue with a Minimum Years Supply of Food** if you can. Long term foods like grains, legumes, rice, oats, etc. will be priceless when a famine hits. Learn how to store them best for long term and also how to use and prepare them. Be sure and include honey, salt, cooking oils, powdered milk, and so forth.
- **Store some Cash** if you can. If the banks suddenly closed, having even a little cash on hand for quick items needed can be super helpful. Store in small bills, like ones and fives. Cash may only be good for a little while after a collapse – but having some on hand would be wise. Ultimately, you cannot eat cash or precious metals; so food will most likely end up being the best commodity to invest in.
- **Build your Faith.** While realizing that danger is coming or an emergency is upon us and being fully aware of needing to be ready; it is also just as important if not more so to believe that God is in control and to be aligned with Him. Having Faith in Jesus Christ and trusting Him can and will be the foundation that pulls us through these traumatic situations that are surely coming upon us. Let us fill our lamps with the oil of service, love and obedience so that our hearts won't fail us and we will know where to find peace when things are chaotic.

The world is facing a test right now which requires acute situational awareness. The many signs of the last days are before us, and it's imperative for each of us to know Jesus as the only One who can redeem us from the days to come. "And when these things begin to come to pass, then look up, and lift up your heads; for your redemption draweth nigh" - Luke 21:28.

Original article: http://www.diypreparedness.net/how-to-recognize-and-overcome-the-normalcy-bias-in-these-last-days/
Image of taking a picture of meteor found on: veryfunnypics.eu

Quick & Mobile Rolling First Aid Kit for your Home

Original article here: http://www.diypreparedness.net/quick-and-mobile-rolling-first-aid-kit-for-your-home/

For years I had the same home-made First Aid Kit in a big long tackle box. I felt pretty good about it, but as time has gone on, I knew I needed to update it. Upon looking around, I decided to also build another kit and organize it better. When I saw this rolling cart, I knew I had to do a kit that could be mobile and hold more things.

My biggest motivator is knowing that in an earthquake, it would be days and possibly weeks before help might arrive and I wanted to have things on hand to help my family and others.

This "tool box" is called: Keter Master Pro Sliding Box. I got it on Amazon for around $55. The price seems to fluctuate and I've seen it for less on Walmart.com and Homedepot.com. Do a search for the "Keter Master Pro Sliding box".

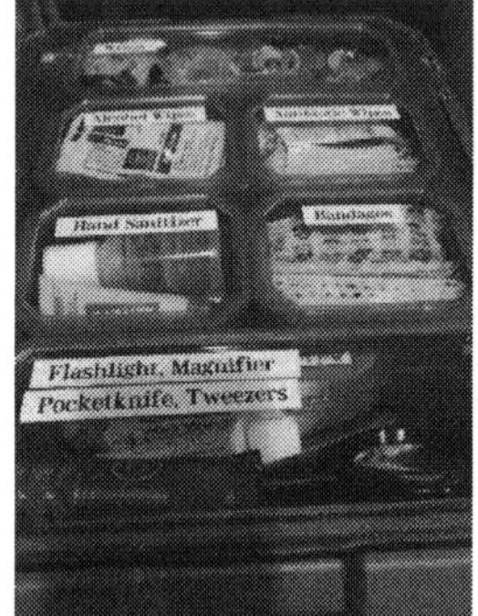

The top compartments slide open with a bin inside for bigger things. It is lockable, not too rugged of a lock but I think it would do well enough to keep unwanted little hands from exploring the contents when you have it out. For the top portion, I keep books and resources on the left and

Above is a closer look at the top right. It has small red compartments that are removable. This is where I put my Quick-Grab items like band-aids, hand sanitizer, antibacterial packets, tweezers, and other small tools. I love to label everything so I can get it quickly. I put in a multi-tool pocket knife and added safety pins (not on the label). Since making this blog post I've also added in the flashlight area: safety pins, Splinter Out, thermometer, nail clippers, tape measure and a tick remover.

These are the books I am storing in the top left of my Rolling First Aid Kit for now. Polly's Birth Book is one-of-a-kind booklet that covers pregnancy and birth - a GREAT resource. The RNotes is another great resource with descriptions and pictures of what to do in various medical situations. It can be used for triage like situations when you need help understanding symptoms and how to treat them. The duct tape book has drawn pictures of how you can use duct tape medically. Now I need to make sure I have duct tape in there! Lastly, it's smart to have a notebook and pens/pencils to write down information and/or keep notes on any injuries or person's you treat.

These are the items inside the bin of the Rolling First Aid Kit. Items in plastic containers are labeled so when you are going through this in a hurry, you can quickly look at the labels to find what you need. I feel like labeling is imperative. You can never have too many gauze and dressings. Exam gloves are also very important.

This is the "spread" of what I have in my Rolling First Aid Kit (minus the pack of N95 masks). I love having organizers so I don't have to rummage through items to find what I might need. I tried to put items in categories to be able to find more quickly. I used plastic containers I found at Walmart where the lid snaps closed effectively. I didn't want containers where the lids might slip off or come off too easily and make a mess. Since making this blog post, I've also added a Waterbag/enema kit.

In the biggest container I have pain relievers (aspirin, ibuprofen, Tylenol), allergy medicine, cold and flu medication, cough and congestion

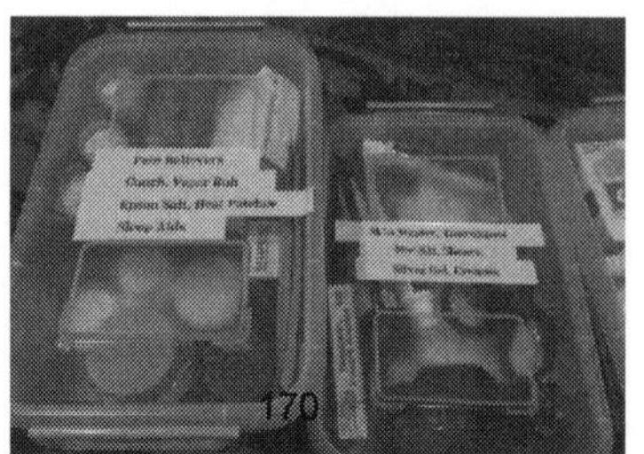

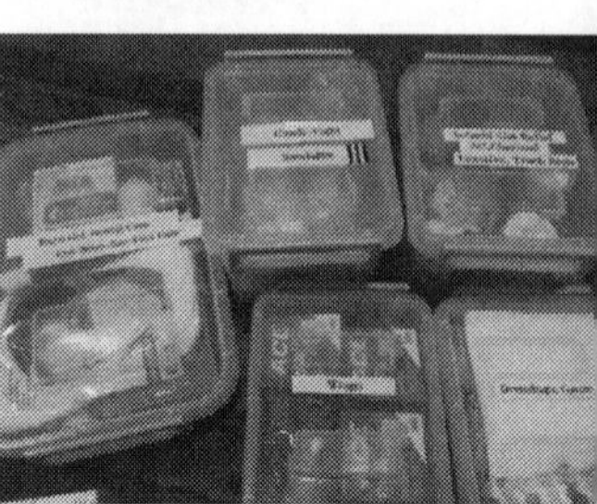

syrups, Halls cough drops, vapor rub, bag of Epson salt, large and small heat patches for painful muscles, and sleep aid pills. The next biggest container I have a skin stapler, stapler remover, box of simple tourniquet/forceps/scissors, anti-itch cream, Hemorrhoidal ointment, Silver gel, and first aid shears which can cut clothing off quickly when needed.

In another container which was the same size as the last one I keep Burn Jel (This works awesome), Dental care items like dental pick and mirror, dental fillings repair, dental topical anesthetic. Also things for the eye/nose/ear/foot care: nasal strips, nasal relief spray, eye patch, ear plugs, athlete's foot cream, Moleskin, liquid corn and callus remover. And some simple face masks I got at Dollar Tree.

A smaller and taller container has 4 Cinch-Tight bandages. These are great for treating wounds that are hemorrhaging. A must have for every kit, I think! Look up YouTube videos on using Cinch Tight or the Israeli bandage. I think there's one called the hook or H bandage that are also similar. It's important to see how they work.

The other smaller and taller container has items related to stomach and digestion: activated charcoal capsules, antacid, gas relief, laxative, Pepto bismal, and a small pack of trash bags (also from Dollar Tree).

The two smallest containers have Ace wraps and sensi badages (the kind that sticks to itself when wrapping up a wound or area); and different sizes of gauze and dressings. The orange rolls there are padded aluminum splints. You can unroll it and form it to the limb needing the splint, getting it just as you need it. Then bend the width of the splint to make it firm and immovable. This is a great resource for your First Aid Kit and is like those used in many ER rooms. Also a bite and sting kit is important. And petroleum jelly.

FIRST AID KIT - in ROLLING BOX	
Flashlight / Magnifier	Skin Stapler / Staple remover
Thermometer / Splinter-Out	Tourniquet/Forceps/Scissors
Multi Pocketknife tool	First Aid Shears
Tape Measure / Safety Pins	Mini Sewing Kit
Tweezers / Nail clipper	Anit-itch/Clotrimezole cream
Tick Remover	Silver Gel
	Hemorrhoidal Ointment
Hand Sanitizer	
Bandages	
Alcohol & Antibacterial Wipes	Asprin / Ibuprophin
Carmex	Ibuprohin
Sensi-Wraps / Ace Wraps	Allergy Medicine
	Cold / Cough syrup
Finger Splints	Clear congestion syrup
Water Bottle - Enema System	
Padded Aluminum Splints	Halls cough drops
Exam Gloves	Epson Salt
Colloidal Silver	Vapor Rup
Petroleum Jelly	Sleep Aid
Bite & Sting Kit	Cold / Flu Medication
Q-Tips and Cotton Balls	
	Burn Jel
Cinch-Tight Bandages	Nasal Strips
Activated Charcoal capsules	Nasal Relief spray
Antacid / gas relief / laxative	Eye Patch
Dressings & gauze	Ear Plugs
N95 Face Masks	Athletes Foot Cream
	Moleskin
Polly's Birth Book	Liquid corn and callus remover
Duct Tape 911 Book	Dental mirror/pick
First Aid Book	Dental fillings repair
Rnotes - Clinical Pocket Guide	Dental Topical Anethetic
Notebook and Pens	Face Masks

Exam gloves are important to have on hand. You can get some excellent exam gloves that are non-latex at Costco in a two pack for $20. Cotton balls and swabs can be easily gotten at Dollar Tree. I also like keeping some colloidal silver on hand as it has helped my family get over many illnesses and even cured my daughter's strep throat. The one pictured here is called St. George Nano Silver, but there are other kinds and brands that are effective.

Other items you might want to consider having in your first aid box or preps:

- Items you might need during a baby delivery like: hemostats (clamping cords), resuscitation masks ranging in sizes, and an infant suction bulb.
- Reusable nitrile gloves that can be disinfected and used over and over.
- Perineal Irrigation bottle – to clean out a wound with clean water.
- Triangular bandages

One way to determine what you might want in YOUR kit, is to think of what disaster or possible trauma would MOST LIKELY occur in your area or even just to your family. So for me, I'm thinking earthquake. When there is a big quake, I know we won't have access to help for days/weeks. The most common injuries from an earthquake are broken bones, crush injuries, blunt force trauma, penetrating wounds and contusions and head trauma.

Top 10 Natural Medicines To Have In Your Emergency Preps

If there comes a times when we are not able to get to or access a hospital or doctor; we will have to rely on our own know-how and medications for health issues. There are many things we can have on hand for times like this and even times like now. It's a good idea to try and become more reliant on ourselves than institutions for our health care as much as possible.

From my own study and combined with notes from a webinar titled: "What if there were no medicines tomorrow?" featuring Professional Herbalist and Traditional Naturopath, Laurence Smith; I have this list of ten items to have on hand for just such times.

*** Disclaimer - I am in no way associated with Laurence Smith, or any of the products he mentions, or any company's listed or pictured here. I am simply sharing information I found very helpful ***

1. Colloidal Silver and Colloidal Silver Gel

Silver is like a second immune system. It has a broad spectrum it reaches with no resistance build up. It's a first line of defense for bacteria and viruses, and considered the first of the top ten health "ammunition" to have in your armada. It has many topical and internally. The webinar talked about Silver Shield and Silver Shield Gel which provides a finer particle sized silver giving a higher bioavailability rate and no risk of heavy metal contamination. I personally have used colloidal silver to ward off sicknesses and strep throat. It's one of the best things to keep in your medical and health preps.

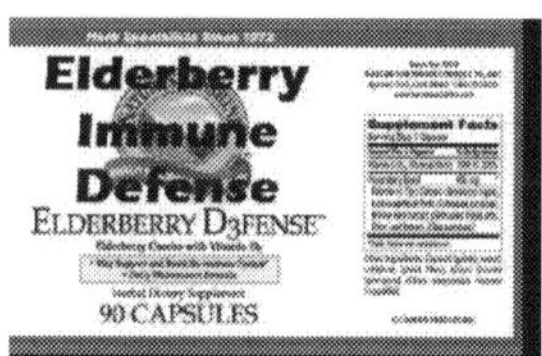

2. Elderberry Immune Defense

A second most powerful and potent immune defense. Elderberry is the best antiviral. Take this when you begin to feel a cold or flu coming on - like even a tingle in your throat. Take often to keep sickness away. Try looking for this herb with Vitamin D added, like Elderberry D3fense from Nature Sunshine which was the product recommended in the Webinar.

3. Olive Leaf Extract

Besides being a natural anti - bacteria, fungi, viral, yeast herb; Olive Leaf Extract is known for helping you live longer. There are many benefits of Olive Leaf Extract that have been known for ages and now proven by scientists. It helps lower blood pressure, keeps arteries healthy, helps lower blood sugar levels, helps prevent tumor growth (anti-cancer), protects the brain and central nervous system by suppressing inflammation, can help prevent arthritis. These top three items are all a powerful defense against sickness, bacteria and viruses.

4. Mullein (Lambs Ear)

Officially known as Verbascum Thapsus, Mullein is a fuzzy leafed biennial plant. It is known as the herb of the lungs. Powerful as a respiratory remedy; it has been used to treat asthma, coughs, tuberculosis and other respiratory related problems. Not only that, you can use it as a mild astringent, expectorant, and anti-inflammatory. You can treat hemorrhoids, bruises, burns, gout and clear your ears out with it. Mullein can be ingested, or used topically.

5. Hawthorn

Hawthorn is good for the heart, like a cardiac tonic, it strengthens the heart. Hawthorn berries can make your heart beat stronger and even normalize a heartbeat. They have also been used to benefit the circulatory system altogether and treat high blood pressure, high cholesterol, angina, and congestive heart failure. Hawthorn has been used for many centuries.

6. Capsicum

This is a hot pepper, like cayenne, which contains the active principle capsaicin which is used to cool pain. You can apply directly to a wound or swallow. It can be used for pain from inflammation, psoriasis, muscle spasms, and even dry mouth. In the webinar, the presenter said he used this on a woman to stop a nose bleed and just seconds after she swallowed some capsicum, her bleeding stopped.

7. Yarrow

Yarrow is a healing herb and a great go-to source for helping children as well as adults. It can ease fevers and shorten the length of colds and flu's, and help you relax during an illness. When used topically, it eases skin rashes and itching. Good for cuts, abrasions, and stopping cramps; yarrow is shown to have an effect on every organ in the body and thus it brings balance to your system by harmonizing it.

8. Activated Charcoal

Similar to regular charcoal, activated charcoal is made specifically for medical purposes. It can treat poisonings, lessen gas, treat bile-flow issues, and lower cholesterol levels. Basically, it is effective at trapping chemicals and preventing their absorption. You can even put activated charcoal in a straw and use cloth on each end, and use it as a water filter. The same thing with two face masks; put some activated charcoal in-between the masks and tape them together and you have a mask that will filter out poisons and poisonous contaminants as you breathe. This is a great item to keep in your cabinet and emergency supply kit. For a great video on all the ways you can use BULK activated charcoal, check out the Healthy Preparedness blog post and video: http://healthypreparedness.blogspot.com/2015/08/activated-charcoal-internal-external.html

9. LBS II (Lower Bowel Stimulant)

LBS is a lower bowel stimulant and support. It can help production of digestive fluids and bile, and help you have a bowel movement. It also helps you have better digestion. This is important when your body is needing to get rid of toxic waste, and especially if you do not have access to a doctor.

10. Slippery Elm Bark

Native to North America, the Slippery Elm tree can get up to 60 feet tall. Bark from this tree is collected in the spring for many medical purposes and has been used for years. It relieves coughs, sore throats, colic, diarrhea, constipation, hemorrhoids, irritable bowel, stomach issues, and even expels tape worms. You can apply it to the skin for burns, wounds, cold sores, boils, abscesses, toothaches, and as a lubricant to ease labor.

So these are just the top ten items that could be extremely useful in an emergency situation or in day to day health care. Best of all, you don't need prescriptions for these, they are all natural and good for you. Many of these items are things you can find in the wild or make yourself. I'm finding that learning about these things helps me feel more confident in my own ability to help my family.

Original article found here: http://www.diypreparedness.net/top-10-natural-medicines-to-have-in-your-emergency-preps/

Using Buckets and Bins To Organize Your Preps

There are so many lists of things to gather and have on hand. One way to organize and store these various "Prep" items is using buckets and bins.

BUCKETS

A 5 gallon round bucket is a common, very useful and sturdy container that can be sealed tight with a gasket lid. Buckets come in other sizes and they have different grades, food grade typically being stamped with a number 1, 2, 4, or 5.

For long term food storage, the best kind of plastic bucket to utilize is a high density polyethylene (HDPE) which is one of the most stable and inert types of plastic and is a food grade #2. PETE, PP (Polypropylene) and LDPE are other kinds of plastics that are also okay for food storage and use the food grade #'s of 1, 4 and 5 typically. If you run in to a plastic bucket with a # 7, it is a bio plastic which are synthesized from a plant-based source like corn. However, not all #7 buckets are bio-plastics. So you may want to stick with buckets labeled with a 1, 2, 4 or 5 for storing food. ** TIP - Be sure and store a bucket lid opener with your buckets to make opening them much easier.

You can also purchase a gamma lid for your 5 gallon bucket, making it easy to open and use the contents. Not all your buckets need a gamma lid, just the one or two that you are using the most often and need to get the contents in and out more frequently.

4 Gallon SQUARE Buckets

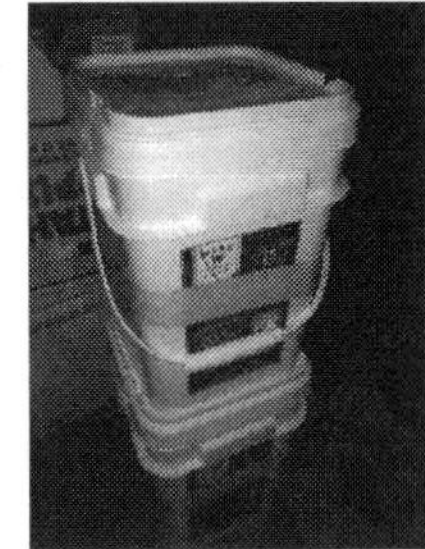

Another way to store your preps are these 4 gallon square buckets with gasket lids (you can get non gasket lids, and even gasket lids with hinges) from the Industrial Container and Supply Company in Utah. This is a great way to store food or non-food preps.

I've decided to use colored duct tape to help identify what's inside (blue for hygiene, yellow for fire, etc.). And a printed list of what's inside taped to the lid. I've put most things inside in ziplock bags or vacuum sealed bags.

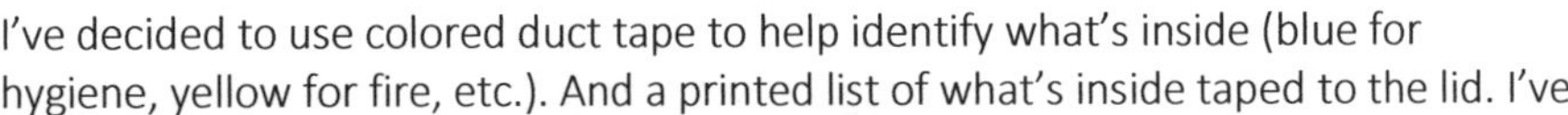

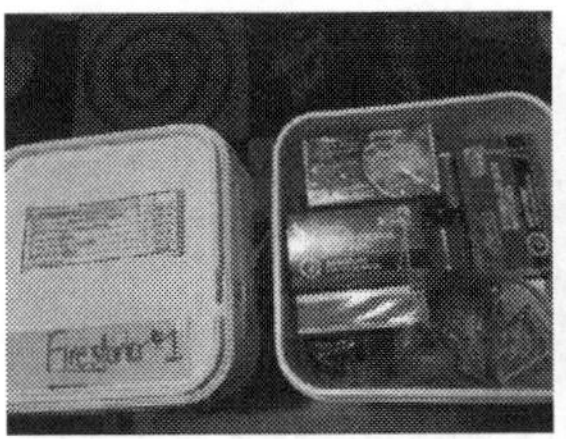

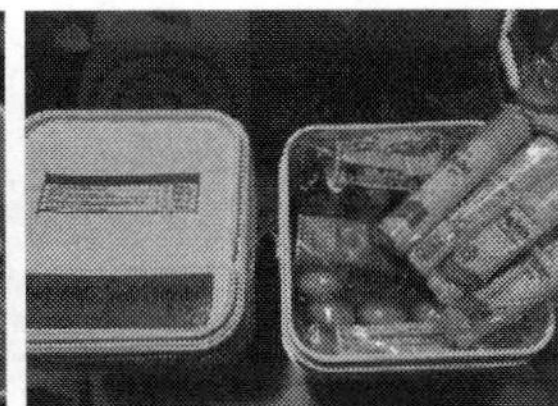

I'm thinking I will do this to store a lot of my non-food items. These are for items beyond the 72-hour-kit time frame. In preparing "every needful thing" and the "necessities of life" as counseled by several prophets. In the event that stores cannot be reached or are closed, power outage, call to gather or bug out, and so forth.

BINS

Bins are plastic containers that have lids and come in various sizes and are usually stackable. There are different brands and durability of bins. Some material weather better in different temperatures and have better fitting lids, although the more durable bins are usually more expensive as well. I have found that the clear plastic bins I've used seem to end up breaking and cracking first. We've gotten blue bins and brown bins from Wal-Mart that we've had for several years and have fared okay. The lids snap on each end, but do bend with the contents up in the middle not always keep things sealed inside.

Recently, we've purchased bins like this, which seem to be much more thick and durable than previous ones we've been using these last ten to fifteen years. ** TIP - Always label what is inside your buckets and bins. Have labels clear and easy to read.

Some of The Many Ways You Can Use 5 Gallon Buckets

1. Store and organize your preps
2. Use as a homemade clothes washer (http://www.foodstoragemoms.com/wash-clothes/)
3. Use as a port-a-potty. Get a toilet seat cover/lid that fits right over it. (http://chadperson.com/recess/2010/05/bucket-toilet-lid.html)
4. Use a portable survival garden. You can move it easily to where there is sunlight using the handle. You can use them for composting.
5. Make a water filtration system using two buckets. (http://www.cheaperthandirt.com/product/CAMP-352)
6. Use to harvest rain water, or to even collect water from a stream.
7. Turn one on its side for an animal den or shelter.
8. Use in building things; mix concrete or other things inside it.
9. Use buckets to cover plants in the winter.
10. With the lid on, you can use it as a seat or stool.
11. Use it to carry dirt, wood, tinder, etc. while camping or gardening.
12. Carry and transport about anything like fishing gear, cleaning supplies, tools, etc.

Ways You Can Use Storage Bins

1. Turn it into a sink. Some even install a little drain to it.
2. Give a child or pet a bath in a large bin
3. Use as your firewood container when camping
4. Use as a bed or home for animals or a pet.
5. Keep clothes, towels, bedding and other items dry.
6. Use as a catch all for shoes before entering a home or tent.
7. Keep all your medical supplies together.
8. Use as furniture if needed (coffee table, chair, bench, etc.)

What To Store in Your Buckets and Bins

- Food Storage Buckets - Bulk wheat, rice, beans, etc.
- Food Storage Buckets - Ready to eat Meals, Freeze dried packets, just add water meals, MRE's
- 72 hour kits - one bucket per family member
- Water Bottles Bucket - one bucket per family member filled with water bottles
- Dishes: plates, bowls, silverware
- Prepping Dishes: large bowls, spoons, spatulas, rubber scrapers, whisks, measuring cups
- Pans: Dutch oven, iron skillet
- Spice Bucket: spices, gravy mix, baking soda, yeast, bullion
- Disease Control Buckets: toilet seat/toilet paper
- Shower Bucket: Solar shower bag, bar soap, face cloth, lotion, shaver, towels
- Tool Bucket: Spare tools, hammer, screw driver, measure tape, glue
- Quarantine Bucket: disposable overalls, gloves, masks (must have to treat sick people)
- Laundry Bucket: plunger, soap, line and clothes pins
- Cleaning Bucket: Scrubbers, cloths, soap, aprons, hand towels, all purpose cleaner
- Utility Bucket: tape, bungees, cutters, rope, wire, glue
- Fuel Bucket: propane stove, 1lb propane bottles
- First Aid Bucket: ointment, bandages, medications, braces, stomach ailments, flu remedies
- Hygiene Bucket: shampoo/conditioner, toothpaste, make-up, q-tips, lotion, poison ivy lotion
- Sewing Bucket: thread, needles, scraps of material
- Candle Bucket: left over candles, new candles, bag of wicks, matches
- Media Bucket: personal Media player(s), Uplifting movies, Music on iPod.
- Library Bucket: books, scriptures, photos

- Game Bucket: cards, dominos, dice, chess
- Baby Bucket: cloth diapers, bottles, blankets, pins
- Military Bucket: binoculars, netting, ammo belt, knives, radio, 2-way radios
- Office Bucket: paper, notebooks, pens, pencils, crayons
- Weapons Bucket: guns, ammo, stun guns, etc.
- Money Bucket: precious metals, cash, copies of family papers, passports, etc.
- Shoe Bucket: Boots, flip flops, sandals, tennis shoes
- Bedding Bin: sleeping bag, wool blanket, pillow, camp blanket
- Clothing Bins:
- Winter Clothing: overalls, gloves, beanies, cap, long underwear, wool socks, long sleeve T's, long sleeve shirts, jeans, coat, sweatshirts, vest
- Summer Clothing: swimsuit (showers), shorts/capris, short sleeve shirts, sunglasses, socks, underwear, belt, hat/visor.

Original post: http://www.diypreparedness.net/using-buckets-and-bins-to-organize-your-preps/

Helpful Links

TEACHING YOUR KIDS: For some great strategies in teaching your children about the signs and events of the last days in a way that doesn't instill fear, but helps build their faith - here is an article that you may might very helpful: http://www.diypreparedness.net/preparing-your-kids-for-disasters-and-events-of-these-last-days/

STORING GLASS / CANNED FOODS: If you've been looking for ways to store your home canned foods safely, here is a blog post showing one inexpensive way to store your jars that can keep them more protected as well as easy to transport in case of a bug out: http://www.diypreparedness.net/store-your-glass-jars-canned-food-safely-and-affordably/

ITEMS TO STOCK UP ON: Here is a great list of items that would be most essential after a disaster or economic collapse. These items would be great to have on hand for us and for bartering: http://www.diypreparedness.net/items-to-stock-up-on-for-barter-after-disaster-or-economic-collapse/

EVENTS TO FOLLOW AN ECONOMIC COLLAPSE and HOW TO PREPARE NOW: This article shows what events would happen after a national financial drop, and how you can prepare now: http://www.diypreparedness.net/events-to-follow-an-economic-collapse-how-to-prepare-now/

MAKE YOUR OWN ALTOIDS SURVIVAL TIN: If you've ever wanted to put together your own survival tin, it's all laid out in this blog post. You can put these in your 72 hours kits, car glove box or in your purse to always have these survival items with you: http://www.diypreparedness.net/diy-altoids-survival-tin-for-family-bug-out-bags/

ORGANIZE YOUR OWN FIRE-STARTING KIT: Have all your essentials for making fire together in a kit for easy retrieval and use in making a fire should the need arise: http://www.diypreparedness.net/basics-of-fire-starting-diy-fire-starter-kit/

HOW TO BOTTLE BACON: Learn how to can bacon at home in this simple tutorial blog post, including pictures: http://www.diypreparedness.net/canning-bacon-how-to-bottle-bacon-at-home/

WAX AND STORE REAL CHEESE: Preserve hard cheeses for your food storage and enjoy real cheese during an emergency. This article will show you how: http://www.diypreparedness.net/waxing-cheese-at-home-real-cheese-food-storage/

David's Prep Tips

"The best storehouse system would be for every family in the Church to have a supply of food, clothing, and, where possible, other necessities of life." Pres Monson, Sep '13

I wanted to share a few things I've learned as I've prepared to gather to a Place of Refuge. Some of these tips I feel were inspired, some of them were luck, and some of them were learning after trial and error. This is not a comprehensive list, but rather, it has some things that I did research on and I feel I can recommend them (and maybe save you time. Some of these items are expensive, but my thinking was that money is only useful for things like this and it won't be worth anything in the not too distant future.

General Tips: Amazon Prime: Assuming you are going to buy more than 10 items from Amazon, you will want to get Amazon Prime. It costs money, but you will more than make up for it by having free shipping. And having 2-day shipping is very, very nice. If you plan ahead, you can just do the free trial of Amazon Prime and order all your things at once. But comparatively, it's not much

Food: I have bought food from the Church and at least six other preparedness companies. If looking for prepared meals, one of the best purchases was a pallet of 36 six-gallon buckets of prepared meals from Costco online. Not only is it a massive total of 2,592,000 calories, the meals look good. And the price per calorie is the best I've seen (comparing pre-packaged, long term meals). What I did is I emptied all the mylar-resealable pouches out of the buckets, placed them in boxes I got from the Church Home Storage center ($0.95 each), and then filled the buckets with wheat and rice. Because all 36 buckets are food-grade and come with gamma lids, I was able to just pour bags of bulk wheat from the Church Home Storage Center ($6 per 25 lbs!) This alone would have given me all the food I need for my whole family.

Cost: $3,499.99 including home delivery. They also have a variant with some buckets substituted for freeze dried vegies and fruit.

Cooking Pot: Instead of a pressure cooker, I got an insulated thermal cooker from Saratoga Jacks. There are many similar thermal cookers on Amazon. If you get the Saratoga Jacks one, get the option where the inner smaller pot has the extra thick bottom. This site also sells lithium battery packs, hanging LED lights and essential oils.

Water Filter: I really like the Sawyer mini (100,000 gallons, 0.1 micron, 99.99999% of bacteria; 99.9999% of protozoa) for the price (~$17.00). It works much better than the life-straw kinds. But I also like this Survivor filter (indefinite gallons, 0.01 microns!). Besides the primary filter, it also has a carbon filter, which will improve the taste and smell of the water. It advertises the removal of 100% of all bacteria and protozoa, 100% of all viruses, and 99.99% of all chemicals and heavy metals. It has a pump, bobber and hoses for pumping water quickly. Cost: ~$65.00. Both may be purchased on Amazon.

Shelter: Without a doubt, the best price I've seen for a good tent is a refurbished, insulated, military style tent at thecampingstore.us. Just note that these are very heavy tents. Talk to Brandon Hunter and he'll help you out.

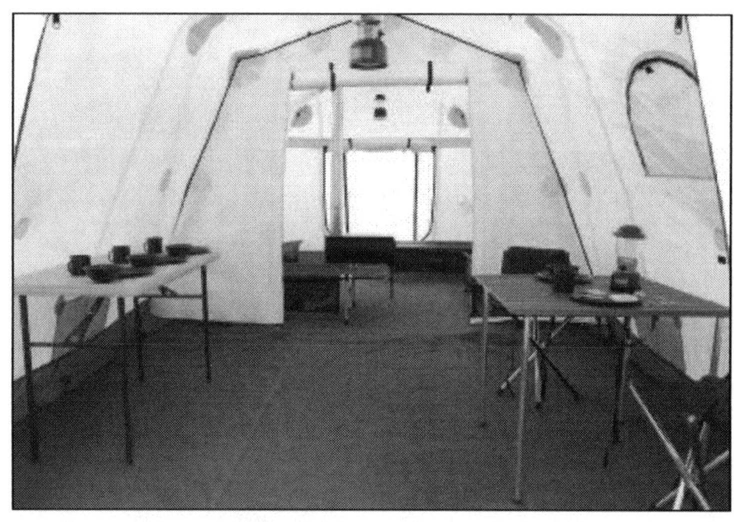

Arctic Oven: But if you don't buy one of Brandon's I would highly recommend an Arctic Oven tent. Yes, they're expensive. But as far as preparations go, having a good tent may be the best thing you can allot your money to (next to food, water and having a reserve of money). These Arctic Oven tents are much better than a canvas wall tent. They have two walls – water/wind-proof outer, and a very condensation proof inner wall. Not only are you warm, but you're dry. And it's almost impossible to over-stress the importance of protecting against condensation. When it gets cold, there are a lot of people that are going to discover that everything in their tent is wet. Consider this my warning to you. Arctic Ovens are the tent of choice for some Arctic expeditions, but they will work great for the other three seasons. If you buy multiple, each tent after the first is 10% off. Sizes range from 3- to 15-man tents. They are compatible with wood-burning stoves (sold on their website; also check ColoradoCylinderStoves.com, Kni-Co.com, and OutfittersSupply.com; you can buy an oven attachment on Amazon.com...for those that want to bake some bread or even a pie.) Save more money and instead of buying the floor saver ground cloth (in picture) go to Home Depot and buy indoor/outdoor carpet for ~$0.45/ sq. foot.

Testimonials: "I'm from the Northwest Territories, Canada. ...This is my second season with your Arctic Oven. What a treat!!! I went from freezing in a canvas wall tent (and having to get friends to put it up for me) to being toasty warm in your tent - that took less than an hour to put up. What a pleasure... All were very impressed. Kudos for a great product." – *Linda*

"It is more of a secure cabin feel to me than it is a tent. Just can't be beat for warmth and wind resistance. Had it in Kodiak for 7 days of sideways rain. No problems." *Tom Zimmerman*

"We used our Arctic Oven tent on the northern part of the Tibetan Plateau (~5 km high) during late October when the permafrost is already frozen. Temperatures were as low as -30 degrees C at night. The insulating capabilities of the tent kept us warm enough to get a comfortable sleep **even without a stove.** The tent works very well in extremely cold conditions." *Carmala Garzione – University of Rochester, Dept. of Earth and Environmental Sciences*

"I spent 14 days in Nunavut, Canada, inside an Arctic Oven. All I can say is -50 degrees, on top of 8 feet of ice with 35 mph straight line winds and zero visibility . . . no sweat for Arctic Ovens! *Casey Keefer/Dropped: Project Alaska*

UV Protection: Most tents are not made to endure UV rays for years on end. To fix this, pick up a couple bottles of Nikwax Tent & Gear Solar Proof. It will extend the life of you tent from about 18 months to many year. It also makes things water-resistant. Cost: ~$18.00

Tent Space: Tent space will be at a premium. You can save room by hanging up nets on the ceiling, clotheslines along the walls... and you get these hanging organizers at Ikea or Amazon. You can also buy Disc-O-Bed Cam-O-Bunk Cots, which will save a ton of room over normal cots. They come in adult or child size. The con is they are expensive and heavy. But they are easy to put together and are very sturdy. They also come with hanging side organizers. If you don't get them but want a cot, be sure to get one that doesn't squeak whenever you move (a common complaint with cots).

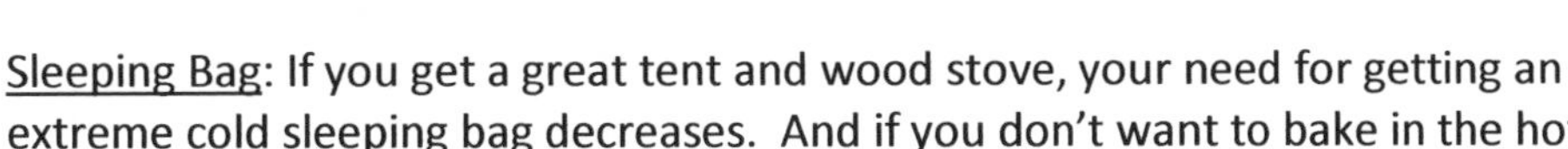

Sleeping Bag: If you get a great tent and wood stove, your need for getting an extreme cold sleeping bag decreases. And if you don't want to bake in the hot summer, I recommend getting a modular sleeping bag (or at least bring extra blankets). I love this military set (called the MSS-3) and was astounded that I could buy it refurbished for just

over $50! I loved this bag; it's warm, it's cool, and now it's inexpensive. I got it at MidwayUSA.com, but they always seem to sell out fast. So also check Ebay.com. When both layers are combined, it is rated for -30° and comes with a compression sack.

If you want an extreme sleeping bag, the brand I recommend is from Wiggys.com. Remember what I was saying about condensation in tents? This means people will be sleeping in damp sleeping bags and blankets that will never really get dry. Wiggy's has amazing insulation that also pulls water away. According to one man who got soaked in rain while camping, instead of removing his clothes, he went into his Wiggy's sleeping bag with his clothes on. The next morning, his clothes were all dry and the outer layer of the bag was wet. It works so well, the company sell strips of their insulation you put in winter boots to pull the moisture out and dry for the next day. They've had a 20% sale on sleeping bags for a long time and a bonus deal where you get free winter pack boots (see boots below). They sell modular versions, and a wide range of temperature ratings...from +40° F to -80° F. The one pictured to the right is a Wiggy's Hunter Antarctic (FTRSS) Rectangular Bag (Cost $264, plus almost 2-3 free pairs of pack boots). With the three combinations of using it, it can be for temps of +35°, -60°, or -80° F. It comes with a camp pillow and compression sack.

Winter Clothing: Clothing is one of the few specific things mentioned by President Monson to get. For whatever reason—warranted or not—I have based all my winter gear purchases with the idea that I will be out all night in the bitter cold keeping guard over our tent city. Spending several hundred dollars now will be nothing to what I—or those I share with—will feel in the coming years. I hate being cold! Here's a few tips.

Arctic Boots: You may find a less expensive or more versatile boot than these, but you probably won't find a warmer one. I bought these Baffin boots (see left) several years ago when I was a scout leader in Alaska and we were preparing for our winter overnighter in the mountains. I vowed my toes would be cold no longer and so I splurged and got these. That campout was ridiculously cold but my feet were the only part of my body that never got cold! At one point my feet actually got too warm and I needed to change my socks. They are rated for -148 degrees ... so you aren't going to wear these on a chilly fall day. They have women's versions as well. Just look for "Baffin Impact insulated boot." Cost: about $155.00

Wiggy's also sells these winter Pack Boots for $120 (see right). I have four pairs, but they were all free! They have a deal online where you get a free pair for the first $200 you spend, and an additional pair for each additional $100 spent. One lady I know bought two sleeping bags and got seven free pairs of boots! They have the same excellent moisture wicking properties I described in sleeping bags.

Snow jacket: I'm really happy with this arctic under-parka insulation from Wiggy's. It's not just comfortable, it's extremely comfortable. I love how it covers the neck and fills in all the space around my body (much like down does). But down doesn't keep you warm when it's wet. I saved a ton of money by just getting the L-12 insulation and not buying the outer parka shell. They have a great description on their site as to why their insulation is so good and I recommend reading it; it was very informative for understanding cold weather gear and other insulations (like foam clothing). Like their sleeping bags, not only can it be washed, they actually encourage you to wash it. A great product! I did notice, however, that when the insulation is compacted (like when I'm lying on my back), I can start to feel the cold seep through. Standing up, I didn't feel any cold in a wintery night with 23 mph winds.

Cap and neck Gaiter: Wow! Perhaps the greatest buy I accidentally came across is the -60 degree Windblocking Arctic Thermal Hat, and Windblocking Arctic Thermal Straight Neck Gaiter. I tried out my gear in 23 mph winds in below-zero temps, and of all my expensive gear, I was most impressed with the relatively inexpensive cap and gaiter! I didn't feel a tinge of cold coming through—not in the wind, and not while laying my head in the snow for a half an hour. I wish they made more clothing items with this material. These products are toted as 100% wind proof; I was skeptical but they worked flawlessly. The cap is advertised as the "warmest hat on the Planet," and although I got the lightest neck gaiter they sell, I think the only way it could be better would be if it covered more area (which the colder rated ones do). I highly, highly recommend these! (Note: I love their Thermal Moisture Wicking Liner Socks too; they are amazing) Cost: Cap = $45.99 and Gator: $26.99 at tadvgear.com/page34.htm

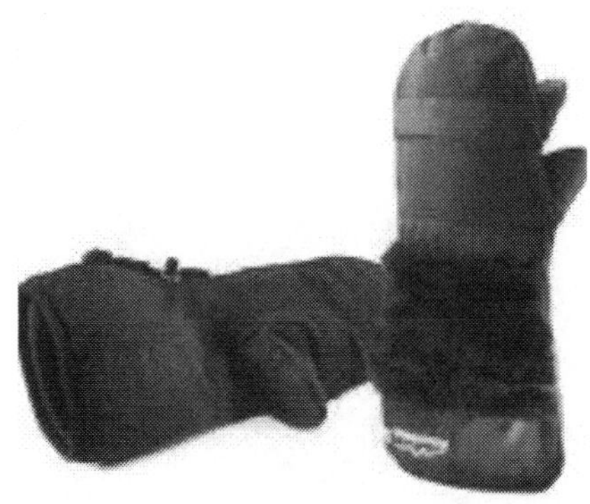

Mittens: Did I mention I hate being cold? I have two arctic/Iditarod racing mittens that work much like a warming pouch; your hands will never get cold in them, but you won't be able to handle much with them because they are so bulky. One of my mittens is from Technical Advantage Gear (same company that makes that cap and neck guard) and I don't really recommend them. They are too big for my liking, and I got the smallest size! The other pair is from Norther Outfitters and is rated to -60°. I got the smallest size and they fit just a little large (I have medium size hands). I can wear low-profile gloves and slip my hands in these. They were very, very warm, however, the large opening doesn't seal and it let cold air get to my wrists. I accidentally got snow inside and I was surprised at how well it absorbed the water; I really didn't feel it. However, they have an odd detail that I like: there is a digit sticking out of the palm where you can slide your index finger into to give you added dexterity. This would allow you to pull the trigger on a gun without removing your mittens, for example. Wiggy's also sells various gloves and mittens. Their

warmest ones come with inner insulation covers for your hands. Both these and the Northern Outfitters brand have a fluffy area meant to wipe your nose with. They also have a draw string to close up the opening around your forearm. I don't have the Wiggy's kind, so I can't really say if I'd recommend them, but because of the deal they have, you can get more free boots buy buying them! They are both very expensive (about $125.00 for Northern Outfitters and $133.00 for Wiggy's), but for that money you are guaranteed to never have cold hands and fingers! And that is a great blessing!

Goggles: Get goggles! If you don't want your eyes to freeze in the blowing snow and cold wind, you need goggles. I bought these ones (they are meant for snowmobiling) and they work great. The have double-layered visors (to reduce fogging up), extended foam, and micro fleece which is moisture wicking. I wanted the nose guard to add extra wind protection for my nose when uncovered. They also have a large viewing area. But you don't need these ones ... ANY goggles will be so much better than nothing. (If interested, these are called Dragon Alliance NFX Ionized Snow Goggles)

Timberland Pro Boots: I spent a lot of time going to half a dozen shoe stores to find a pair of boots that will last me through the years of tribulation. Without a doubt, these are the winners of my search, and I am excited to recommend them! I bought an equivalent pair for my wife (Called "Titan"; pictured at bottom right). Honestly, this may be the most valuable review you'll get from me. The Timberland Pro line of boots have some kind of "anti-fatigue" padding that feels great. Besides that, they are waterproof (a must!), are anti-microbial, ice/slip resistant, have a composite toe (lighter than steel but just as strong), and the outside toe area is covered in a tough rubber for increased wear and abrasion resistance. (They are also electrical shock and oil-slip resistant, but I don't imagine those things will be important.) I liked the looks of the "Endurance" brand more (and it had some attractive features, such as steel toe, rubberized heal and puncture resistant sole), but I settled on "Boondock" kind because it had even more stitching and looked more durable. But either would be great. They have cold insulated versions of the exact same shoe (minus the composite toe), but you don't want your feet cooking in the summer and if you just have a good pair of warm socks. You can buy them at Amazon. The men's are true to size but we found we had to get the wider women's size. Cost: Men's: $215.00, Women's: $108.00

Kids Shoes: If you want a rugged waterproof shoe for toddlers, I found these for a really good price online at Basspro. But I haven't seen them in a while. Cost $39.99. They're called RedHead Roark Jr Hiking boots. Be sure to get waterproof boots for your kids! It's a must-have attribute for your shoes.

Socks: I know they are expensive, but Darn Tough brand of socks are extremely comfortable, made of merino wool and may just last for the rest of your life (unless you live to the age of a tree). But I'm not kidding; they may last for decades...let alone the years of tribulation. Think of it this way: a few good pair of socks will be one of the most important items you will own. Everyone I know who has them loves them. And while researching socks, this brand kept coming up at the top of the pack in very extensive reviews of multiple brands of quality socks. I highly recommend you cast a blind eye to the price and buy several pair for you and your family. You can find all sorts varieties, cushions, lengths and for hot or cold on Amazon.

<u>Lumberjacking:</u> Cutting firewood won't just be a good idea, it will be an urgent matter of surviving the long winter ... which we won't have much time to prepare for. These are the tools I got to make this go as quickly as possible.

I got a Two-man Crosscut Saw from crosscutsaw.com. They looked to be the best quality AND at the best price I could find.

Woodchuck log lifter. This one is very expensive but the others I researched seemed to bend/brake when hoisting large logs. This one is very thick and sturdy. You can get it on Amazon for $105.00

Fiskars X27 Super Splitting Axe, 36-Inch: The reviews of this thing on Amazon are beyond positive. Another great looking tool is the Smart-Splitter log splitter from Baileys. It has a wedge on a track that you just throw down. Instead of swinging an axe, you let gravity do most of the work. Cost: $55.00 and $99.00

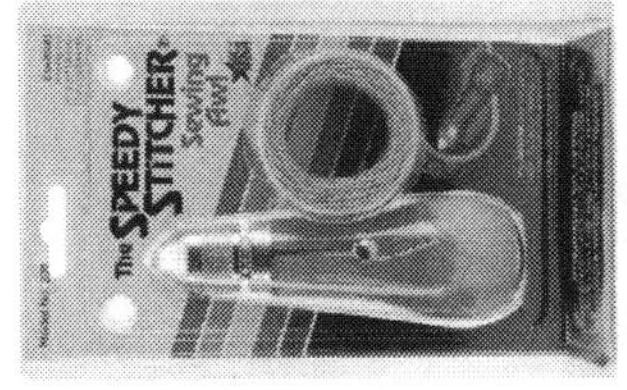

Fire gloves: I'm very impressed with the quality of these gloves. Who needs a wimpy pot holder when you can reach into a fire and grab a log with these guys! I bought the red welding ones, but I think these black hearth ones would be better. Cost: $24.66

Speedy Stitcher Sewing Awl: If you think you are going to need to sew tents, canvas, shoes, leather, etc., you will need an awl

Bandanas: Don't buy handkerchiefs, buy bandanas. They are more versatile. I got the tan ones. As a general rule, you don't want white handkerchiefs in dusty environments. I found a 12-pack on Amazon for $13.12.

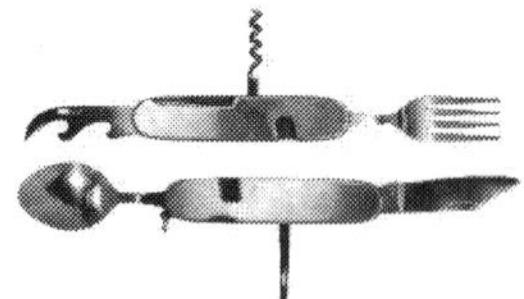

Utensil: A pretty nifty eating utensil. The quality is not very good, but if you can find a better quality version, I would recommend something like this. I like how it separates to allow you to cut with the knife and fork. Cost: $4.24 on Amazon

Laundry: I bought this paint bucket for doing laundry. You can't tell by the picture but it has a sloped, ridged side that will allow you to agitate your clothes ... just like a wash board. It's as though it was made for this! $10.00 at Lowe's.

On a similar vein, I found out from an Amish department store how to make your own laundry detergent for real cheap. Don't bother ordering from them; you can get all the ingredients you need for dirt cheap. Buy one box 20 Mule Team Borax (76 oz. box); Arm & Hammer Washing Soda (55 oz. box); and 5 bars Fels-Naptha soap (5-1/2 oz. each) and combine them. You'll need a cheap cheese grater to reduce the Fels-Naptha bars. In one small bucket you'll have enough detergent for 800 loads of laundry. Buy a box of Oxy-clean booster for your white clothes.

Zodi Outdoor shower: If you want to step up from a spray bottle, this is a quality product that I recommend. You can buy a version with a propane stove attachment (at Emergency Essentials), but this one is cheaper, and I figured I could just heat my water in a pot then pour it into the container. I've used it and it works even better than I expected. Because it's all stainless steel, I've even placed it right on top of my wood stove to let it warm the water. It easily pressurizes and sprays water a good 18 feet. It stores 3 gallons which has always been more than I've needed. $133.00 on Amazon. Consider a basin & shower curtain contraption to take showers in your tent.

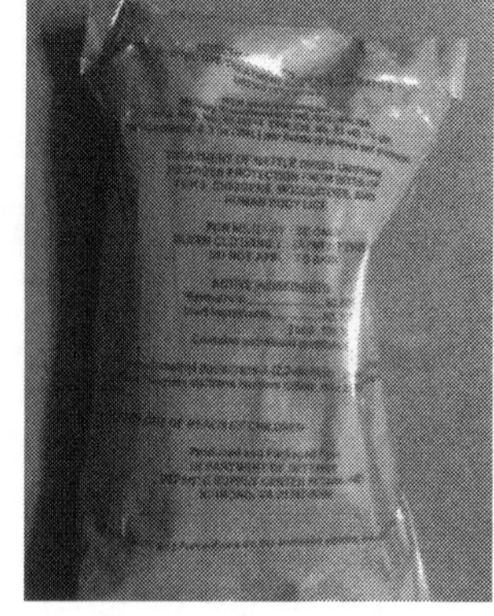

Pestilence: I have had the impression (from the Spirit, I believe) that besides ticks and mosquitos, those of us in the camps may have to deal with plagues of lice/other pestilence (so you may want to pick up some lice kits at Walmart). I plan on treating my family's outside layer of clothing with the USGI Permethrin kits the military has used for decades. You can't just soak clothes in permethrin; it needs to be a special treatment.

Using this kit, once treated, the clothes will be permanently treated and will protect you from ticks, lice, chiggers, and mosquitos. One Army study showed that even after 50 washings, individuals wearing the clothing had 96% less ticks on them than non-treated clothing. It works! These kits are not normally available to the public, but I found them from some guy on EBay for about $7.50/ kit. Decades of studies have been done to prove they are safe. It adheres so tightly to the fabric that only miniscule amounts come off. And of that, and even tinier amount can be absorbed through the skin. I've done the research and absolutely believe it's safe; the risk of lime disease or mosquito-borne illnesses will be an immeasurably greater concern. However, you should know that some people who are sensitive to such things believe that permethrin is very dangerous. For what it's worth.
LED Lights: This was a pretty good deal. 10 mini LED key lights for $3.64 and free shipping on Amazon. I got 20 white ones, 10 red and 10 green (Red is good for not blinding others in the night, and green light does not travel far to be seen by others). The quality isn't the best, but they work and are quite bright. They have a switch which will keep them on without depressing the button (like how a flashlight works)

SunLight Solar Powered Lanterns: This is one of my favorite products I've come across. For camping, lanterns are much more useful than flashlights because they give off light in all 360 degrees. These lanterns last 12 hours when charged, inflate/deflate for easier storage, are waterproof, recharge by sun with a solar panel on top, and have a built in lithium battery that's resistant to fire/over-heating and which performs better in extreme climates than normal batteries. And once charged, they hold that charge for 3 years! You can buy 3 for $19.99 at www.sunlightlantern.com

Spry Xylitol Gum: To help with teeth, I bought xylitol gum (not only does xylitol not feed the bacteria that is thought to convert sucrose to acid, but it inhibits the bacteria from building the plaque it uses to adhere to your teeth). I bought one of these and found that it no longer appears to have titanium dioxide (or at least it was removed from the ingredients list.) This is the best price I've found. Cost: 600 pieces for $40.00

Sunglasses: I am happy about my scratch resistant, anti-glare, fog-resistant, polarized sunglasses I got at the optometry desk at Costco. They were about $50.00. I really wanted something with a scratch resistant coating. You can also search for tactical sunglasses to find other good options. It may be best, however, to get a bunch of inexpensive ones.

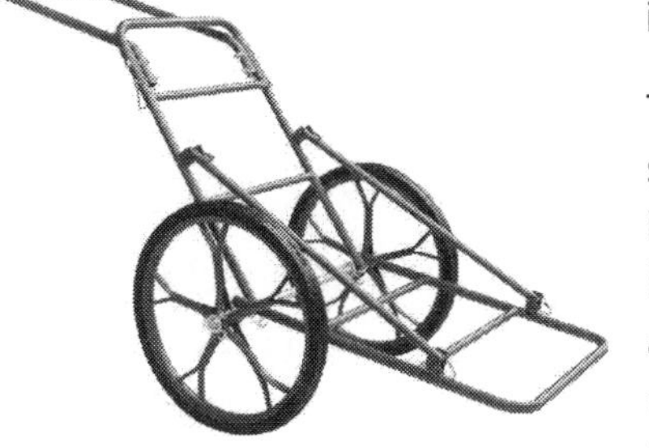

TMS 500lb Deer Cart Game Hauler: You'll probably want something to help you carry your things around. A deer cart is made to do this. They are lightweight, can carry huge loads, and if you get no-flat rubberized tires, they will go over all types of terrain and last a good amount of time. In my mind, they are a necessity. This is the one I got. $52.26 + $20.24 shipping on www.Amazon.com

Guns: It's difficult to recommend one gun because different calibers of ammunition are used for different purposes. This Chippa X-Caliber Survival Rifle can shoot 12 different calibers of ammunition, making it extremely versatile. It folds in half for easier carry, and has a durable type of foam stock which makes it lightweight. It has picatinny rails for scopes, lights. Comes with 8 steel adapters for shooting those different types of ammo.

Bioenno Power BPP120 Rechargeable Battery Pack: If you don't have anything electronic you're bringing, you won't even need this. But this is a good option if you are. I'm not convinced this is the best battery pack out there, but I wanted to get a Lithium-iron-

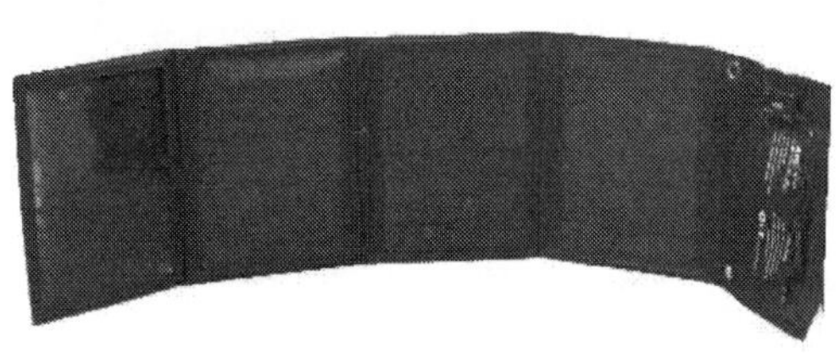

phosphate battery because they won't overheat, give off no harmful fumes, are much more lightweight, hold their charge better than nickel or lead-acid in cold climates, and over time, is able to be recharged thousands of times more often before wearing out, charges faster, and holds its charge over time better (phew!). This particular one is only 120 Watt Hours of Capacity, which is fine more my needs, but the output is limited; you aren't going to be able to run a hair dryer or electric wheat grinder off it. It charges with a 28watt max, 15-volt solar panel (which is not common, so you may not be able to use just any solar panel you'd like. You can get these on Amazon or eBay. NOTE: It don't think it will be too long before we may not have any electronics, due to EMPs from high-altitude nuclear explosions or the sun. Battery: $204.99 Solar Panel: $110.00 (check eBay)

<u>Coleman Portable Water Heater</u>: I haven't used this yet, but it may be worth considering if you want to have on-demand hot water in 5 seconds. It has an internal rechargeable 6V battery for the pump and pulls water from any container you can put the hose in. It also requires common 16.4 oz. camping propane cylinders; 40-gallons of hot water/cylinder. You can crank up the heat and get very hot water out of it.

<u>Toilets</u>: Here are two toilet options if you don't want to use a common bucket. Cabela's Camp Commode Camping Toilet is a lightweight collapsible folding chair with a toilet seat. It firmly holds either plastic bags or a buckets

underneath. It has a shelf and a place for a roll of toilet paper. Some people love this thing (I don't personally have one). Online or at the store at Cabelas for $100 (which seems too expensive to me).

Camco 41541 Portable Toilet is a sturdy toilet system. It uses a bellow flush system and has sealing slide valve to lock in odors and protect against leakage. It has a very high, 5-star review on Amazon. There are two variants with different sized holding tanks (either 2.6 or 5.3 gallon). This thing recently shot up in cost and is now $83.00 (unless you want to buy a used one ☺)

Washroom: Consider making a wash room with sandbags for the walls. This 1000ct of bags costs $222.00. You'll also need a couple wide boards from Home Depot to both flatten each layer of bags, and to provide some beams for the roof. Get a tarp for the roof, some ties, and consider buying garage door insulation for the roof. Buy a couple PVC pipes wide enough to channel a wood stove pipe and an air vent to fuel air to that stove. You will need a round tipped shovel (not flat) to fill the sandbags. I've seen an ingenious way of propping them open by using a stool, removing the cloth seat, and clamping the bag to the two bars with some strong carpentry clips. For the ground, where the shower is, you will want good drainage. You could lay a few inches of smooth stones underneath a rubber mat with holes. The stones could be shoveled from the river into a metal grate wagon. This will allow all the dirt and small stones to be sifted out, and you can easily haul it back to camp. I plan on using a home hot water heater basin (about three feet in diameter), a shower drain and the requisite pipes for plumbing the shower run-off. For the sink, I bought the key components of the foot-powered sink at deluxecamping.com, but I had Michael Robertson custom fit mine to fit the fish-cleaning sink (which he was happy to do) It works great! This can be found at deluxecamping.com.

David's 72 hour Pack List	
1	Backpack
1	Thermarest sleeping pad (w 2 straps)
1	Machete w/ scabbard
1	LED Pen light (on outside)
1	Hand Sanitizer – 1 fl oz (on outside)
1	Camelbak attachment (w/ water)
1	Water filter (Survivor or Sawyer mini)
1	Ripcord pants w/ riggers belt
1	Moisture wicking shirt (long sleeve)
1	Pair boots (water proof, anti-fatigue, composite toe, anti-microbial)
2	Pair socks (Darn Tough brand)
1	Set garments (nylon mesh top/bottom)
1	Fleece jacket
1	Set heavy thermals, top and bottom)
1	Sun hat (full brimmed)
1	Fleece cap
1	Set Frogg Toggs rain top & bottom
1	Handkerchief (tan)
1	Pair insulated work gloves
1	Pair lightweight gloves
1	Emergency blanket
4	Sets hand/toe/body warmers
1	Inflatable solar lamp ("SunLight")
1	Toiletries bag
2	-- Aqua Towels
1	-- Toothbrush with loaded paste
1	-- Dental floss
1	-- Nitrile gloves
1	-- Sm Bottle shampoo/conditioner
1	-- Sm Bottle body wash
1	-- Sm Hair Brush
1	-- Stick Deodorant
1	-- Extra bottle hand sanitizer (1 fl oz)
1	-- Bag antacid (10 ct)
1	-- Sm tube hand lotion
1	-- Set toe and fingernail clippers
1	-- Tweezers
5	-- Single use eye drops

1	Pack Kleenex
2	Stick chapstick
1	Pack moist wipes
1	Pack Readybath washcloths
1	Trashbag
1	Pair earplugs
1	Sm Emergency radio (w/ batteries)
1	Handset 2-way radio (rechargeable)
1	Emergency whistle, compass, waterproof matches combo
1	Signal mirror
1	Lightstick (12 hours)
1	Road flare
1	Knife
2	Paracord (bracelet)
1	Plastic magnifying sheet (for fire)
2	Pen
1	Notepad
1	Grease pencil
1	N95 breathing mask
1	First Aid kit
	-- Ibuprofen, diarrhea medicine , quick clot bandage, bandaids, ice pack, fish hook kit, tape, gloves, breathing mask, moleskin, thermometer, triangular bandage, q-tips, disinfectant wipes, scissors, safety pins, tweezers
1	Tourniquet
14	Potassium iodide tablets
1	Travel bowl (with lid & 4x Oatmeal)
1	Multi utensil tool (spoon, fork, knife)
1	MRE (w/ meal, spoon, matches, etc)
4	Easy prep meals (freeze-dried/MRE)
1	Block emergency rations (coconut)
4	Snacks (fruit & energy bars)
1	Pack chewing gum
1	Pouch cash, small bills, & blank check
1	Pouch important documents (passport, SS cards, birth certificates)
1	Harmonica
1	Dog tag (ID info)
1	Inventory list/tag

1	Backpack
1	Inflatable sleeping pad
1	LED Pen light (on outside)
1	Hand Sanitizer – 1 fl oz (on outside)
1	Paracord bracelet (outside w/ clip)
1	Jestcream whistle (outside)
1	Internal water bladder (w/ water)
1	Pair Jeans/rugged pants
1	Long-sleeved Bahama shirt
1	Pair boots (water proof, anti-fatigue, composite toe, anti-microbial)
2	Pair socks (1x thermal, 1x Coolmax Darn Tough brand)
1	Set Garments (in plastic bag)
1	Sweater/coat
1	Set heavy thermals, top and bottom
1	Sun hat
1	Extra thick thermal windblocking cap
1	Set Frogg Toggs rain top & bottom
1	Pair medium weight gloves
1	Handkerchief (tan)
1	Emergency blanket
1	Neck Gaitor/scarf
1	Toiletries bag
2	-- Aqua Towels
1	-- Toothbrush with loaded paste
1	-- Dental floss
1	-- Extra bottle hand sanitizer (1 fl oz)
1	-- Menstrual cup
2	Sets hand/body warmers
1	Stick chapstick
1	Pack moist wipes
1	Pack Readybath washclothes
1	Trashbag
1	Pair earplugs
1	Handset 2-way radio (rechargeable)
1	Match case (hurricane matches)
1	Lightstick (12 hours)
1	Plastic magnifying sheet (for fire)
1	Pen
1	Notepad

1	Grease pencil (in ziplock bag)
1	N95 breathing mask
6	Laundry detergent packs
1	First Aid kit
	-- 28x potassium iodide tablets, Quick seal cut spray, gloves, bandage tape, bandages, gauze, safety pins, antiseptic ointment, 8x eyedrops, Silver water spray, silver gel ointment, 18x herbal pills (6 elder berry, 6 olive leaf, 6 yarrow – viral, bacteria, toxins), ibuprofen, children's Motrin w/ syringe, thermometer, eye patches, 2x scissors, pencil, tweezers, CPR face shield, duct tape, iodine, blister agent, glacier gel, wilderness medicine book, suture kit, 1 wrist and 2 finger Sam Splints
1	Foldable sewing scissors
1	Travel bowl (with lid & 4x Oatmeal)
1	Multi utensil tool (spoon, fork, knife)
1	MRE (w/ meal, spoon, matches, etc)
3	Easy serve meals (freeze-dried/MRE)
1	Block emergency rations (coconut)
4	Snacks (fruit & energy bars)
1	Pack chewing gum
1	Case silver coins (20 ct)
1	Inflatable solar lamp ("SunLight")
1	Candle
1	Pack Kleenex
1	Dog tag (ID info)
1	Inventory list/tag

1	Backpack
1	Hand Sanitizer – 1 fl oz (on outside)
1	Insulated water bottle (w/water)
1	LED Pen light (on outside)
1	Long-sleeved shirt
1	Pair jeans/rugged pants
1	Set wicking thermals (top & bottom)
1	Pair waterproof hiking boots
2	Pair socks (1x thermal, 1x Darn Tough)
2	Underwear
1	Wool/knit cap
1	Pair cold weather gloves
1	Coat/sweater
1	Scarf
1	Sun cap
1	Pair sunglasses
1	Set Frogg Toggs rain top & bottom
1	Emergency blanket
2	Sets hand/body warmers
1	Toiletries bag
2	-- Aqua Towels
1	-- Toothbrush with loaded paste
	-- Children's dental floss/picks
1	-- Extra bottle hand sanitizer (1 fl oz)
1	-- Bottle tearless shampoo/wash
1	-- Chapstick
1	Pack Kleenex
1	N95 breathing mask
1	Travel bowl (with lid & 4x Oatmeal)
1	Multi utensil tool (spoon, fork, knife)
1	Inflatable solar lamp ("SunLight")
1	MRE (w/ meal, spoon, matches, etc)
3	Freeze-dried meals (just add water)
4	Snacks (fruit & energy bars)
1	Dog tag (ID info)
1	Inventory list/tag

#	Toddler & Family Duffle Bag
1	Duffle bag
1	Camelpak (filled with water)
1	Insulated water bottle (w/ water)
1	Long-sleeved shirts
1	Pair Carhartt overalls
1	Set wicking thermals (top & bottom)
1	Pair waterproof boots
2	Pair socks (Darn Tough)
1	Wool/knit cap
1	Pair gloves
1	Set ski overalls & ski jacket
1	Sun cap (with neck guard)
1	Pair Sunglasses
9	Diapers
1	Pack wipes
1	Sm Roll trash bags (for diapers)
1	Trash bag
1	Emergency ponchos
1	Emergency blanket
2	Sets hand/body warmers
1	Toiletries bag
2	-- Aqua Towels
1	-- Toothbrush and paste (age 2+)
	-- Children's dental floss/picks
1	-- Bottles hand sanitizer (1 fl oz)
1	-- Bottles tearless shampoo/wash
1	Pack Kleenex
1	N95 breathing mask
1	Travel bowl (with lid & 4x Oatmeal)
1	Multi utensil tool (spoon, fork, knife)
1	MRE (w/ meal, spoon, matches, etc)
2	Bag of 5-person meal (boiling water)
4	Snacks (fruit & energy bars)
1	Biodegradable dish soap
1	Toilet bag (with gel)
1	Laundry bag (green)
1	Charging base for 2-way Radios
1	Power inverter for radios (for car)
1	Kelly Kettle kit

Musings on President Monson's Message to the Church

In the words of the Prophet, "We live in turbulent times." He said this in the September First Presidency Message -- the message the Lord wants shared by Home Teachers to every member of the Church throughout the world. That alone is significant!

Yesterday, it hit me like a rock what he meant in his story at the beginning of his message. For those that read his message, "Are we Prepared?", President Monson begins with an odd story about a chicken ranch. I just discarded the story as a cute sentimental memory that vaguely had something to do with the Church farms. That is, until the Spirit impressed me -- rather forcibly, I might add -- that this was a parable with deep significance. The key to understanding the parable – which has to do with getting us prepared -- is to realize that the members of the Church are the chickens and the workers are the general Church leadership – especially the First Presidency and Quorum of the Twelve. Here's his story:

> "In the vicinity where I once lived and served, the Church operated a poultry project, staffed primarily by volunteers from the local wards. Most of the time it was an efficiently operated project, supplying to the bishops' storehouse thousands of fresh eggs and hundreds of pounds of dressed poultry. On a few occasions, however, being volunteer city farmers meant not only blisters on the hands but also frustration of heart and mind.
>
> "For instance, I shall ever remember the time we gathered the Aaronic Priesthood young men to give the project a spring-cleaning. Our enthusiastic and energetic throng assembled at the project and in a speedy fashion uprooted, gathered, and burned large quantities of weeds and debris. By the light of the glowing bonfires, we ate hot dogs and congratulated ourselves on a job well done.
>
> "However, there was just one disastrous problem. The noise and the fires so disturbed the fragile population of 5,000 laying hens that most of them went into a sudden molt and ceased laying. Thereafter we tolerated a few weeds so that we might produce more eggs."

He then goes on with his message, which is, in my own words: 1) Don't assume the Church has food for you; we have been telling you to get your own supply, 2) You need more than food; you need clothing and the "other necessities of life," 3) He chides the members who have not done so, but instead "have a supply of debt and are food-free," and 4) Counsels us to set aside money and get out of debt "as quickly as you can."

I believe that President Monson is trying to tell us that he is caught between the need to warn us about preparing for the future, and the sensitivity of the saints to be alarmed that something bad is on the horizon. He could use words of "destruction and fire," but that would be counterproductive; the "fragile population" of members would stop living their lives in a productive, one-egg-a-day kind of way. Once some chickens get it into their minds that the sky is falling, their lives will become unbalanced and fearful.

So instead of telling us WHY we need to prepare, he tells us HOW we need to be prepared. And those that believe he's a true prophet, will just have the faith and prepare regardless of the details.

I already listed above HOW we need to prepare. But I want to focus on one detail that was curious to me.

President Monson said that it would be best for "every family in the Church to have a supply of food, clothing, and, where possible, other necessities of life." In reading an old talk by President Benson, I found this exact quote. Exactly. Even the four commas are in the same deliberate places. However, there is one change: President Benson said that where possible, we should have fuel. Our current prophet expanded this to not just include fuel, but recognized that there are other "necessities of life" for which we must have on hand. Some of these things we can easily identify. But some of these "necessities" require us to know "WHY" and for what we are preparing for. For this, I believe you must either use the Spirit of revelation to you, or the accounts of other inspired individuals whose words don't risk causing the membership of the Church to go into a sudden molt.

When something is mentioned in all the cannons of scripture, I believe it is not just a coincidence, but has an intended extra measure of significance. In the Bible, The Book of Mormon and several times in the Doctrine and Covenants, the Lord has told us that He wants to gather us to safety, even as a hen gathereth her chickens under her wing. But in all three accounts, He laments that there are those that simply "would not." We need to listen to His mouthpiece -- the Prophet -- and prepare, so that when the call from danger is declared to the Church, we will be ready. In the First Presidency Message before this month's, we were reminded of the law of the harvest; we reap what we sow ... nothing more.

I'm convinced that we will live to witness the Second Coming, in our lifetimes, assuming we live to a normal age. This being the case, we are going to see miracles that even surpass those witnessed by the Children of Israel when they were called to gather and leave Egypt. But before He comes, there will be serious calamities for which we must prepare.

President Monson's closing words are these: "Are we obedient to the commandments of God? Are we responsive to the teachings of prophets? ... We live in turbulent times. Often the future is unknown; therefore, it **behooves** us to prepare for uncertainties."

Notice he didn't say "The future is always unknown, therefore ..." If anyone has had the future revealed to them, he has! And he is telling us that it would "behoove" us to prepare.

And then he closes with this interesting and ominous warning: "When the time for decision arrives, the time for preparation is past."

Notice again that he didn't say, "When the time for **calamity** arrives, the time for preparation is past." This is what we would expect would be said. But he used the word "decision." "When the time for decision arrives, the time for preparation is past." This is because, I believe, there will be a decision for us all to make which, at the time it is presented, all our preparation must be pre-accomplished.

David Randall Smith

The Call to Flee Nauvoo – A Foreshadow of Our Day

These details are from notes I took from a BYU Church History class in 2003 or 2004 (the professor was Susan Easton Black).

After Joseph Smith's death, Brigham Young was busy preparing the Church for an exodus from Nauvoo to the Rocky Mountains. The Church members, in general, knew they were going to leave, but didn't know when. The "wise" were preparing to flee. The leaders of the Church gave the saints a list of things they needed to get before it was time to go, and when that time came, only those that had obeyed and got the things on that list were allowed to leave in the first wave of Saints.

One of the great endeavors -- beginning 10 December 1845 -- was that the Temple was very busy endowing as many members as possible.

According to Sis. Black, everyone thought Brigham Young was going to call the Saints to flee in the Spring of 1846. But on a much earlier, February 4th, 1846, he gave the call to "Flee Babylon by land or by sea." To Brigham Young, Babylon represented was the United States. This time is when songs like "Ye Elders of Israel" were written with the words: "Oh Babylon, Oh Babylon, we bid thee farewell; we're going to the Mountains of Ephraim to dwell!"

To give you an idea of how quickly they left, the temple was going to close immediately, but at the request of some Saints, they fit in some more endowments -- the last of which was performed 7 Feb, 1846 -- just three days later.

The prepared saints had purchased wagons, but they were not initially covered. But when Orson Hyde went on a political mission to Washington D.C. while advocating for the Presidency of Joseph Smith, Joseph Smith had instructed him to buy 5,000 yards of canvas -- which was supposed to be used for building a tabernacle. Because a tent temple wouldn't provide protection, the tabernacle was never built. And because they had all this extra canvas, they cut it up and placed it on top of the wagons that first left for the valley. Thus their wagons became "portable tabernacles." These saints had the power of God attend them.

The Saints were warned to flee, because they were in real danger. Sis. Black made it a point to say that there were actually three waves of departing Saints. The first group left in February (earlier than most everyone thought) in portable tabernacles (their wagons) and with the general authorities. The second group left in April, but they had no general authorities with them. The third group left in September, freezing and running for their lives. This third group was poor, sick, and they struggled mightily through that winter.

One other thing of note: It was on the 7th of September, 1846 (which was a Monday) when a Major Parker gave the order that the Mormons must depart Nauvoo. He was sent with an army to enforce the expulsion of the Mormons. On 10 September, their force totaled more than one thousand. The Saints put up a remarkable fight, but on 17 September, the remaining saints fled during a winter so bitterly cold the Mississippi River was frozen over. Carrying their only possessions with them, these saints walked on foot across the frozen river, exiting the western border of the United States. Thus, whether they prepared and followed the prophet or not, they were all eventually forced to leave "Babylon."

****

Now let me just highlight some of the shadows I see for our day:

- The political issue today will likely cause persecution of the saints similar to what the saints in Nauvoo experienced. (You must read Elder Robert D. Hale's prophecy in the Oct 2013 General Conference about future persecution we will suffer – just like the persecutions of the early Saints – and how to be strong; https://www.lds.org/general-conference/2013/10/general-conference-strengthening-faith-and-testimony?lang=eng)

- Brigham Young gave the Saints a list of things to gather in order to be eligible to leave with the first wave of saints. President Thomas S. Monson gave us a similar list of preparations which we may need to follow in order to leave with the first wave of Saints (see the September 2014 First Presidency Message, "Are We Prepared?"; https://www.lds.org/ensign/2014/09/are-we-prepared?lang=eng).

- The great work at the time in Nauvoo was Temple work -- particularly to endow as many members as possible -- and the temples were opened non-stop, 24 hours a day. We too have seen a hastening of temple work leading to the call to flee, but just like with Brigham Young, the time will come when temples will be closed (perhaps due to persecution) and the work will be halted for a time.

- Many believe the Call to Gather will occur in the Spring, just as most believed in Brigham Young's day. What remains to be seen is if our call to flee comes sooner, as it came in February for the Nauvoo Saints. Christ warns us to be ready (Matt 24:43).

- Just like in Brigham's day, most of the Saints who flee will go to the Rocky Mountains for safety. Here are two prophecies: Brigham Young: "An inland Empire will be established in these valleys of the mountains, which will be a place of refuge for millions of people to gather to, when the great day of the judgements of God comes upon the earth, and the righteous come here for safety. Our people will go East, West, North and South, but the day will come, when they will be glad to come back. We will be shut out from the rest of the world." Prophecy of Heber C. Kimball: "I am very thankful that so many of the brethren have come in with handcarts; my soul rejoiced, my heart was filled and grew as big as a two-bushel basket. Two companies have come through safe and sound. Is this the end of it? No; there will be millions on millions that will come much in the same way, only they will not have handcarts, for they will take their bundles under their arms, and their children on their backs, and under their arms and flee" (Source: Journal of Discourses, 4:106).

- Once the call from Brigham Young came to flee, they left almost immediately within days. This is similar to various dreams and visions of the Call to Gather in our day.

- The early Saints who left in the first call to gather were provided canvas covers on their wagons. In our day, many people who have had dreams/visions about the gathering saw that there were thousands of white canvas tents that were provided by the Church (for just one example, see "Dream of Plagues," http://visionsandtribulation.blogspot.com/2013/12/the-dream-of-plagues.html). There are accounts of people that work for the Church that have seen warehouses full of tens of thousands of white canvas tents the Church owns. As are the temples today, these tents will be like tabernacles of safety (as was shown in the Dream of Plagues).

- The Nauvoo saints fled in three waves. Dreams and visions of the future tell there will be three waves of saints who flee in our day. Just as was the case in Nauvoo, these people also describe that the third group of fleeing Saints will be destitute and walking, taking only what they can carry with them. It is yet to be seen if these saints will also flee in the dead of a terribly cold winter. But those who have had dreams of this often (but not always) describe a terribly cold, early, and long winter following the call to gather. As Christ forewarned in His prophesy of the future calamities of Jerusalem and of the Latter-days, "Pray ye that your flight be not in the winter, neither on the sabbath day" (Matt 24:20).

- The Nauvoo Saints fled an army commissioned to expel the Mormons. Dreams and visions of our day show that ALL people were fleeing invading foreign armies (primarily Chinese in the West, and Russian in the East).

David Randall Smith

~Personal Revelation and Directing Others~

I think it would be beneficial to state a few pearled principles of revelation. Because if you are not confused, you will certainly run into someone who has been or will be.

The question is: can one person receive revelation concerning another? The answer is always "yes." And I'm not talking about parents for children and presidents for their stewardship. A person who is not in a presidency may receive personal revelation that *CONCERNS* a complete stranger. ...Not revelation *FOR" a complete stranger, but that *CONCERNS* that stranger. And this actually happens all the time.

Next question: Can a person receive personal revelation about the future administration of the Church and the President of the Church. The answer is "yes." And this too has been happening frequently. It's the exact same principle I just stated above. You can have a vision or dream about the Prophet calling the whole Church to gather (for example).

However, a person who receives revelation about another or about the Church, does not have the authority to *DIRECT* another person on God's behalf --even when that revelation comes from God. The authority to *DIRECT* only comes 1) from God directly to the individual being directed, 2) from God to a parent/guardian for a child, and 3) from God to an individual in a presidency which is over that person being directed. (And the level of direction must be in harmony with that Presidency)

You see, the principle of *receiving revelation* and *directing* are different and this is what many members often confuse. They consider the conditions to the right to revelation as the same conditions surrounding the right to direct. Hence you will often hear it said that God would never give Julie Rowe a revelation concerning the guidance/direction that must eventually come from the Prophet. People that teach this don't understand; they are combining two different principles.

Julie Rowe and Hector Sosa Jr.., and such-and-such a random person can see in vision what the Prophet will one day announce and tell the Church. They have, and they do. As you know, they can't direct the Prophet, nor can they speak for the Prophet. (And these two specific individuals are extremely careful to point out that they don't make that claim.) Does this mean that their revelation isn't pertinent? No. If it came from God, it is absolutely true! It just isn't binding on others. (But if it's true, why wouldn't you take it seriously?)

So what do we do when someone claims to have received revelation concerning us (think Julie Rowe and others)?

Answer: If God wants you to be DIRECTED -- or to act -- according to that revelation, then you -- or someone who has authority to direct you -- has the right to also receive that revelation. Does that mean you or they are *entitled* to receive that revelation? Not necessarily. But you are not required (or accountable) to act on that dream/vision/inspiration until you, or someone else that can direct you, receives that message. Make sense?

A word of caution, the still small voice is a legitimate way that God can direct you. When I listened to Julie Rowe for the first time, I felt the Spirit. I didn't have a vision ... but I felt the confirming witness. From that point on, I had the DIRECTION from God FOR MYSELF ... and I was ever after accountable for that knowledge. I didn't need to obey Julie Rowe... I needed to obey the Spirit to me.

President J. Reuben Clark stated, "We can tell when the speakers are 'moved upon by the Holy Ghost' only when we, ourselves, are 'moved upon by the Holy Ghost.'" This is REALLY important everyone! It's how you discern truth, and keep from being led astray. This principle will become increasingly important in the future.

We all know these authors, NDE'ers, dreamers and visionaries do not replace the prophet. "We do not think these authors have replaced the prophet, we do not think these books have replaced the scriptures, we do not think all visions are literal, we don't believe all visions/dreams will come to pass (but may just be a warning), and [this is my favorite part] we don't need to be reminded to have discernment."

That said, we know that whatever the Prophet tells the Church will be guidance on which the members are accountable to act on. Because of this, if Julie Rowe, et al., encourages you to do something that the Prophet has already counseled us to do, we are obligated to do so. Not because of Julie, but because of the Prophet.

Nobody should accuse another of treating Julie Rowe as a prophet when they are actually complying with something that she AND the Prophet has already told us to do. The current prophetic guidance on temporal preparedness is to 1) get short- and long-term food, 2) water, 3) clothing, 4) "other necessities of life" and 5) to have a reserve of money (not just get out of debt). Many items fit in the category of "other necessities of life" and we should seek the spirit and personal revelation for ourselves to tailor this guidance and know what these items are for us.

As James E. Faust said in a great talk on revelation: "We have been promised that the President of the Church will receive guidance for all of us as the revelator for the Church. Our safety lies in paying heed to that which he says and following his counsel." James E. Faust, Oct 1989

David Randall Smith

Earthquake Preparedness Ideas
by Becky Edwards

-Anchored our storage shelving to the wall if they weren't already.

-Used bungee cords in front of the shelves to keep the food and stuff on the shelves.

-Hung our scouting backpacks on nails on the wall rather than storing them on the basement floor, in case of flooding. Also moved the luggage onto shelving rather than the floor.

-Used Quake Hold museum putty to anchor the backs of frames to the walls and trinkets to shelves.

-Anchored a tall bookcase to the wall, and I pushed the books to the back.

-Moved the glass jar foods from the pantry into a cardboard box on the pantry floor.

-Moved prep gear from the basement to our missionary son's bedroom upstairs to avoid potential flooding.

-Protected my canning jars in the basement by creating cardboard dividers in the boxes that didn't have them. Putting those boxes closer to the floor.

-Installed seismo-latches on the kitchen cupboard doors that only lock when a shaking occurs.

-Had an FHE last spring and another one a couple days ago about how to respond to an earthquake and how to turn off water, gas, and power. Also practiced climbing out of a high window using a rope ladder.

-Today my husband realized how much broken glass our shower door would create, so I bought a shower curtain and rings at the dollar store. Not as pretty but who cares?

-I'm putting my 72-hour kit in my van because I have a couple out-of-town overnight commitments in the middle of August and I want to be able to walk home if it happens while I'm gone. I'm also praying that the Lord will let me know if I should cancel my plans. So far I feel fine about going.

-I plan on un-stacking some of the bins and buckets that we have stacked in piles so they aren't as likely to fall over.

-Updated our 72-hour kits with fresh food and clothes.

-Put a shoe box under each person's bed with shoes and a flashlight in case of earthquake in the middle of the night and we need protection from broken glass.

-I had a prompting to pray for the Lord to place shields of protection and angels around our home and our preparedness stuff that we have worked so hard to gather. We invited our children to pray for that too. I know that even if every other house on our street got flooded or ruined some other way, God can protect our home if it's His will and if we ask fervently for it.

Emotional Process of Being Awakened to the Signs of the Second Coming

Written by Sara Low

Steps:

1) **DOUBT**
    a. Believing the prophesied events will not happen in your life time
    b. Rejecting the message and/or the messenger
    c. No feelings of urgency so it can't be true
2) **REALIZATION**
    a. You've received a spiritual witness of the urgency
    b. You've read many visions, prophecies, dreams, etc. that have awakened you.
    c. You mourn for the wickedness of the world. Mourning the destruction of so many people. Mourning for the pain the earth is experiencing.
    d. Realizing your spiritual preparation has been a bit complacent and needs to be re-addressed in a serious way.
3) **FEAR**
    a. Worrying about the physical events that are meant to come, calamities, plagues, destruction, and infirmities.
    b. Feeling you're the last person to know what is going on.
    c. Worrying about your current preparations or lack thereof.
    d. CAUTION! This is when depression can set in. This is exactly where Satan wants you to sit and marinate, in paralyzing fear and depression. Don't let him win your soul! We all know who will overcome and WIN this battle in the end. Now is the time to pick your master, get to work, and don't look back.
4) **ANXIETY**
    a. Lying awake at night worrying about what is to come and how it will all play out.
    b. Worrying about no time to prepare.
    c. Worrying about your children and what will happen to all of you. Worrying about your grown children and grandchildren. You wonder how you can get the parents of your grandchildren to see the urgency.
    d. Expressing anxieties to others to see if you're going CRAZY!
5) **NINJA PREPPER MODE**
    a. Accepting the fact it will happen and it's time to get going on the preps!
    b. Looking in every possible place for ways to get organized and get your life in order.
    c. Life priorities completely change at this point. You realize your planned for and hoped for future is not likely to happen. (It's time to cash out the 401(k) you won't need it anyway.)

d. You overload on trying to learn every possible skill available. This could include purchasing a gun, learning how to make bread from wheat, ways to sanitize water, the shock that comes when you realize how much toilet paper you're going to need to store.
e. It's time to exercise like there's no tomorrow, because tomorrow may be VERY different or not at all. And, there will likely be a lot of hiking in your near future.
f. You consider learning to eat a lot less so your food storage will last longer if you're trained to not eat very much.

6) SAMUEL THE LAMINITE MODE

a. Tell everyone you know to read the books, study the scriptures, study the brethren's words, watch the news, pay attention.
    i. You quickly learn who you can and can't tell. Some are willing to listen, most are not. You recognize "the look" you get when they shut down and stop listening.

7) BUYING SUPPLIES

a. You look for every good deal on Wheat, Oats, Powdered Milk, Beans, toilet paper etc. You add as much as humanly possible to your food supply.
b. You look for every possible place in your home to store water. Purchase the 55 Gallon drums as well as fill up every empty bottle in the house.
c. Your biggest concern is a sturdy, heavy, weather resistant tent that will keep warm and be big enough for all your toilet paper.

8) SELLING

a. You look at every useless thing in your home and consider selling it to make room for more supplies as well as earn money to buy those supplies. Who needs a couch anyway?

9) SPIRITUAL FOCUS

a. For some this is the very first step, as it should be. If you're spiritually in-tune and able to receive spiritual guidance, you'll know what you need to do for your family.
b. The TV is shut off, the music is changed, the world is shut out. Spiritual preparation is now a HUGE Priority and you can't understand why others aren't preparing in this way.
c. You seek the guidance and direction of Priesthood leaders. You receive blessings of comfort.
    i. Some leaders are not yet awakened don't let this discourage you. Keep studying!

10) STUDY

a. This is when you can't get enough information. You want to read every possible book, study the scriptures non-stop, read every talk ever given. You are starving for truth and search everywhere for further light and knowledge.
b. Your 'to-read' list is four pages long.

c. Your temple attendance has tripled! You can't do enough there and can't learn enough, the thirst can't be quenched.
d. You search all the news outlets to see the signs unfolding.

11) ENOS MOMENT

a. You pray for others, you hope the Lord will open their eyes and they will see the urgency of getting ready for what is coming.
b. You worry about people who are buying cars, buying boats, buying new houses and furniture. You realized a long time ago that purchasing anything that won't sustain your life is useless!
c. You worry what side your loved ones will stand on when the great divide happens.

12) PEACE

a. You have come to the realization that the Lord is in charge. You place everything in his hands and trust in His plan and in His timing.
b. You do all you can every day to prepare a little more and help a few more people. You have faith that everything will work exactly as it should.
c. This is also when gratitude takes center stage. You begin to focus on all the beautiful blessings you've been given in your life. You see the Lord's hand in everything happening. You recognize all the simple things you've been so abundantly blessed with; a warm bed, running water, a hot shower, clean clothing, plenty of food, a beautiful family, many comforts and luxuries that make this mortal life enjoyable.

13) PURE EXCITEMENT

a. You realize the Second Coming is the biggest and most amazing event to ever happen in all of history throughout the eternities.
b. THE SAVIOR IS COMING!!! You weep with gratitude that He will save, He will provide, He will bless, He will rescue, He is in charge. Your efforts are worth it. HE is worth it!

The Jewish Calendar

By Cynthia Ligouri

A friend of mine, who is a Book of Mormon scholar and a historian, once shared a story with me. He had a good friend who was a Biblical scholar, and an Orthodox Jewish Rabbi. My friend told me that he shared a copy of the Book of Mormon with him. After the Rabbi had read it, he came back to my friend and told him "You don't know what you have. This is a Jewish book." The way this man was able to tell that the Book of Mormon as a Jewish book, was he could see the Hebrew Calendar and Holy Day celebration cycles that are imbedded into the writings of the Book of Mormon. For my friend and most other Mormons, that is a facet of the writing that is hidden from our view because of our never having learned of it. (Story shared with permission, but with request for anonymity.)

Christ was a Jew. He was a Rabbi. He taught in the Synagogue and He taught in the Temple. Not understanding these things makes it harder for us to "have ears to hear and eyes to see". Our leaders have repeatedly told us that the Lord works in patterns and to watch for them. The Hebrew calendar is one of these patterns that he uses. If we understand that calendar, we will have access to more layers of meaning in both the Old and New Testaments, as well as in the Book of Mormon.

1) Jonathan Cahn, *"The Mystery of the Shemitah"* summary: His premise is that there are harbingers of judgment in last days. His perspective is that of a Rabbi, Messianic Jew, Levite and born again Christian.

   What is the Shemitah?

   Just as in the creative period and the pattern of the Sabbath, the Shemitah pattern was followed by the Jews anciently and today, we also follow the same pattern in how our week is organized. (Exodus 31:12 – 18) The Jewish calendar takes this cycle another step.

   This same six/one cycle continues not only for weeks, but years as well. The seventh year (Sabbath year) is called the Shemitah. It translates from Hebrew to literally mean the release, the fall, the shaking and/or the collapse. The law related to the creation or identification of the Shemitah was given to the Jews at the time of Moses and Mt. Sinai. For every six years in which we work, anciently farm, on the 7th year the Lord expected His people (the Jews – to whom this was given) to rest. (Leviticus 25:1-5) Fields were to lay fallow, people were only supposed to harvest what grew naturally. In addition, this would bring with it a forgiving of all debts. (Deuteronomy 15:1&2) If this year was kept and dedicated to God, a time in which His people were to draw closer to him, at its end, the people who obeyed would be blessed. If the people did not obey, they would come under judgment.

Seven Shemitah cycles brings the Jubilee year, which is the calendar cycle that is the foundation of the Bible and seven Jubilee years is a Super Jubilee.

All of these cycles – Shemitah, Jubilee and Super Jubilee were all completed on Elul 29 5776 or September 12-13, 2015. The Super Jubilee cycle is the first since the Birth of Christ.

2) Here are a few talks/articles/references by the General Authorities and others that support the importance of Jewish Holy Days to the Latter-day Saints today. These include a link to a paper and a compilation of LDS historical events in relation to the Hebrew calendar and holy days by a Jewish convert to the Church, Mariena Tanya Muchnick.

"A Message from Judah to Joseph" by Pres. Ezra Taft Benson - https://www.lds.org/ensign/1976/12/a-message-to-judah-from-joseph?lang=eng

The Restoration of Priesthood Keys on Easter 1836, Part 1: Dating the First Easter by John P. Pratt - https://www.lds.org/ensign/1985/06/the-restoration-of-priesthood-keys-on-easter-1836-part-1-dating-the-first-easter?lang=eng

"The Restoration of Priesthood Keys on Easter 1836: Symbolism of Passover and Elijah's Return, part 2 – by John P. Pratt - https://www.lds.org/ensign/1985/07/the-restoration-of-priesthood-keys-on-easter-1836-part-2-symbolism-of-passover-and-of-elijahs-return?lang=eng

"The Golden Plates and the Feast of Trumpets" by Lenet Hadley Read - https://www.lds.org/ensign/2000/01/the-golden-plates-and-the-feast-of-trumpets?lang=eng

"Rosh Hashanah and General Conference" by Mark Paredes - http://www.jewishjournal.com/jews_and_mormons/item/rosh_hashanah_and_general_conference_39100906

"What is the Spiritual Significance to Mormons of Rosh Hashanah and Yom Kippur?" by Mariena Tanya Muchnick - https://judaicaworld.wordpress.com/what-is-the-spiritual-significance-to-mormons-of-rosh-hashanah-and-yom-kippur/

Major LDS Events That Have Fallen on Hebrew Holy Days compiled and comments by Mariena Tanya Muchnick (Baker) - http://www.jewishconvert-lds.com/lds_events-jewishholydays.pdf

"Orson Hyde's 1841 Mission to the Holy Land" by David B Galbraith - https://www.lds.org/ensign/1991/10/orson-hydes-1841-mission-to-the-holy-land?lang=eng#pop_001-91910_000_005

Orson Hyde's Dedicatory Prayer - http://www.nyx.net/~cgibbons/orson_hyde_prayer.html

3) The Jewish calendar is ancient and has its roots in biblical commands regarding the observation of the Holy Day/Feast Days of the Jews. The months were religiously significant to the Jews and enabled them to commemorate the important events of their history in unity, regardless of where they lived. Each month's beginning was considered holy. To ancient Israel, the moon became a spiritual symbol of the nation itself; the sun eventually became symbolic of the Messiah (Malachi 4:2). Since the moon produces no light of its own, the symbolism is especially appropriate: Israel was supposed to reflect the Messiah's light to the world."

"It appears that Heavenly Father honors the building of his Church by having events coincide with several Hebrew holy days and other important dates that were specifically given by God to his earliest prophets as recorded in the Old Testament. This coordination between ancient and modern occurrences can be seen as a theme of restoration and restitution of all things anciently in force, a time when the Lord may "gather together in one all things in Christ, both which are in heaven and which are on earth; even in him." (Ephesians 1:9,10)." Munchnick, *Major LDS Events That Have Fallen on Hebrew Holy Days*.

From Orson Hyde's prayer in Israel in 1841:

To you, our friends of modern Judah, we declare, "We are Joseph, your brothers." We claim kinship with you as descendants from our fathers, Abraham, Isaac and Jacob. We belong to the same family. We, too, are the House of Israel.

We are brothers and sisters to the Jews. Our church is the restoration of the church that Christ Himself set up on the earth in the meridian of time. The traditions of the Jews as well as the commemorations in their calendar begin with Creation story. The Jews have never left the calendar behind, but have continued to observe it and will continue to until the Gospel is completely restored to them and the Savior has returned.

False Prophets

"According to Joseph Smith, 'False prophets always arise to oppose the true prophets' (Teachings of the Prophet Joseph Smith, sel. Joseph Fielding Smith [1976], 365). If they don't oppose them, then they aren't a false prophet. The sure way Christ taught us to recognize a false prophet is 'by their fruits.' Here's a great talk by Elder Ballard all about false prophets."

So I've pasted the link to that talk below. Elder Russell M. Ballard was very clear about what constitutes "false prophets". None of the NDEs or dreams/visions I have read fall in to this category. Instead, they help build faith, help remind us to follow the prophet, be obedient and prepare! I know that there are NDEs/visions/dreams of false prophets out there, but I completely stay away from them.

I have listed two different things: A) is the INVERSE of what Elder Ballard spoke about, aka what DOES NOT constitute a false prophet and B) what Elder Ballard said DOES constitute a false prophet.

A) PEOPLE ARE NOT FALSE PROPHETS IF :

1. They PROMOTE faith and testimony and DO NOT "lie in wait to ensnare and destroy faith and testimony."

2. They DO NOT CLAIM to have received direct revelation from the Lord FOR THE CHURCH, and DO NOT CLAIM independent of the order and channel of the Priesthood.

3. They DO NOT espouse an obviously false doctrine.

4. They DO NOT presume to have authority to teach the true gospel of Christ according to their own interpretation.

5. They DO NOT claim, without authority, endorsement to their products and practices.

6. They are NOT self-appointed declarers of the doctrines of the Church who seek to spread their false gospel and DO NOT attract followers by sponsoring symposia, books, and journals whose contents challenge fundamental doctrines of the Church.

7. They DO NOT speak and publish in opposition to God's true prophets and DO NOT actively proselyte others with reckless disregard for the eternal well-being of others.

8. They DO NOT rely on sophistry to deceive and entice others to their views [they simply share the message they were prompted to share].

9. They DO NOT "set themselves up for a light unto the world that they may get gain and praise of the word; but they [DO] seek the welfare of Zion."

10. They are NOT "proud and self-vaunting, who read by the lamps of their own conceit; who interpret by rules of their own contriving; who have become a law unto themselves, and so pose as the sole judges of their own doings."

11. They DO NOT declare Joseph Smith a duplicitous deceiver.

12. They DO NOT challenge the First Vision as an authentic experience.

13. They DO NOT declare the Book of Mormon and other canonical works to not be ancient records of scripture.

14. They DO NOT attempt to redefine the nature of the Godhead.

15. They DO NOT deny God has given and continues to give revelation today to His ordained and sustained prophets.

16. They DO NOT arrogantly attempt to fashion new interpretations of the scriptures to demonstrate that these sacred texts should not be read as God's words to His children but merely as the utterances of uninspired men, limited by their own prejudices and cultural biases.

17. They DO NOT argue that the scriptures require new interpretation and DO NOT ARGUE that they are uniquely qualified to offer that interpretation.

18. They DO NOT deny Christ's Resurrection and Atonement, and DO NOT argue that no God can save us.

19. They DO NOT reject the need for a Savior.

20. They DO NOT attempt to reinterpret the doctrines of the Church to fit their own preconceived views, and DO NOT deny Christ and His messianic role.

21. They DO NOT attempt to change the God-given and scripturally based doctrines that protect the sanctity of marriage, divine nature of the family, and the essential doctrine of personal morality.

22. They DO NOT advocate a redefinition of morality to justify fornication, adultery, and homosexual relationships.

23. They DO NOT openly champion the legalization of so-called same-gender marriages.

24. They DO NOT attack the inspired proclamation on the family.

B) PEOPLE ARE FALSE PROPHETS IF:

1. They "lie in wait to ensnare and destroy faith and testimony."

2. They claim to have received direct revelation from the Lord to the Church, independent of the order and channel of the Priesthood.

3. They espouse an obviously false doctrine.

4. They presume to have authority to teach the true gospel of Christ according to their own interpretation.

5. They claim, without authority, endorsement to their products and practices.

6. They are self-appointed declarers of the doctrines of the Church who seek to spread their false gospel and attract followers by sponsoring symposia, books, and journals whose contents challenge fundamental doctrines of the Church.

7. They speak and publish in opposition to God's true prophets and actively proselyte others with reckless disregard for the eternal well-being of those whom they seduce.

8. They rely on sophistry to deceive and entice others to their views.

9. They "set themselves up for a light unto the world that they may get gain and praise of the word; but they seek not the welfare of Zion."

10. They are "proud and self-vaunting, who read by the lamps of their own conceit; who interpret by rules of their own contriving; who have become a law unto themselves, and so pose as the sole judges of their own doings."

11. They declare Joseph Smith a duplicitous deceiver.

12. They challenge the First Vision as an authentic experience.

13. They declare the Book of Mormon and other canonical works are not ancient records of scripture.

14. They attempt to redefine the nature of the Godhead.

15. They deny God has given and continues to give revelation today to His ordained and sustained prophets.

16. They arrogantly attempt to fashion new interpretations of the scriptures to demonstrate that these sacred texts should not be read as God's words to His children but merely as the utterances of uninspired men, limited by their own prejudices and cultural biases.

17. They argue that the scriptures require new interpretation and that they are uniquely qualified to offer that interpretation.

18. They deny Christ's Resurrection and Atonement, arguing that no God can save us.

19. They reject the need for a Savior.

20. They attempt to reinterpret the doctrines of the Church to fit their own preconceived views, and in the process deny Christ and His messianic role.

21. They attempt to change the God-given and scripturally based doctrines that protect the sanctity of marriage, divine nature of the family, and the essential doctrine of personal morality.

22. They advocate a redefinition of morality to justify fornication, adultery, and homosexual relationships.

23. They openly champion the legalization of so-called same-gender marriages.

24. They attack the inspired proclamation on the family.

Beware of False Prophets and False Teachers - M. Russell Ballard

Beware of those who speak and publish in opposition to God's true prophets.

lds.org | By M. Russell Ballard

35122269R00119

Made in the USA
San Bernardino, CA
15 June 2016